Sexual Unfolding

SEXUAL UNFOLDING

Sexual Development and Sex Therapies in Late Adolescence

LORNA J. SARREL, M.S.W.
*Assistant Clinical Professor of Social Work in Psychiatry
and of Obstetrics and Gynecology, Yale University
School of Medicine*

PHILIP M. SARREL, M.D.
*Associate Professor of Obstetrics and Gynecology
and of Psychiatry, Yale University
School of Medicine*

WITH A FOREWORD
by Ruth W. Lidz, M.D.
Clinical Professor of Psychiatry,
Yale University School of Medicine

and Theodore Lidz, M.D.
Sterling Professor of Psychiatry, Emeritus,
Yale University School of Medicine

Little, Brown and Company
BOSTON

*To the memory of
our fathers, Macy and Bert,
and to the future of our children,
Marc and Jennifer*

Contents

Foreword

Lorna and Philip Sarrel have, in a sense, written a book about two sexual unfoldings: the development of sexuality in the adolescent and young adult, and the transition of college youth through the sexual revolution. Thus, aside from furnishing a superb guide to how to offer sexual counseling services to a university community— for the Sarrels' efforts and influence have extended beyond the student body—the volume will, we believe, also attain importance as a record of what happened when a generation of students met the sexual revolution with few precedents to follow. The sexual revolution did not happen simply as a reflection of a change in the sexual moral code fostered by awareness of the relativism of ethical values, the breakdown of parental guidance and example, the impact of the sexual stimulation of children by television, or even the slow victory of the Freudian concept that sexual repression formed the basis of the neuroses as well as many other human woes. It required the ability provided by the pill and IUD to separate intercourse from conception with a high degree of reliability; the knowledge that one could, and even had the legal right to, obtain a safe and relatively simple vacuum-extraction abortion in case of need; and the removal of most of the lifelong effects of venereal disease by antibiotic medications. The antiestablishment rebelliousness that accompanied the Vietnam war may have hastened the day.

In any event, the sense of freedom to engage in sexual intercourse with a friend or friends to whom one is not committed in a permanent or even an extended relationship, instead of relying on petting or masturbation, has greatly altered the mores of American youth. Whether sexual encounters leading to orgasm through intercourse and heavy petting have actually increased may be debatable, but the openness and acceptability with which couples share their thoughts and feelings about sex and have sexual relations for love, recreation, and diversion have certainly changed. One hears sighs from the older faculty, "What a boon to happiness; would that I had been young now rather than a generation or two ago!" But sexual freedom has not brought freedom from neuroses or from conflicts about sex and sexuality—at least not yet.

With sexual freedom and enlightenment, youth found itself beset by new insecurities, self-doubts, and impulsions to perform sexually as well as the freedom truly to make love to one's true love. At Yale what had been largely extra-university problems—how college men would conduct themselves with girls or women from town, Smith, or Vassar; how Yale men would manage the pseudomacho reputation flaunted on the banners in some dormitory rooms, "When better women are made, Yale men will make them"—became an important intra-university matter in 1969 when women were admitted to Yale (with the unspoken expectation that henceforth when better Yale men were made it would largely be Yale alumnae who would make them). The women were admitted to all twelve Yale colleges where they would live in the same buildings and sometimes even share the same bathrooms with their male colleagues. College men and women were to assume the responsibility as adults for their sexual behavior, just as for any other behavior. However, conferring the title of Yale Woman and Yale Man did not turn the entering youths into adults, and in the area of sex most were less prepared for assuming adult responsibility than in other areas.

Nevertheless, the transition to undergraduate coeducation at Yale and also to the new sexuality went surprisingly well. And it was the Sarrels, together with an enlightened administration under Kingman Brewster and a farsighted university mental health service under Robert Arnstein, who were major factors in easing these transitions; shall we say, they were the accoucheurs of the new era in sexuality at Yale.

The book is largely a product of the Sarrels' experiences with university students over the past 10 years, an experience built upon Lorna Sarrel's excellent training in social work and Philip Sarrel's recognition early in his career as an obstetrician and gynecologist that many women sought the opportunity to discuss sexual difficulties with their gynecologists—few of whom could listen or discuss such matters usefully. Some of what the Sarrels teach, use in therapy, and write about herein derives from their work with Masters and Johnson, but such teachings have been transformed by a couple who, able to communicate easily with each other, have been able to hear as well as listen and in hearing learn from each person who has come to learn from them. The book is a well-thought-through text on adolescent sexuality, on teaching college students about sexuality, on providing contraception, on when to use behavioral techniques, on how to counsel, and on how to engage in a therapeutic relationship—not a book on sex, but on how to provide guidance for the sexually perplexed.

But it is more. The book is a very human document which lifts it far beyond the ordinary or the expected. It forms a model for the practice of patient-oriented medical care. The reader will note how the Sarrels regularly and naturally develop a relationship with each student or patient who comes to them—taking time to learn about the woman who comes for contraception, for example, but also about her partner and his needs and feelings about the technique the woman will use—a relationship that enables both partners to return for help if needed and that saves both time and suffering in the long run. The book has more to impart than facts and experiences, it conveys the dedication, warmth, and thoughtful interest in the patient and client without which a sexual counseling service cannot truly succeed, but also the constant renewal through learning that has made these authors such fine teachers. The book offers the reader the opportunity to learn from them.

Ruth W. Lidz, M.D.
Theodore Lidz, M.D.

New Haven, Connecticut

Preface

This book is an outgrowth of our work at Yale University as sex educators, counselors, therapists, and researchers. For the past 10 years we have had the privilege of learning about and learning from the thousands of Yale students who have shared their thoughts, feelings, problems, and creative energies with us.

Several different influences have determined our approach to our work. We brought with us backgrounds in social work, obstetrics and gynecology, and, in particular, experience with adolescents. From the beginning, we both paid attention to body issues and psychological issues simultaneously. We feel that our insistence upon *not* splitting the mind and the body is probably the most significant aspect of our work and hope this book substantiates our conviction.

We came to a department of psychiatry, which was created more than 50 years ago, to respond to the mental health needs of the Yale student population. For 10 years we have been learning about psychodynamics and psychotherapy from the therapists within this department and have integrated their findings into our daily work.

Our specialized skills in sex therapy began when, in 1971, we had the opportunity to work and study with William H. Masters and Virginia E. Johnson. That one month of intensive training gave us a basic understanding of male and female sexuality and the ways in which a therapist can help a couple develop understanding, sensitivity, and trust in a relationship. The perspective on sexuality that we gained from Masters and Johnson has proved invaluable in our work with students. A great deal of the material in this book is derived directly and indirectly from their teachings.

We have relied heavily upon our understanding of the students we have talked to in our office and in the classroom, and have made extensive use of their individual stories and case histories. We have been scrupulously careful to protect the confidentiality of individual students by altering names, dates, places, and minor details without, we hope, destroying the unique reality and complexity of each person's or couple's life experience. Where we have used extensive material about a given student or couple we have asked for and received permission to do so. We are very grateful for these permissions.

We wish to express our gratitude first to our students. They trusted us and we them. They taught us and in return, we believe, we have made some contribution to enhancing the quality of their lives. Without them there would have been no book.

We thank those administrators at Yale who were helpful in the creation of The Sex Counseling Service and who have continued to support it.

A special word of gratitude is reserved for Dr. Robert Arnstein, Director of Yale's Division of Mental Hygiene within the University Health Service. His division stands as an example of excellence in the field of student mental health. His initiative and support enabled us to start the Sex Counseling Service in 1969—a rather daring venture at that time—and he has continued to offer support and guidance over the years. Dr. Arnstein was also generous in reading and making valuable comments on the manuscript.

We want to acknowledge our special indebtedness to Drs. Ruth and Ted Lidz who have been role models and mentors for many years. We greatly appreciate their reading of the manuscript, their intelligent criticisms, and their writing of the foreword.

We want to thank Dr. Sidney Berman who has taught us a great deal about the psychological makeup of many of the people we have seen. Through him we have learned about body image and the significance and relevance of the Draw-A-Person Test in sex therapy.

Our thanks also to Professor Haskell Coplin of Amherst College, a friend, colleague, and source of inspiration, for reading and commenting on the manuscript.

Last, but by no means least, we want to thank Ms. Jackie Smaga, our secretary and administrative assistant, for typing the several different versions of the manuscript. Ms. Smaga also helped considerably with organizing the reference material. No matter how great the stress we created, Jackie has always been cheerful, efficient, and able to get us through the crisis.

Financial support received from the Josiah Macy, Jr. Foundation enabled Philip Sarrel to spend a sabbatical year at the university at Oxford. During that year a significant part of our time was spent gathering material for this book and initiating the writing process. We wish to thank the Josiah Macy, Jr. Foundation Faculty Scholar selection committee for making the award and also wish to thank Dr. John Bancroft and Prof. Michael Gelder for providing for us while at Oxford.

L.J.S.
P.M.S

Sexual Unfolding

Introduction

This book is meant to be a distillation of our experiences in the fields of sex therapy, counseling, and education from the late 1960s to the present. Since our experience has been largely, though not entirely, with college and university students, this is the group we focus on. We have tried to write primarily for professionals working with students, other late adolescents, and young adults. We feel confident about our clinical material and have little or no hesitation in writing about the day-in-day-out work we do. Where we have ventured into abstraction and generalization, we are less confident. We offer our ideas tentatively, in the hope that they may be useful as a conceptual framework for the clinical material.

Because this book draws so heavily upon our particular professional experiences, we feel that the reader should know something about who we are and the nature of our work. These days we both call ourselves "sexologists," but we arrived at this professional identity almost without meaning to. Lorna Sarrel received a masters degree in social work, beginning a professional career in medical settings and continuing this work for six years. At present, Lorna Sarrel has the title of Co-Director of the Human Sexuality Program and Assistant Clinical Professor of Social Work in Psychiatry at Yale. Philip Sarrel is a medical doctor, trained as an obstetrician-gynecologist, and is an Associate Professor of Obstetrics and Gynecology and Psychiatry at Yale. While still a resident in Obstetrics-Gynecology (1964) he started a special clinic for teenage unwed mothers. It was his work with these girls and their boyfriends that prompted his first venture into sex education. Soon afterward he organized the first course in human sexuality for Yale medical students. During two years in the Air Force he continued to expand his interest in sex education, starting noncredit sex education courses for Mt. Holyoke, Smith, and Amherst students [1].

Together, we led small group discussions that were an integral part of these courses. It didn't take long for students to start telephoning us at home, asking for advice about abortion, contraception, and sex. This was our first experience of the largely unmet need for sex counseling on a campus.

Our timing was fortuitous. It was the fall of 1969. We were returning to New Haven at the same moment that Yale college was going co-ed. The student health services wanted to provide gynecologic care for the incoming undergraduate females. We suggested that we provide that care but in a unique way—a service called sex-counseling, located within "Mental Hygiene" (Yale's slightly quaint term for psychological services). We have run the Sex Counseling Service (SCS) since then (seeing more than 2,500 students between fall of 1969 and spring of 1977), and taught courses in human sexuality for Yale students and at many other colleges and universities. After two years of working as a student sex counseling team and teaching sexuality at Yale, we had the privilege of being trained to do sex therapy by Masters and Johnson at the Reproductive Biology Research Foundation (1971). Since that time, we have done Masters/Johnson sex therapy with over 200 student and nonstudent couples. What we learned from Masters and Johnson has been the core for all of our clinical work. Even when we are not doing sex therapy in their format, we use their basic concepts and the understanding of human sexuality that they imparted.

Although the primary focus of our work has been with a university subgroup, nevertheless, an important dimension of our professional experience is its multicultural nature. As a result of working within the Yale community, we have listened to people from a wide variety of the world's cultures and subcultures, since Yale faculty and graduate students come from every continent. Because the undergraduate population during these years has increasingly included students from different American subcultures and minority groups, we also have the beginnings of an understanding of sexual development among these young adults. Five years' experience working with ninth grade teachers in an inner city high school, developing and delivering a sex education program for more than five thousand 14- to 18-year-olds, has yielded some understanding of sexual issues in this population also.

In 1975-1976 we lived in Oxford, England and had the chance to teach our methods of treating sex problems, to learn about their somewhat more behaviorally oriented therapy and to see English couples [1]. We also taught sex therapy to a group of Danish and Swedish psychotherapists (in Copenhagen) and learned something about sexual problems in those countries.

However, the majority of our clinical work has been with a select and small subgroup and we want to emphasize the real limitations this puts on our observations. We are describing and deriving generalizations from a group of late adolescents and young adults, predominantly white, middle-class, intelligent, achievement-oriented, and verbal—at a particular moment in time (the early and mid 1970s). We honestly cannot say how relevant our experiences and concepts will be in other settings and other years, but we wouldn't have bothered writing at all if we didn't believe that there is a great deal in common among American students today. Our experiences at many different schools across the country have persuaded us that, although there are important regional differences in attitudes and behavior, the underlying themes and conflicts in growing up as a sexual person today are much the same for students in Vermont, North Carolina, Nebraska, and California. Our more limited experiences abroad, in England and Denmark particularly, suggest that, again, in spite of cultural differences, the basic processes are similar.

In 1973 there were seven million young people attending colleges and universities in the United States—nearly half of all the youth in that age group. This contrasts with 1963 when there were four million students and 1953 when there were only two million. This means that college students today represent a mainstream and not a minor tributary. In concerning ourselves with the personality and emotional life of college students, we are following in a tradition of concern for the quality of life and for humanistic values as a vital and appropriate part of education—a tradition which extends back to the Greeks, but a tradition that is sometimes eclipsed by other concerns and other philosophies of education. In the 1950s and much of the 1960s, education in the United States was focused on turning out highly skilled technicians. The epitome of this attitude was expressed in a statement by a past president of the American Association for Higher Education:

Whether or not a student burns a draft card, participates in a civil rights march, engages in premarital or extramarital sexual activity, becomes pregnant, attends church, sleeps all day, or drinks all night is not really the concern of a collegiate institution . . . Colleges and universities are not churches, clinics, nor even parents. They are devices by which a limited number of skills, insights, and points of view are communicated to the young in the belief that possession of these somehow aids the individual to become a more skilled worker [2].

It is interesting to note that the educational "extras" in the above statement—churches, clinics, and parents—are viewed as the preventers of "wrongs" that students might commit. This is an awfully negative view of churches, clinics and parents! A more humanistic philosophy of education sees these, and the entire educational process, as promoting human potential and fostering development in many areas—body, intellect, emotions, values, citizenship. Humanistic education is education of a person for all facets of life, not simply for a work role.

Books such as Nevitt Sanford's *Where Colleges Fail—A Study of the Student as a Person* (1968) have highlighted the need for colleges and universities to concern themselves with the student as a maturing adolescent who is in the midst of major personality development. Even Arthur Chickering, author of the quote above, acknowledged this when he wrote of seven dimensions of a student's development: competence, emotions, autonomy, identity, interpersonal relationships, purpose, and integrity.

One rather cynical observer of the college scene thinks that students are simply marking time. Bennet Berger maintains that a postindustrial society uses universities as storage bins for a large group of people it doesn't know how to fit in and that the adolescent "search for identity" gives students something serious to be preoccupied with instead of working [3]. Kenneth Kenniston sees it differently: Because our society is characterized by rapid change and confusing role expectations, socialization is not effective in preparing children and youth for their adult lives. Kenniston has remarked that "Socialization is the main problem in a society where there are known and stable roles for children to fit into: but in a rapidly changing society like ours, identity formation increasingly replaces socialization in importance" [4]. Robert J. Lifton has also focused on the need for a new personality type, "protean man," who can be flexible in choice of work and change career one or more times in adult life [5].

Kenniston, Lifton, and others suggest that there is a greater need today than ever before for a core individual identity which is both secure and flexible. But the fact that future role models are unknown or, when known, in conflict makes identity formation more difficult than ever before. In an essay written in 1962, Kenniston mentioned that there was a shift among college youths away from a work-role oriented future toward a vision of life centered on personal and interpersonal fulfillment. He found many students who planned to have large families and thought that much of their satisfaction in life would come within the context of their family life. Without knowing it, Kenniston provided a perfect example of the role confusion and dizzying pace of change to which young people must somehow adapt. Within five to seven years of this essay, the Zero Population Growth movement in the United States (with an assist from the Women's Movement) helped to foster a negative sanction on large families, and a great many young people began to speak of never having children or at least limiting the number of biological offspring to one or two.

But Kenniston's generalization about youth seeking fulfillment through the personal and interpersonal rather than through "success," status, and money is still valid for many students. The majority of students at least pay lip service to these values. There is widespread discontent with the traditional forms of family life, the isolated nuclear family, sex-role stereotyping of husband and wife, and the high divorce rate. This discontent is not preventing most young people from marrying eventually and leading lives not so very different from their parents, but it does lead to a lot of talk about, and some experimentation with, alternative life styles: communes, "open" relationships, the importance of a special emotional bond between partners (rather than the "conventional" more pragmatic and/or religious view of marriage), the possibility of a fulfilling life as a homosexual "out of the closet," and the positive values of bisexuality.

That there has been a sexual revolution in attitudes is undeniable. There are few moral absolutes left in the sexual sphere. Even if a student feels that he or she will not have intercourse before marriage, this is not felt to be a norm for all. Pluralism, moral relativism, and the "consenting adult" philosophy prevail. But this doesn't mean total amorality. There are still some standards almost all young people seem to accept in theory. Sex should not involve coercion. If two people don't want to have a baby, they shouldn't have intercourse without contraception or they should be prepared to have an abortion. Sex should be pleasurable for both partners. People should have some knowledge about sex and their bodies.

Beyond these fundamental areas of shared belief there is a tremendous range of feeling and opinion on almost every aspect of human sexuality and a tendency to publicly discuss the subject in a way which would not have been possible 20, or even 10, years ago. When one of us (L. S.) was a student at an all-female college in the Northeast in the late 1950s the only official recognition that sex existed as a human activity was a "hygiene" examination—a test taken by almost all students as a way of avoiding a dreaded one-credit hygiene course. In her freshman year the exam consisted of one essay question, "Discuss the dangers of sexual promiscuity." Presumably those students who could conjure up the most lurid and terrifying consequences got the highest grades. She always regretted not writing something like, "One might come to enjoy it so much, one's studies might be affected."

Men were not allowed to visit dormitory rooms and there were dozens of other regulations including a semiofficial one which said that pregnant students would be kicked out. But no college official ever acknowledged that the rules and regulations were for the purpose of controlling sex among students. This official "silent treatment" was matched in the 1950s by a private silence. Roommates did not confide about having intercourse, masturbating, orgasms or lack thereof. They talked *some*—just enough to know that there was something sexual happening with most of us but not enough to relieve the guilt or to inform accurately. We were left to struggle it out, each of us more or less alone, with our dates, boyfriends, steadies, or fiancees.

Meanwhile, at an all-male college to the north, the fraternity houses each had a "pit" in the basement—a mattress-filled place where couples necked and groped in the dark alongside other groping couples. In those years some 50% of the male students visited a prostitute sometime in their four years. The freshman hygiene course "covered" sex (earning it the nickname "Smut I"). There was lots of talk about sex, but most of it was in jokes and innuendo and much of it was plain bragging. Again, there was not enough real talk to inform and just enough to make each young male feel he was terribly inexperienced compared to all the others.

Fifteen years after the fact, two of these men discussed an event of their sophomore year—this time honestly. They had gone to a nearby city to "get laid." One was supposedly the experienced man-of-the-world, the other, naive and virginal. The worldly one went into the bedroom first and emerged with a smile of pleasure and triumph. His friend went in next and he too came out of the bedroom smiling. Fifteen years later each could confess that he had been impotent!

They could speak the truth now because they were older and had some sexual self-confidence and also because the times had changed and being self-revealing was now all right. It is probably not coincidental that their mutual disclosure took place after they attended a lecture and discussion on human sexuality for Yale undergraduates.

Public and private candor have grown alongside one another. One or both of us have been personally involved in sex education courses at many colleges since 1967—Mt. Holyoke, Smith, Amherst, Brown, Dartmouth, Yale, Wellesley, Cincinnati, Nebraska, North Carolina, Washburn, Northwestern, Rockford, Indiana University, and Emory [6]. Probably the majority of American campuses have had some officially sanctioned sex education course or public debate in the past five years. In many instances student initiative and demand have been the impetus and the "Establishment" has had varied reactions—from enthusiastic support to resistance. In 1971 we were invited to speak at a special week-end conference on human sexuality sponsored and organized by the students' association at the University of Nebraska. We found, on arrival, that the Nebraska State Regents were attempting to take out a court injunction to stop the entire proceeding. They were unable to get the injunction, but the week-end was pervaded with an aura of fear and caution lest the Regents retaliate, as students told us they had threatened, by closing down the vocational advisory office for students. We also learned that one of the primary student organizers of the program, a sophomore girl, had been thrown out of her home and told never to return because of her role in planning the week-end.

A *New York Times* article of March 23, 1975 entitled "Sex Week at U. of Alabama Stirs Only Token Protests" describes a "Sex Week" at the University of Alabama.

Tuscaloosa, Ala., March 23—The University of Alabama, probably best known as the place where Gov. George C. Wallace stood defiantly in the schoolhouse door to block the admission of two black students in 1963, seems an unlikely setting for the showing of obscene movies and a lecture by a star in a pornographic movie.

Nonetheless, the university today went quickly into the sixth day of an officially sanctioned Sex Week—a series of films, lectures and dramatizations dealing with a variety of explicit sexual themes.

"At first," said Al Goldstein, who is editor of *Screw* Magazine and probably the nation's best-known hard-core pornographer, "at first I thought I was being set up for something.

"Can you imagine a hairy New York Jewish pornographer walking onto the campus of the University of Alabama with a filthy movie under his arm to show the students—and then give them a lecture? Even my shrink said not to come."

Mr. Goldstein and his "filthy movie" were received with hardly more than a flutter from college officials and only token complaints from the community.

There have been protests from the religious community, but no pickets, no arrests and no censorship. . . .

The university administration has judiciously kept a low profile, although official approval was necessary to guarantee the $3,000 in students' funds that the week will cost.

Another week-long campus conference at the University of Colorado devoted some of its time to sex. Russell Baker described his reaction in his *Observer* column in *The New York Times:*

All will surely be ready for the great American sexual feast, judging from the enthusiastic attendance at every panel concerned with the flesh and its troublesome demands. The level of student sophistication about politics would bore a barber, but on matters sexual most of the campus appears fully qualified for the Ph.D. They packed rooms in which sex was to be discussed in all its aspects and confidently lectured those middle-aged panelists whose views of the matter were ill-informed.

So much seriousness about sex is undoubtedly a healthy sign of maturity, but after a week's exposure to it one cannot help wondering whether sex really shouldn't be a bit more frivolous than the World Bank and the United States Senate.

It could be a trend to make us all yearn for a return to the good old days of kidnapping the dean and firebombing the physics lab.

That such scenes can and do take place on campus after campus is really quite remarkable, although it already seems almost routine and humdrum. What is remarkable? To begin with there is the students' demand to know—to be fully informed on a subject which has previously been left in the shadows by a kind of collusion between the generations not to say too much. Secondly, there is the official recognition of the right to be sexually informed and a willingness to go beyond allowing sex to be discussed to actually sponsoring, supporting, advertising and sharing in the public discussion. It seems that the establishment has begun to accept the idea that knowledge about sex doesn't lead to abuse and promiscuity but can actually promote growth and a respect for the human meanings of sexuality. We are finally beginning to believe what Margaret Mead told us in 1954:

The more society obscures these relationships, muffles the human body in clothes, surrounds elimination with prudery, shrouds copulation in shame and mystery, camouflages pregnancy, banishes men and children from childbirth, and hides breast feeding, the more individual and bizarre will be the child's attempts to understand, to piece together a very imperfect knowledge of the life cycle of the two sexes and an understanding of the particular state of maturity of his or her own body [7].

It is remarkable too that the knowledge sought and given is not restricted, as it once was, to the plumbing of reproduction, the fact that condoms prevent VD, and intercourse leads to pregnancy. These campus discussions range wide and deep, including the gamut of feelings about sex—pleasure, lust, fear, tenderness, anger, and jealousy. They are sometimes astonishingly personal, usually without being embarrassing. One "lecturer" in such a discussion told the students that every year of his adolescence on Yom Kippur (the Jewish Day of Atonement) he vowed to give up masturbation. When the format is a small group there is even more freedom to be self-revealing and to ask questions (see Chapter 10 on sex education).

The very seriousness of the campus discussions about sex, which Russell Baker chided so well, is also rather remarkable. Sex education has so often been greeted with nervous laughter, and, in the past, there was a kind of gleeful pleasure in getting around the rules—fooling the old folks and the dorm housemother. Now, "eyeball to eyeball" with the older generations, young people want to talk, debate, and refine their ideas.

Philip Slater has said that a concern for the moral basis of their behavior seems to characterize students today—not that they adhere to their parents' sexual norms; they tend to violate them regularly and without much guilt, but "every act must have . . . a moral foundation." The concern for moral standards does seem fairly widespread and genuine. In the intergenerational debates about sex it often seems as if the young man or woman is debating with a parent, but in an adult to adult way, with a frankness about their own and the elder's sexuality that would heretofore have seemed impossible between child and parent.

It certainly shouldn't surprise us that such debates and discussions are serious. In the high schools and at the universities, more young people than ever before are having sexual experiences, and at a younger and younger age. They are doing so at a time when norms are changing very rapidly and when most rules have evaporated or become outdated. They have surely begun to discover for themselves that sex is not just fun and good feelings but is a part of themselves and their relationships, something powerful in its intensity that can be easy and a source of pleasure but can also hurt and confuse. In this understanding, they far surpass the youth of former generations. Even if half of all the talk is just an attempt to rationalize behavior, we should respect the enormous need to come to terms with sex, especially if, as Kenniston suggested, it is the world of private and interpersonal experience that really matters to young people today.

We would not agree with Russell Baker's feeling that there is too much seriousness about sex on college campuses today. Probably there is not yet enough. It is the serious students who show up for seminars. Other observers of the college scene have stressed the absence of serious thought about sex. Sanford, in his otherwise fairly liberal view of the American student "as a person" seems to say that the sexually active student is usually immature, sick or irresponsible: "[A] large proportion of the students seen by college psychiatrists and at planned parenthood clinics are those who act out their problems through unconventional sexual behavior. . . . [I]t is not easy for a girl to be the image of sexual freedom and at the same time a fully developed person" [9]. Richard Hettlinger, who has written extensively about sex and students does not take as dim a view as Sanford, but he does not think campus sex is an example of postconventional, self-chosen morality but more an expression of adolescent rebellion against the Establishment. True freedom, Hettlinger says, means "not blindly reacting but questioning" [10].

Part of the difference of opinion between us and Hettlinger may be a matter of which campuses we are seeing most closely because there are undoubted regional variations. There is, of course, the problem inherent in any generalization. Obviously, on any given campus there will be a wide divergence in sexual behavior, attitudes, and values. It may be a matter of closing either the right eye or the left to substantiate one's viewpoint. We suspect, however, that a campus milieu can be substantially affected by the administration, the health services, the chaplains, and the faculty. At Yale, where there is a multifaceted program in sexuality that touches a high proportion of the student body, the milieu is more one of care than carelessness, where relatively few students have intercourse without contraception, where the noncredit course in human sexuality is well attended, and a high percentage of students choose to come to the Sex Counseling Service to talk about the meaning of sex in their lives.

References

1. Sarrel, Philip M. and Coplin, Haskell, "A Course in Human Sexuality for the College Student," *American Journal of Public Health*, Vol. 65(5), May 1971.
2. Chickering, Arthur W. *Education and Identity*, San Francisco, Jossey-Bass, 1974, pp. 2-3.
3. Goode, Elizabeth, "Drug Use and Sexual Activity on a College Campus" in *American Journal of Psychiatry*, Vol. 128, April 1972, pp. 1272-1276.
4. Kenniston, Kenneth, *Youth and Dissent*, New York, Harcourt Brace Jovanovich, Inc., 1960, p. 73.
5. Lifton, Robert J. and Olson, Eric, *Living and Dying*, New York and Washington, Praeger Publishing Co., 1974, pp. 143-145.
6. Sarrel and Coplin, [1].

7. Mead, Margaret, *Male and Female*, New York, Dell Publishing Co., Inc., 1949.
8. Slater, Philip, *Pursuit of Loneliness*, Boston, Beacon Press, 1970, p. 80.
9. Sanford, Nevitt, *Where Colleges Fail—A Study of the Student as a Person*, Jossey-Bass, San Francisco, 1967, pp. 132, 138.
10. Hettlinger, Richard, *Sex Isn't That Simple*, New York, Seabury Press, 1974, pp. 27-28.

Part I

BECOMING SEXUAL

I

The Concept of Sexual Unfolding

Adolescent sexuality is like an evolving complex, kaleidoscopic jig-saw or crossword puzzle in which the pieces, the clues, the questions, the struggles and explorations, and the answers may change shape and colour before the full pattern is formed. Changes in one area influence another. There are causes and effect, actions and reactions, expected and unexpected. There are obsessions and digressions, progressions, and regressions. There are times of triumph, glow and gloom. There are times of excesses and interactions, times of stillness and reflection.

SIMON MEYERSON [1]

There is something special and fascinating in seeing young people move through the years of college and graduate school. When they are freshmen you have to force yourself to call them "men" and "women"; the words *boy* and *girl* want to come out instead. And then, by about their senior year or some time in graduate school, most of them *are* men and women. If you don't know the individual very deeply, the process seems to happen smoothly, almost magically, like time-lapse photography of a flower opening.

17

But, of course, the process is anything but smooth and magical, and not everyone accomplishes the transition in these years.

In recent decades there has been a growing body of literature about the transition to adulthood as it occurs in our society. There are important areas of consensus now about some aspects of adolescence. Virtually all observers agree that the years from puberty through the early 20s involve major psychological changes.

A list of the major changes which take place during the years between puberty and adulthood would include the following: (1) intellectual growth, and in particular, the capacity for abstraction and theory building; (2) moral growth, which for college students usually means a moral relativism evolving toward personally held "universal" principles; (3) a more or less permanent choice of life-work and avocational interests; (4) an evolving sense of one's sexual identity; (5) increasing independence from one's family of origin and an ability to be intimate and loving with a friend (lover). One might also want to add (6) spiritual growth and (7) an altered relationship to the community—seeking oneself and being seen as an adult participant in community affairs. Clearly these areas overlap and mutually influence one another. But rates and direction of change can differ from one aspect to another. For example, many a bright, career-minded and high-achieving college student remains emotionally immature and may have many ego deficits outside a particular sphere of intellectual function. Or, in another instance, intellectual function may be impaired when unconscious sexual fantasies invade what should be a conflict-free ego sphere.

Sexual Unfolding

In running a Sex Counseling Service (SCS) for students we have focused our interest on and have learned most about issues 4 and 5 on the preceding list—the evolving sense of sexual identity and the increasing capacity for intimacy (both emotional and sexual). We believe that this concentrated focus has taught us something which is worth sharing, namely a fairly close-up view of the processes by which some young people form that aspect of their identity we call the sexual. Because the term *sexual identity* is too narrow, but *identity* itself is too wide, we have gradually come to use the term *sexual unfolding* or simply *unfolding*.

By *unfolding* we mean a process made up of innumerable experiences during adolescence, by which a person becomes aware of himself or herself as a sexual being, a male or female, who relates to oneself and others, sexually, in some characteristic ways. When unfolding is successful the person becomes capable of satisfying sexual and psychological intimacy with another (nonfamily) person (or persons).

In deference to the human need to enumerate and subdivide we have attempted another list—this time a list of the processes involved in sexual unfolding. In offering such a list, we realize the degree to which we, ourselves, are culture and class bound. Our entire discussion is heavily value laden but we are not pretending to speak for anyone other than the students we know and work with. For this group, at least, unfolding involves (not in any special order):

1. an evolving sense of the body—toward a body image that is gender specific and fairly free of distortion (in particular about the genitals);
2. the ability to overcome or modulate guilt, shame, and childhood inhibitions associated with sexual thoughts and behavior;
3. a gradual loosening of libidinal ties to parents and siblings;
4. recognizing what is erotically pleasing and displeasing;
5. the absence of conflict and confusion about sexual orientation;
6. an increasingly satisfying and rich sexual life, free of sexual dysfunction or compulsion—(for the majority, but not for everyone, this would also include a satisfying auto-eroticism);
7. a growing awareness of being a sexual person and of the place and value of sex in one's life (including options such as celibacy);

8. the ability to be responsible about oneself, one's partner and society, e.g., using contraception and not using sex as exploita-
   tion of another;
9. a gradually increasing ability to experience eroticism as one
   aspect of intimacy with another person (not that *all* eroticism
   occurs, then, in an intimate relationship, but that this fusion of
   sex and love is possible).

In lectures and in counseling, people seem to respond well to
the term *unfolding;* it somehow fits with their understanding and
experience of sexual development during adolescence. The dictionary sheds light on why this word may ring true when used in
a sexual context. Its meanings are subtly sexual: to bring out of a
folded state; spread or open out: unfold your arms; to spread out
or lay open to view; to reveal or display; to become unfolded:
open; to develop; to become clear, apparent or known; and in music, to develop is to unfold, by various technical means, the inherent possibilities of a theme.

The major problem with the word *unfolding* is that it may suggest a process in which everything is given at the start, awaiting
only the right moment to open and become known, like Sleeping
Beauty awaiting the prince's kiss. Adolescent sexual awakening is
nothing like that. There are givens, to be sure, and they are very
important: There is one's biology and all of one's past experiences.
But the process is one of dynamic, even dramatic, interaction with
the world outside—with family, peers, lovers, therapists, and doctors to give a partial list—and current events sometimes alter the
previous gestalt in major ways.

We find ourselves in a philosophical position somewhere between those who emphasize the overriding significance of infantile experience and a biologically determined "sex drive" and some
sociologists, most notably John Gagnon and William Simon [2],
who claim that sexual expression is entirely a function of social
learning.

In the past several decades there has been a movement away

from an overly simplified view of an inborn sex drive. We now realize that certain life-experiences are needed to actualize biological potential. Renee Spitz found that infants raised in a foundling home may show none of the usual childhood interest in sexual play [3]. Primate studies have supported the idea that social experiences are crucial in developing sexual capacity. Harlow showed that male primates need months or even years of practice to develop a mature pattern of copulation. If the primate is deprived of the ordinary childhood sex play and experimentation he will be unable to copulate even though aroused by a receptive female [4].

Mature sexual behavior is not a biological given and can never be understood apart from its particular social and historical context* [5]. But we must not allow the pendulum to carry us so far that we revert to an epistemologically outmoded view of the mind as a tabula rasa. If Freudian concepts of the oral, anal, and phallic stages seem too deterministic, we cannot deny the special importance of the organs of perception in the interchange between our bodies and the environment. And, in highlighting the great significance of social experiences that the culture defines as "sexual," we don't need to go so far that we deny the importance of the biological changes of puberty. Gagnon and Simon have warned that an overemphasis on a search for continuity with prior experiences is "dangerously misleading" [6].

Sexual unfolding is a process which takes place over time. Without belaboring the obvious, this must be stressed because time is a crucial variable. Historical and cultural differences are major determinants of timing. In one society we might need to focus the majority of attention on the sexual behavior of ten-year-olds, whereas, if we were studying the Irish living on Inis Beag, we would need to place more stress on the sexual and social experiences of men and women in their mid- and late 20s or even 30s. Within our own country, changes in courtship patterns and premarital sexual behavior have gradually lowered the age of sexual

---

* See the work of Ford and Beach, the Harlows, and others in primate studies, and the anthropologic data and the writings of people like Bandura (see [5]).

awareness and experimentation. Even biology changes with time and we must take into account the younger and younger age of pubarche.

In the United States today adolescence is considered to span roughly ages 12 through 20. Blos' and Lidz's further division of adolescence into early, middle and late is helpful, as is Kenniston's term *youth* to describe that segment of the population which today prolongs its "adolescence" into their 20s, and sometimes to 30. Even within the time frame 12-to-20, in the mid-twentieth century United States, there are regional, subcultural, and individual differences. In any high school class of 15-year-olds there will be great discrepancies in emotional and physical maturity, in sexual knowledge and experience, and in self-understanding.

Although the timing of specific experiences is quite variable, most American adolescents today experience a fairly prolonged, sequential introduction to sexuality that includes a myriad of inputs. There are the body events and changes of puberty. Socially there is a progression from 12-year-old disco parties and kissing games, through early group interaction and pairing, some groping in cars and on couches, perhaps masturbation and some sex play to a gradually increasing intimacy and closeness with one partner at a time. There is also a world of "information" that enters the young person's life, from friends, media, church, school, parents, pamphlets and sex manuals, porno books and X-rated films. And, along the way, there are issues to be coped with such as contraception, having a pelvic exam, a VD scare, and perhaps a pregnancy or an abortion. In the life story of the individual, the sequence and timing of such events *relative to that person's physical and emotional development and his or her prior learning about sex* will determine the course of the unfolding process.

Private Body Experience and Sexual Unfolding

All awareness begins with our own bodies. Each person has a mental representation of his or her own body—its size and shape, how it or parts of it move in space, etc. This mental representation has elements which may be quite stable and other aspects which are subject to change from year to year or even from moment to moment. What matters, from a psychological point of view, is not the bodily reality but the "perception" of reality—the personal meaning—for a given individual. The composite of these perceptions is called the "body image," and it is made up of unconscious, preconscious, and conscious elements.

Female

There are very important differences in body image between boys and girls which go beyond the usual "vive la différence!" Psychoanalysts have long noted the dissimilarities in boys' and girls' resolution of the oedipal conflicts. The little girl doesn't ever repress her oedipal fantasies during latency to the same extent as the boy. Greenacre [7] and others have stated that some bisexual identification is part of latency for most girls. Blos notes that in early adolescence the girl still maintains illusory ideas about the existence of a penis. Her body perceptions, especially so far as sexual characteristics are concerned, are still extremely vague [8]. The "Draw-a-Person" test can give graphic representation to this gender-identity blurring. The authors of *Human Figure Drawing in Adolescence* found that a considerable number of 13-year-old girls showed lack of certainty about having a female body either by drawing a male first or by drawing a sexually ambiguous figure and spontaneously labelling it as a "tomboy," "boy-girl," or "neuter." By contrast, boys of this age nearly always draw an identifiable male figure first [9].

Puberty, and its concomitant bodily changes, obviously can present a sequence of dramatic changes in body image. Any one of these changes can be a source of anxiety and self-doubt. For example, along with early breast development and the growth of pubic and axillary hair, most girls experience the onset of a vaginal discharge because of the increase in circulating estrogen. This is a normal, physiologic discharge but it is seldom, if ever, discussed in sex education books, lectures, or films and is often a source of great anxiety for girls. Retrospectively, college students can usually recall this discharge and the particular meaning it had for them. "My underwear was always stained by the discharge. Between the ages of 12 and 14, I must have changed three or four times a day. Out of habit I still take a dozen or more pair of underpants with me when I go away for a week-end." The student who said this had received instruction about menstruation in the fifth and sixth grades, but as the estrogen-induced secretion had not been mentioned, she felt there was something abnormal about her body and didn't dare tell anyone. We were the first to hear about it because we had mentioned this pubertal change during her office visit for an annual gynecological check up. Some girls feared an infection or a more serious disease like cancer or VD. One student arranged an emergency appointment for her younger sister to see us with her mother because the sister was convinced the discharge was a sign of cancer. Considering the uncertain body-image of the girl at this age, it is not surprising to learn that some recall thinking that this discharge was semen, although how this might be so was very vague in their minds. The near universality of this premenarchial discharge and the anxiety associated with it suggest that a discussion of normal vaginal discharge should be included in sex education materials, whether for young people or professionals and should also be included in medical/sexual history taking.

Breasts, too, cause anxiety. Girls worry about when they develop, their size and shape, the existence or nonexistence of hair around the areola, inverted nipples and breast assymmetry. Even in this era of liberated, braless young women and a concept of fashion that makes small breasts an asset, masses of girls and women feel devastated by "flat-chestedness." We were made aware of the extent of concern about small breasts through a monthly magazine column we wrote. We kept a tally of questions asked and, much to our surprise, found that, second only to questions about female sex response and orgasm, were letters expressing a desire to have larger breasts.* In 1974-1975, the total number of questions about

* Slightly more than one third of all questions received concerned "cosmetic" problems while slightly under one third concerned female sex response. It must be considered a biased sample of the total female population since the column appeared in a magazine about fashion and beauty but it is interesting to note the

the body was 161. Of these, 106 were about breasts. The letters vary from expression of mild concern to severe, almost crippling worry about lack of "femininity" and sexual attractiveness because of small breasts. Feelings about breasts tended to generalize to feelings about the entire self, expressed in statements like, "I have become obsessed that I am horrible." The following excerpt is typical of the feelings associated with this issue:

I have always had small breasts. It didn't concern me too much except I never dated any boy, always fearing they would notice if I went swimming. But now here's my biggest problem. Recently, I fell in love with a young man and he loves me and he brought up the subject of having sex. Sex! How can I let him see my ugly body, especially my breasts! God only knows if my breasts weren't so small and ugly I'd not think twice for I love him so, but I'm afraid of him seeing me. Will I ever get over this fear? I haven't consulted any doctor because I'm even afraid to let them see me! I feel so unfeminine and deprived, especially when I see other girls who have nice breasts. I'm afraid I shall never be able to have a normal sex life.

The extent to which our culture has fetishized the breast as a symbol of female sexuality is well known and the woman who doesn't resemble a center-fold can suffer from lowered self-esteem because she doesn't, literally and figuratively, measure-up. Research on body image has shown that there are shared group norms regarding ideal dimensions for body parts and that a person's attitude toward a body part is significantly determined by deviation of that part from the norm [10]. But the young woman's feelings about small breasts cut much deeper than a need to compete in the arena of sexual attractiveness. The full breast has come to stand for all aspects of female sexuality, in particular, sexual responsiveness, although such a correlation has no basis in truth.

It is interesting to speculate on the pervasive nature of this concern. Desmond Morris puts forward some arguments in favor of

---

range of cosmetic concerns among young women today. In addition to concerns about breasts, we have received questions about the following: stretch marks, body odor and genital odor, body hair, genital anatomy, overweight, varicosities, tallness, pubic hair, acne and shortness.

the idea that the protruberant human female breast has evolved *not* primarily for sucking purposes but as one of a set of frontal body formations whose function is primarily that of sex-signalling. Breasts signify that the sexual system is more or less matured and indicate whether the person is masculine or feminine. Morris also speculates on the possibility that breasts mimic the buttocks and serve a further role in sex-signalling parallel to the role of buttocks in primates who copulate with the male facing the female's buttocks [11].

Be that as it may, in our culture breasts have an overdetermined value as sexually symbolic objects. The pubescent girl may hate her breasts because they serve as a constantly growing reminder, to herself and others, that she is maturing and that she is female. On the other hand, she may welcome these growing representations of adult femaleness. The breasts then may serve a crucial role in helping to focus and reorganize the prepubescent body-image and the felt absence of "adequate" breasts could, in some instances, undermine the evolution of adult-female body-image. Obviously the breast does not play this role in all cultures. Japanese women traditionally bound their breasts, attempting to appear quite breastless. It is interesting that along with so many other Western ways, Japan has also imported the cult of the large bosom.

This is not to say that young girls with large breasts have no problems; they do. After one magazine column in which we wrote about the concerns of the "flat-chested," we were deluged with letters from big breasted girls and women. They complained about the physical difficulties involved: pain, problems sleeping on their abdomen, and interference with athletics. They also complained about being viewed as sex objects by males. Some attention is nice, but too much focus on the breasts is embarrassing and, given today's feminist perspective, annoying, perhaps even infuriating. The young adolescent girl who feels she is a sex object has a difficult time learning to believe that males can be interested in her as a person, not just as someone with large breasts. It may be harder for her to traverse the path of sexual unfolding toward intimacy.

The focus on body parts to differentiate male from female is part of many diverse cultures, and is often included in initiation rites at puberty. For example, among the Gusii (of the South Nyanza district in Kenya) there is a genital operation performed at puberty on females during which the female's desire to be male is openly indulged and expressed in both words and behavior. Following this rite, she is identified, to herself and others, as female [12].

Blos documented the importance of real body features during adolescence in his study of cryptorchism in prepubescent males. The fact of undescended testicles, especially if "aggravated by the environment" (for example, a male sibling who flaunted his "superior" genital apparatus), resulted in vague and distorted body image [13].

The phrase *if aggravated by the environment* reminds us that a single factor is rarely sufficient, in and of itself, to determine the course of sexual unfolding. The age of onset of puberty must be understood in the context of family and peers. Studies have shown that, among girls, to be the very earliest in the peer group to enter puberty creates lowered peer status while to be slightly ahead generates high status. Late developers have the lowest peer status of all. It is the context of physical events which determines their meanings for the individual.

MENSTRUATION. The onset of menstruation is of profound significance in the life of a girl. So much has been written on the subject that we see no need to review its multiple implications. We would like to focus on three aspects of menstruation: the first period, irregularity of periods, and the use of tampons.

The first period is special in many ways. As the single most significant bodily change signalling transition from girl toward woman, it is a time of strong feelings (whether positive, negative, or mixed). The way in which it is experienced can have important ramifications for the process of sexual unfolding. If a girl's family and peers take a positive attitude toward the onset of menstruation it will help the girl to integrate the experience. Unfortunately, the biology of menarche is not always an ally in this regard. It is not often mentioned, but the first period is often heavy and prolonged, and contains clots and brownish-black discharge; it is very unaesthetic. This is because for the majority of girls, the first period is anovulatory and these are some of the hallmarks of an anovulatory cycle. The girl's idea of a menstrual period is not likely to include these realities and many are shocked. She may have been looking forward to menstruation—but not to this mess. If the girl's prevailing emotions were negative, she will be confirmed in her anger about having to grow up and cope with such unpleasantness or about having to bear this female "curse." In this enlightened age, when menstruation is supposed to be "normal and natural," heavy bleeding or pain can be seen as abnormal. There is a need to present a realistic picture of the kind of experience menstruation can be. Even those whose menses are normally regular may feel that their pattern is abnormal because it doesn't fit the textbook description of menses, i.e., a 28-day cycle. We have heard a great many students verbalize their worry about future fertility and/or degree of "femininity" when they have felt their menses to be abnormal. When periods have been absent altogether and hormonal regulation is part of the medical history, the feelings are intensified, and several women have used very strong words to express these feelings, such as "I thought I was a real freak—no breasts, no periods." Here again, the menses serve as a major outward sign of normality and gender identity and reinforce future sex-role expectations. As with breasts, the absence of this body confirmation may have a major effect on self-image.

In this day and age, in the United States and much of Europe at least, the vast majority of females use an internal menstrual absorbent or tampon. Thus, with menarche or soon thereafter, most teenage girls have their very first experience with something entering and leaving their vaginal space. In our clinical practice we have come to appreciate the importance of this experience in sexual unfolding. When there are no problems with inserting or removing a tampon, the girl learns some important lessons about her body. She gains a much greater clarity about her own vagina which, until then, was almost certainly represented in her mind in the vaguest way. She learns the location of the opening, some sense of vaginal size, distensibility, sensitivity or lack thereof, and ease of object penetration. She has a special kind of permission to touch and explore and even to look at her own genitals because she is doing it for a purpose. Many girls see their own genitals in a mirror for the first time when they are trying to learn to insert a tampon. It can be speculated that dealing with the realities of menstrual flow helps females to become desensitized to many aspects of body function such as unpleasant odors and messiness and with the idea of body-boundary penetration.

When tampon insertion is unusually difficult or impossible or when it is associated with pain the girl will miss out on most of the opportunities for positive learning and will, at the same time, incorporate negative ideas about her vagina. Girls who try repeatedly to insert a tampon, but continue to fail (often in spite of very determined efforts and the assistance of an older sister or a friend), tend to believe that they are not constructed normally. At pubarche (the time at which the earliest pubertal changes begin), the vagina and uterus are small structures, not very changed from their size in a small girl. By the time of menarche, enlargement has begun but the vagina is still smaller than it will eventually be at the end of the teenage years. If a girl tries to insert a tampon in the first year or so of her periods she may have difficulty or it may be impossible because of the smallness of the vagina. Even at a later time there may be so much apprehension and tension associated with the attempts at insertion that, in addition to ordinary difficulties such as correct angling, the girl's pubo-coccygeus muscles may involuntarily tighten, making the vaginal opening too small for the tampon to enter. This is an early experience of vaginismus in response to "threat" of penetration. In the histories taken from women with the problem of vaginismus, this kind of difficulty with a tampon is frequently elicited.

Sometimes a girl will be able to insert her first tampon with relative ease but when she tries to remove it, it seems to be stuck. In pulling more strenuously the tampon comes out but she experiences very sharp pain and local bleeding. This is caused by a strand of epithelial tissue which bisects the vaginal opening in approximately 4½ percent of adolescent females (see Chapter 8 for full discussion). A tampon may go in easily enough to one side of the strand but tends to push against it with attempted removal. Here the important factor is the early association between an object in the vagina and severe pain. Although it is usually only a single incident, it often has a lasting effect, perhaps because it is in the context of a new experience.

Throughout this book we will be referring to experiences which make a female fearful of vaginal penetration. Negative experience with tampons is one example. We have found that vaginismus (involuntary spasm of the muscles at the vaginal opening) is a vastly more common occurrence than was previously believed. We are referring here to a degree of vaginismus that does not usually make intercourse impossible but does make entry painful and difficult. In our thinking about the fear of penetration we assume a degree of penetration-anxiety in all females from childhood on. Without this assumption it would be very difficult to explain the female's extreme sensitivity to life-experiences associating pain or difficulty and vaginal penetration. The psychoanalytic literature supports the notion that little girls do fear (as well as desire) penetration. An alternative hypothesis would be that all humans are "instinctively" afraid of body-penetration of any sort. In support of this hypothesis is Seymour Fisher's* finding that men are more upset than women by a penetration of their body boundary (e.g., by surgery). Fisher postulates that women are gradually acclimated to body penetration through experiences such as menstruation, sexual intercourse, and the delivery of a baby [14]. To date there is not enough data to make any definitive statement about the meaning of vaginal penetration to females throughout their life cycle.

PELVIC EXAMINATION. Another aspect of life experience for the young female today is the pelvic examination. This may or may

---

* Professor of Psychology at Upstate Medical Center-State University of New York, Syracuse.

not have a significant impact on the evolving body-image. Case histories have taught us that a negative event associated with pelvic examination during adolescence can seriously affect a young woman's ideas about her body, especially her genitals. If the examination is difficult or painful and this is ignored, or the doctor comments negatively, then the patient usually comes away feeling there is something wrong with her anatomically or psychologically. On the other hand, a pelvic examination can be a very important growth promoting experience, particularly if the patient is taught about her own genital anatomy and has the opportunity to see her own vagina and cervix. In our experience with approximately 1,200 female patients this has proved to be a very significant moment. They are sometimes moved to tears (of joy or relief, not pain) and almost all express strongly positive feelings. Many are surprised by what they see. This supports the idea that many females have vague and/or distorted ideas about their internal genitalia. The vagina is often referred to as a hole and a hole is nothing. Seeing the reality of the vagina—its actual size, shape, texture, and color, can provide an instantaneous corrective (although, for some, viewing reality probably does not change the underlying psychic "reality").

MASTURBATION. A great many females consciously masturbate for the first time during adolescence. The Women's Liberation Movement has actively encouraged women to masturbate. In *Our Bodies Ourselves*, the women authors stress the role of self-stimulation in learning about one's own body. "Masturbation is not something to do just when you don't have a partner. It is the first and easiest way to experiment with your body. The more you know about your body, the easier it is to show someone else what gives you pleasure. . . . Loving ourselves doesn't just mean our clitoris and breasts. We are learning to love all parts of our bodies" [15].

To our knowledge, there are no studies of the effect of masturbation on body-image or self-esteem. This would certainly be a fruitful line of research. Most masturbation does involve touching of the genitals and some learning about one's anatomy, physiology, and sex responses inevitably takes place. For those women who include vaginal penetration with fingers or an object, masturbation will also provide some practical as well as affective lessons about penetration.

It is the affective and pleasurable aspects of masturbation that are most crucial. In terms of learning theory, sex is a primary reinforcer and the sexual pleasure experienced during masturbation is a very powerful influence. It can potentially transform negative feelings about the genitals into positive. "I only put my fingers in 'there' or near 'there' when I had to—to put in a tampon or my diaphragm. Then I'd run to the sink and wash myself, quick! That's how I felt for many years. So the thought never entered my head that masturbation could be something that was positive or nice" [16].

To some extent, the role of masturbation in any individual case will be influenced by factors outside of the body-pleasure itself. Where masturbation is fraught with guilt, anxiety, or fear of self-injury, the person's reaction to masturbation is enormously complicated. It may be that no one is ever totally conflict-free about masturbation (although we suspect that the emphasis on the inevitability of conflict may be just another hold-over of our cultural anxiety about masturbation). In a female who is relatively free of conflict, self-stimulation provides an excellent gestalt for positive learning about the feel of her genitals, the odor of vaginal secretions, and the myriad, subtle bodily changes involved in sex response. The female who has never had an orgasm can also experience this highly mythologized happening and learn either that it is much less frightening and cataclysmic than she feared or much less earth-moving, star-bursting, and psychedelic than she dreamed.

It would seem logical that such learning about one's genitals and sexual responses would be very beneficial for sexual response. Kinsey's statistics supported such a hypothesis [17]. He found that among those females who had never masturbated or whose masturbation had not led to orgasm, between 31 and 37 percent had failed to reach orgasm in coitus during the first year and, in most cases, during the first five years of marriage. Those who had masturbated to orgasm failed to reach orgasm in coitus in only 13 to 16 percent of cases.

Barbach's recent work in teaching nonorgasmic women to masturbate [18] has shown that, for these women at least, there is not a simple one-to-one relationship between the ability to masturbate and the ability to respond to orgasm with a partner. But this should not be our only criterion of the "value" of masturbation. As we move towards a view of masturbation as not better or worse than other forms of sexual expression but simply different, we will be in a better position to look at the meaning of masturbation to the individual—the whys and wherefores, the plusses and minuses. At this stage there is only a clinical impression. For what it is worth, our impression is that, for the young women we see as patients, masturbation is a positive, growth-promoting act which often increases comfort with the body, fuses sexually pleasurable sensations with fantasy content (where there is fantasy), and affirms the idea that female sexual response is normal, natural and intensely pleasurable. This, however, does contrast with Kinsey's finding that half of the women who had masturbated had some "psychologic disturbance over their experience. . . . There is no other type of sexual activity which has worried so many women" [19].

Male

GROWTH AND DEVELOPMENT. In boys, the bodily changes of puberty occur over a wider span of time than in girls and there are very marked differences in maturation from one boy to another. Boys are thus very vulnerable to comparisons between themselves and other boys and a large percentage feel that they are atypical. They worry about the myriad outer signs of change—height, pubic and underarm and chest hair, beard, voice, erections. Boys who are small and seem to be behind the others in maturation may take this in as part of their self-concept. "My voice didn't change until I was 15½; it was just one more indication of how different I was." Little did he realize how normal he was for as Kinsey indicates, "at age 15, about 50% of boys have changed their voices while another 50% are in the process of changing or have not yet begun to change" [20]. One half or more of boys aged 12 to 14 develop breast changes which can be a source of embarrassment and anxiety about their masculinity. The derogatory remarks of peers and siblings who see their breasts further reinforce these boys' sense of being less developed than a man should be. This theme of being behind, not measuring up, being different, is so common in the histories of men with sexual dysfunction—almost universal—that it is obviously of great importance.

Those boys who are early maturers have their own problems. The boy who is shaving and having wet dreams at age 10, while his peers don't even have pubic hair feels very out of step—a boy in a man's body. Ejaculation may take him very much by surprise because he has not yet heard about it from peers or had any sex education. It is parallel to the nine-year-old girl who suddenly gets her first period and is completely unprepared for it.

Boys, on average, mature later than girls [21]. Between 10 and 13 the girls are more developed, larger, stronger, and better co-ordinated. Many of the girls have breasts and have been menstruating for a year or two when most boys are just beginning puberty. As Tanner has reported, in the fifth and sixth grades ages (10, 11, 12), the girls' hands and feet have grown and their over-all muscle mass has already begun to increase. A boy who shakes hands with a girl in his class is likely to find a bigger and stronger hand than his.

ERECTION. Erections do not begin in adolescence. There is some indication that male fetuses erect in utero. Boys are frequently born with an erection. In the early months of his life he has erections on and off every eighty to ninety minutes and then this automatic, periodic erection continues throughout his life as part of the sleep cycle. By the end of the first year of life, almost every baby boy has found his penis with his hands and felt it erect [22]. Little boys have erections when awake, at random moments, and touch their erect penises. The erect as well as the nonerect penis becomes part of the boy's body image. At first, the response is not felt as "sexual" but as something less defined.

The record suggests that the physiologic mechanism of any emotional response (anger, fright, pain, etc.) may be the basic mechanism of sexual response. Originally the pre-adolescent boy erects indiscriminately to the whole array of emotional situations, whether they be sexual or non-sexual in nature. By his late teens the male has been so conditioned that he rarely responds to anything except a direct physical stimulation of genitalia, or to psychic situations that are specifically sexual. In the still older male even physical stimulation is rarely effective unless accompanied by such a psychologic atmosphere. The picture is that of the psychosexual emerging from a much more generalized and basic physiologic capacity which becomes sexual, as an adult knows it, through experience and conditioning [23].

As this body experience becomes more focused on "sexual" things it also takes on more of the meanings attributed to sex by the culture. After puberty, erection is more likely to cause embarrassment or to bring erotic implications into an ordinary scene. One student recalled that his family had always skinny-dipped together. He thought he might have had erections at these times when he was younger but never noticed it. By about age 12, however, he started to become acutely conscious of his erections as "sexual" and began to worry that he was being turned on by his own mother.

Erections can happen at any time—in front of the class, at a dance, in the shower with other boys. At such times, a boy may feel anything but pleasure or pride in his response. Instead, he may feel confused or embarrassed or even humiliated. A 15-year-old at the beach with a group of friends suddenly realized the others were staring at him. The bulge in his bathing suit revealed the erection that he hadn't been aware of having. Embarrassed, he dove for the sand and hid his front only to find when he turned over that the seepage from his penis had wet the bathing suit and the sand stuck to it. "I was mortified," he recalled when he described the scene to us. A mixture of positive and negative feelings about sexual response is even more apparent in an adolescent's experience of ejaculation.

EJACULATION. Kinsey felt that a boy's first ejaculation was the single most important happening in his sexual development—a landmark fraught with meanings and implications [24]. It is unforgettable for most males (the way first menses is for females; it is *the* turning point). In taking sex histories from about 500 men we have been impressed by the precise, detailed recall in all but a few cases. Interestingly, when a male first says he cannot recall, he usually "suddenly" remembers at some later time and then it is obvious that his experience was—as you would guess— y important but painful or filled with strong conflict.

First ejaculation happens to boys in these ways: Two-thirds, in masturbation; one-eighth, in wet dreams; one-eighth, in intercourse; one-twentieth, in homosexual contact; the remainder, in petting, animal contact, and spontaneous ejaculation [25].

There is a further Kinsey finding about first ejaculation which is particularly relevant from the standpoint of working with college students. He found that the highest incidence of first ejaculation in wet dreams was in boys who went on to college, while the highest incidence in masturbation was in boys who leave school between the ninth and twelfth grades. Those who most often have their first ejaculation in intercourse (one-eighth of the total) were among the boys who had less than an eighth grade education [25]. Although times have changed, we continue to find these contrasting patterns when we compare our college student sex histories with those of working class men and high school students. As a group, those who go on to higher education start their sexual experiences at a later age and have less coital experience in adolescence than other boys. This does reinforce the feeling of the men we see that they need to catch up to other men sexually. The difference also fits the notion of good boys and bad boys, i.e. those who do and those who don't act out their sexual feelings.

The way in which ejaculation happens the first time is important, as are the feelings surrounding the experience. There is not always pleasure and, when there is, it is never unmixed. If the first ejaculation is in sleep there can be confusion as to what has happened. Some boys fear they wet the bed. Others are nervous about discovery, the messiness or odor, the "yukky" feeling of the ejaculate, or the sense of having done something dirty.

If they realize what it is that took place, they may also feel a sense of pride, glad that they are normal and can do what males should do. One sophomore who had only recently had his first ejaculation in a wet dream was enormously relieved. He said, "It seemed to erase all my former doubts about my being peculiar, not really manly."

If first ejaculation occurs in masturbation, the feelings can be very variable. If a friend shows a boy how to do it, homosexual feelings may surface. Even if he is not aware of homosexual feelings at the time, he may look back on this experience and wonder. The Kinsey statistics on the frequency of such adolescent same-sex encounters has been extremely helpful in alleviating unnecessary worry about the implications of these experiences.

Some boys ejaculate for the first time in a "circle-jerk," where boys group themselves in a circle and see who can ejaculate first or farthest or aim most accurately at a target. The competitive pressure and fear of losing in such scenes is very intense. Anxiety runs high. The idea of losing may cause repulsion. Pleasure is clearly subordinate to other feelings and goals. In some ways the circle-jerk could be seen as a prototype of male indoctrination about sex. Gagnon and Simon [26] have stressed that sexuality is just one more avenue through which sex role behavior is learned and this is certainly a good example of their thesis [27]. The anxiety and competitiveness present in the circle-jerk may persist throughout adolescence and, in fact, throughout a man's lifetime as an inherent part of his sexuality.

When a boy first ejaculates from masturbation in private, one might imagine that this could be a less ambivalent scene than it often is. Perhaps it can be, but there are always some mixed feelings. Some boys are frightened by the experience. The intensity of the physiologic response can be startling. "I thought I was having a heart attack." "It was like a fit I once saw in a TV program." "I thought I had done something to myself—hurt myself so that I couldn't have children." There can be guilt over doing something sinful, bad, dirty, unacceptable to God or one's parents or one's self. Knowledge of the ability to "come," to be sexual in this way, can loom large and threateningly. "Now I could get into trouble by knocking-up a girl." "Is this what sex is like?"

It is fascinating to speculate on why boys' feelings about early ejaculation experiences seem to be so universally ambivalent, while, so far as we can tell, girls are less ambivalent about orgasm in sleep or in masturbation. Boys describing their orgasm experiences before puberty (when they have the orgasmic muscle reflex but do not yet have the biological capacity to form an ejaculate) do not report the anxiety feelings we have heard in the descriptions of early ejaculatory experiences. Could the crucial difference be the fact that ejaculation involves a fluid's leaving the body? The fluid takes on a life of its own. It must be dealt with. It is tangible evidence that something has happened. The ejaculation of a bodily substance is an exchange or interaction with the environment, a body-boundary break and a loss of bodily substance. We know that for centuries there have been deeply felt myths about the value of seminal fluid and the harm one could suffer from its loss. Aristotle believed it contained brain matter! The ejaculate is projectile, like a missile, and can easily be associated in fantasy with an aggressive act. So many different feelings can so easily attach to this 3.6 cc of fluid!

The experience of ejaculation makes a very deep emotional impression. As we will discuss later, in the section on ejaculatory problems, this few seconds of sexual response often becomes *the* fact of sex—what it's all about. The early experiences of ejaculation have an importance out of proportion to other experiences. They are writ large in the psyche. The emotions which accompany the earliest experiences can become a very persistent feature, for good or ill. It is a time of critical learning. So many students who have a problem can recall early feelings and conflict but they usually feel "That's kid stuff" and are surprised to learn that the feelings are still with them, less obvious, less conscious, but still there. Perhaps one reason for this continuity is the continuous nature of ejaculatory experience once it has begun. Rarely is there any significant break in time between first ejaculation and the subsequent establishing of a regular pattern of outlet. Kinsey found that less than 1% of males record a lapse of a year or more between their first experience and the development of regular sexual activity. We have frequently seen the techniques and the associated feelings of the first ejaculatory experience become self-perpetuating.

Masters and Johnson have highlighted the importance of early sexual experiences in conditioning a dysfunctional pattern of response. It behooves a boy or young man to start out in the right way, or at least not in some style which he will later regret. This information should certainly be part of sex education for boys.

In masturbation a boy can learn to ejaculate without erection and from minimal stimulation. We have seen such a technique lead to severe premature ejaculation. We have seen six men who had always masturbated by lying on their abdomen and rubbing against the bed sheets. In each case the men, as pubescent boys, had shared their room with a sibling or adult relative (grandparent, uncle) and had specifically developed a pattern to hide their response. To be seen with an erection would have been embarrassing or led to scolding or punishment. In their early sexual relating with women, they had ejaculated with clothes on, without an erection, and from minimal erotic stimulation.

Through masturbation a boy can also condition himself to have trouble reaching ejaculation (see section on "Ejaculatory Inhibition" in Chapter 7). If he always or usually stimulates himself to a point short of orgasm, he may not be able to reverse this pattern when he wants to.

SEX RESPONSE AND SELF-CONTROL. Both erection and ejaculation (which, by the way, a surprising number of men do not psychologically differentiate as separate entities) challenge the adolescent boy's self-control. We have already mentioned the embarrassment of random erections. There are other ways in which the genitals may seem to take over. Adolescent males often have the humiliating experience of coming in their pants while making out or even just talking to a girl! In spite of a more liberal view of masturbation, many boys still struggle to stop but they rarely win the struggle. They may also struggle against "getting carried away" with a girl—another struggle many lose. A few find themselves behaving roughly, forcing themselves on a girl who is protesting and later feeling terribly guilty. There can be attempted or consummated incest.

For most adolescent males, then, the genitals may be seen as an unruly, runaway creature that must be tamed. A number of black students have been eloquent on the dangers of "giving in" to the body because this would undermine their attention to school work. As we have said, college students, as a group, do "indulge" in sex less and at a later age than those who do not go on to college [28]. They approach life in general and even sex through the intellect. It is a question of mind over matter, head versus body. The figure drawings of students so often reflect the hypertrophy of intellect and lack of body awareness.

BODY VULNERABILITY. We have emphasized the girl's vulnerability to experiences of pain in or anxiety about her genital region (and breasts). Boys too are extremely vulnerable to any injury, illness, surgery, deformity, or perceived peculiarity of their genitals. Probably the most pervasive worry about the penis itself is its small size. Dr. Rubin author of *Everything You Always Wanted to Know About Sex but Were Afraid to Ask* gave a witty description of boys' endless preoccupation with penis size, in the locker room, at the urinal, in the pool—any place they can get a peek and compare. Masters and Johnson showed that flaccid size does not correlate directly with erection size. The man with a smaller flaccid penis will erect more. Erection is the great equalizer. This hasn't stopped boys and men from worrying. One group, in particular, tends to worry about small penis size—the obese boys, because the abdominal fat pad overhangs and partly obscures the penis. They need special reassurance.

Blos has shown that boys with undescended testicles have a great deal of anxiety about it. It can result in ". . . a distorted, vague and incomplete body image which in turn exerts a pathogenic influence on ego development" [29].

Both circumcision and repeated urethral catheterization can have repercussions in a boy's feelings about his genitals. He may consciously feel injured and impaired (an echo of earlier castration anxiety, if one thinks of it in Freudian terms) or he may repress his anxiety and refuse to focus much attention on his penis. Even seemingly minor injuries to the penis or scrotum can stir marked anxiety. One very anxious student had been kicked in a football game and his penis "skinned."

Ignorance about normal genital anatomy causes many boys (and men) to worry about their penis and testicles. Just because male genitalia are "out-front" does not mean they are carefully inspected or understood. Students have been confused and anxious about a remarkably long list of anatomical features. They may worry that the epididymus is a testicular tumor; that the plugged up hair follicles (which form white- or blackheads) are a disease; that their penis is peculiar because it is circumcised and in their peer group everyone is uncircumcised, or vice-versa; they may think the tortuous veins are peculiar or the pigmentation odd; they may worry about the line which runs up the under side of the penis (one young man thought it was the scar from an operation performed when he was an infant and that he had been born with female genitals). These are usually low-level anxieties but they can serve as lightning rods for other kinds of anxieties. These worries also make many boys and young men reticent about being naked, lest someone notice their peculiarity and confirm their worst suspicions.

One aspect of body vulnerability which we did not emphasize in writing about girls, but which is equally true for both sexes, is the way in which *any* injury, illness, or handicap may undermine sexual self-confidence. Worry about one's body in general may spread to a concern about genital function. Or, persistent anxiety about some bodily part or function can, through a kind of symbolism or analogy, become genital anxiety. One student's story is a dramatic illustration.

I've worn glasses since age five. My eyes are very bad. It's meant being poor athletically and having no self confidence as a kid. By college I had never seen a naked woman's picture. I didn't want to see. If a woman saw me I'd be destroyed. My eyes are so bad that I know I wouldn't be able to focus on a woman's body and I probably wouldn't be able to have an erection. It might have been better if I was blind. At least then I would be able to develop my other senses. This way, all the energy goes into my eyes.

Another student with a problem of severe premature ejaculation said that he had been a sickly little boy who grew out of it and became a good athlete. He felt secure in his body and proud of it. At age 13, however, he started to become clumsy, lost his athletic ability, and with it his confidence in his body. It took the doctors a long time to diagnose his problem—a mild muscle disorder which disappeared completely over the next year. Years later, however, the effects of his adolescent illness still echoed when in describing how he felt in bed with his girlfriend he said, "I have no confidence in my body. I feel clumsy."

To summarize: The sexual histories we have taken from young men and women indicate the importance of body experiences in pubescence and adolescence. The pattern of normal growth and development with its inherent differences from person to person and between the sexes, the experiences of menstruation and body penetration, of first ejaculation and subsequent sexual outlet all contribute to and not infrequently play a determining role in the subsequent course of sexual unfolding.

References

1. Meyerson, Simon (ed.), *Adolescence, The Crises of Adjustment*, London, George Allen and Unwin, Ltd., 1975, pp. 92-93.

2. Gagnon, John and Simon, William, *Sexual Conduct*, Chicago, Aldine Pub. Co., 1973.

3. Spitz, Renee, "Autoeroticism Re-Examined: The Role of Early Sexual Behavior Patterns in Personality Formation" in *The Psychoanalytic Study of the Child*, Vol. 17, 1962, pp. 238-318.

4. Harlow, Harry and Harlow, Margaret, "The Effect of Rearing Conditions on Behavior" in Money, John (ed.), *Sex Research: New Developments*, New York, Holt Rinehart and Winston, 1965.

5. Bandura, Albert, "The Story Decade: Fact or Fiction" in Rogers, Dorothy (ed.), *Issues in Adolescent Psychology*, New York, Appleton-Century-Crofts, 1969, pp. 187-197.

6. Gagnon and Simon, [2], p. 16.

7. Greenacre, Phyllis, *Trauma, Growth and Personality*, New York, W. W. Norton and Co., Inc., 1952.

8. Blos, Peter, *On Adolescence*, New York, Free Press, 1962, p. 86.

9. Schildkrout, Mollie S., Shenker, I. Ronald and Sonnenblick, Marsha, *Human Figure Drawing in Adolescence*, New York, Brunner-Mazel, 1972, p. 7.

10. Fisher, Seymour and Cleveland, Sidney, E., *Body Image and Personality*, New York, Dover Publications, 1968, p. 24.

11. Morris, Desmond, *The Naked Ape*, Dell Publishing Co., 1967, p. 70.

12. Brown, Judith K., "Female Initiation Rites: A Review of the Current Literature" in Rogers, Dorothy (ed.) *Issues in Adolescent Psychology*, New York, Appleton-Century-Crofts, 1969, p. 79.

13. Blos, [8], pp. 195-196.

14. Fisher, Seymour, *The Female Orgasm*, Basic Books, New York, 1973, p. 55.

15. *Our Bodies Ourselves. The Boston Women's Collective Health Book*, New York, Simon and Schuster, 1971, p. 31.

16. [15], p. 31.

17. Kinsey, Alfred C., et al., *Sexual Behavior in the Human Female*, Philadelphia, W. B. Saunders, 1953, pp. 172-173.

18. Barbach, Lonnie Garfield, *For Yourself—the Fulfillment of Female Sexuality*, New York, Doubleday and Co., Inc., 1975.

19. Kinsey, [17], pp. 169-170.

20. Kinsey, Alfred C., Pomeroy, Wardell B., and Martin, Clyde E., *Sexual Behavior in the Human Male*, Philadelphia, W. B. Saunders Co., 1948, p. 184.

21. Tanner, James M. "Sequence, Tempo and Individual Variation in the Growth and Development of Boys and Girls Aged Twelve to Sixteen" in *Daedalus*, Vol. 100(4), Fall 1971, pp. 907-930.

22. Kravitz, Harvey, "Hand to Body Part Discovery in Normal In-

fants" presented at Children's Memorial Hospital, Northwestern University Medical School, Scientific Exhibit–American Academy of Pediatricians' Annual Meeting, Chicago, 1973.

23. Kinsey, [19], p. 165.
24. Kinsey, [19], p. 185.
25. Kinsey, [19], p. 190.
26. Kinsey, [19], p. 190.
27. Gagnon and Simon, [2], pp. 19-26.
28. Kinsey, [19], p. 173.
29. Blos, [8], pp. 195-196.

2

Learning in Sexual Unfolding

Perhaps the single most striking thing about the process of sexual unfolding is the amount of learning that takes place. Erikson tended to view adolescent relationships primarily as vehicles of self-discovery and self-definition. Certainly self-discovery is advanced via relationships but there is also a tremendous amount of learning about how to relate, about how to be physically close and sexual with another person, about how to be emotionally close and trusting and share important decisions. So much learning takes place that there is no way that we can possibly cover all its dimensions. We would like to focus particularly on the learning that results from the specifically sexual aspects of relationships as sexuality and intimacy unfold.

Early Dating

For American teenagers the process of learning about and experiencing sex in an interpersonal situation usually begins with a game. Games are familiar territory. Most have played sex games like "Doctor" when they were small. So "Spin-the-Bottle" and "Post-Office" are a comfortable extension of old rules and norms into new territory. For many years after this stage, boy-girl interactions, in groups or twosomes, have a gamelike quality which helps to modulate the anxiety and excitement.

There is a gradual movement away from group activity toward pairing. Most of this pair activity comes under the heading of "dating." Although the boy-phones-takes-out-pays-for-girl variety of dating has waned in recent years, teenagers still go places as a couple (or as two or more couples). A great deal has been written about the meaning of dating and its effect on psychosexual development. Recently professional authors have tended to take a negative view of dating [1-3]. They stress the competitive, exploitative nature of much adolescent dating. They decry the fact that boys use sex to obtain peer-status while girls use it as an item of barter in exchange for popularity or a class ring. The boy is expected (by both himself and his date) to play a sexually aggressive role, while she is supposed to set limits appropriate to her age, the number of previous dates with boys, peer norms in her group, parental rules and her own superego. What she might feel on that particular night is not supposed to enter into it because "getting carried away" is how girls get pregnant.

One pair of authors expressed the opinion that early dating patterns led to social poise and "coolness" which ". . . may become a means to delay, inhibit or distort the psychosexual achievement." The superficial stylized character of early dating, they feel, subverts character by stressing social manners before genuine maturity [4].

This argument misses one very important point, namely that psychosexual maturity can develop through these years precisely by way of the date. Dating interaction tends to become, very slowly, less structured, less peer-controlled, and more intimate. More one-to-one talking takes place, there is some risk of exposure, and, hopefully, some acceptance of idiocyncrasies by another.

This is not to say that American dating patterns provide the best of all possible worlds for sexual unfolding and personality growth, far from it. But the potential exists for dating to be a fairly positive learning ground. In a talk delivered to a conference on sex and religion (in St. Louis in the fall of 1971), Carlfred Broderick, Professor of Sociology now at the University of Southern California spoke of his work with teenagers in which he tried to help them understand the process of dating and thereby negotiate its treacherous waters with fewer bruises and catastrophies. He used a model borrowed from economics, teaching his students that dating was based on a barter system involving trade-offs in which the individual who cared less was at a marked advantage. He was trying to help his students to be more realistic and a bit shrewder about how they play the game. We commented at this time that he might have carried his teaching one step further. Young people should be helped to see what dating interactions are about, but they should also be exposed to the idea that there is an alternative. In other words, why not teach teenagers how they can *stop* playing at barters and instead see the opposite sex as a potential trusted friend rather than as adversary.

Sharing Private Space

Another way of viewing a "sexual" relationship is as the sharing of private space. In order to get close enough to touch, boundaries must be penetrated and barriers let down. A great deal of adolescent sexual behavior can be understood as learning how to share private space for sexual purposes. In a lifetime, most of us allow very few people to handle our bodies. Usually the list includes only parents, doctors, peers (in roughhousing or sports), lovers, and our children. There is a natural reluctance that must be overcome either to enter into another's private territory or to allow this entry. In this sense, an extended handshake can be viewed as a means for sharing private space but at a safe distance. When closeness exists, the handshake often falls away to a hug or an embrace.

The purpose of the touching and the social context do alter the permissible degree of closeness. In certain dances, for example, it is expected that male and female bodies will be in very close contact. In early dating experiences, the question of how close and how much touching tends to be a matter of convention. At age 13 or 14, in the movies, the boy knows that he will probably be allowed (or expected) to put his arm around the girl or hold her hand.

Each new sexual encounter has its gray zone, where the rules are not clear. The convention of the goodnight kiss contains some implicit permission for a prescribed amount of closeness and touching. But he might decide to go a bit further and touch her breast. How will she react if he does? Will he or she put a tongue in the other's mouth? Through negotiating hundreds of such situations, in which conventions help to lessen the anxiety, young adolescents learn how to let another person get close, enter their private space, and touch in sexual ways.

Becoming someone's partner often means a greater degree of body exposure, a frequent source of anxiety for a developing person. In more superficial relationships one can cover up, make love in the dark, or not take everything off. It is not hard to hide what one's most anxious about. Student couples today, however, sleep together, bathe together, share the toilet, etc. As a result, it is not unusual for us to hear that a student, in becoming someone's partner, has suddenly shifted from hardly ever seeing anyone naked or ever being seen naked to a scene in which nudity in each other's presence is taken for granted. Such shifts are not always easily integrated.

Learning about One's Own Body

In the earlier material on sexual unfolding we discussed some aspects of body experience and body image. Now we would like to explore the impact of heterosexual erotic interactions on a person's sense of their own body. We should not be surprised that erotic exchanges with another person can have very significant impact when we consider what happens at the beginning of life. ". . . [B]eing stroked, cuddled, and soothed by touch libidinizes the various parts of the child's body, helps to build up a healthy body image and body ego, increases its cathexis with narcissistic libido, and simultaneously promotes the development of object love . . . There is no doubt, that, at this period, the surface of the skin in its role as erotogenic zone fulfills multiple functions in the child's growth" [5].

Let us use a specific aspect of body-image which was discussed earlier—the frequent concern among adolescent girls and young women about the smallness of their breasts. Over and over again we hear females say something like "My breasts are small but my boyfriend (husband) likes them well enough so why should I complain?" If we try to imagine the experience of the adolescent girl who is worried about her breasts, we can appreciate the potential meanings, to her, of having her breasts touched, looked at, or suckled by a sexual partner. If he responds negatively or ignores her breasts, her worst fears may be confirmed. If, on the other hand, he says "Your breasts are lovely. I like them," or, which is more likely, he simply demonstrates by his actions that her breasts are a source of pleasure and excitement for him—what a powerful message he is giving. He reinforces the idea that her breasts are feminine, that they have value as a sexual-attractor and that this part of her body can be a source of pleasure to herself and someone else. Her feelings about her breasts may not be instantly transformed but here is something very powerful to work against the culturally influenced sense of inferiority.

It is interesting to see that the positive messages from a male or males has little or no influence on some females; they continue to feel upset about their "unfeminine" breasts in spite of positive responses from males. A number of young women have also stated that the self-confidence they derived from a boyfriend's valuing their small breasts was entirely undone when they saw the arousal effect, on their boyfriend, of large-breasted magazine center-folds.

We shouldn't leave out one other possible scenario in which the girl's concern about her breasts undermines her ability to relate sexually. If her discomfort and anxiety about her breasts (or any body part) are extreme she will not be able to relax and enter into the totality of the experience. Her mind may cling obsessively to the thought of her unacceptable breasts and turn the rest of the exchange into a very negative transaction.

Through repeated sexual exchanges a person also learns what feels nice, what is neutral, and what doesn't feel good or is painful. This is an important aspect of self-discovery that plays a vital role, throughout life, in facilitating sexual response.

Gagnon and Simon have been particularly perceptive, in their writing, about the significance of adolescent petting experiences. They point out that petting (and foreplay when coitus is anticipated) may serve as ". . . elements in a ritual drama that allow one or both actors to rename themselves, their partners, as well as various parts of the body in terms of the 'special' purpose" [6].

This concept helps us in thinking about one role served by the progressive initiation of the adolescent into sexual practices—the evolution of a new concept of one's own body and the body of another as having erotic significance. Cultures vary in the particular body parts and the modes of interaction which are labelled erotic (although genitals and the act of intercourse are universally defined as erotic). It is interesting to note that, in America and Europe, at least, the process of learning about the sexual meanings of one's body usually follows a cephalo-cordad (head to toe) progression that in some ways parallels the infant's journey in discovering its own body.

Competence and Mastery

Positive adolescent sexual experiences may influence personality development through increasing the sense of mastery and competence. The world of male-female sex is new, unexplored and frightening territory for the adolescent. The anxieties range on a continuum from "Will I be able to kiss properly?" or "Can I ask him to stimulate my clitoris?" to unconscious and primitive fears of injury and loss of control. Through multiple experiences, each person gradually allays *some* of these fears and anxieties. The more primitive the fear, the more it persists, even in the face of experience to the contrary.

One major area of mastery is becoming familiar with the body and sexual responses of the other sex. The female has usually not seen or touched an erect penis until the first time in a petting situation. Those who have previously seen an erect penis have often done so in an anxiety-provoking context—a brother's penis where incestuous desires and taboos pervaded the scene or the penis of an exhibitionist. Many young women have to overcome revulsion or fear of the penis. Some never get past these feelings. The girl or young woman also must contend with the lubricating fluid that comes from the penile urethra and with ejaculation. Here she will be influenced by her feelings about body fluids and odors in general and by her attitudes toward males and sex. Through repeated associations of a penis with giving and receiving pleasure the female moves toward positive, or at least neutral feelings about the penis. It is probably helpful if she has had this opportunity before she has intercourse.

The boy or young man has similar problems in becoming comfortable with the female body. He is usually ignorant about female genital anatomy and the processes of her sexual response. Myths about "wetness" usually lead to a search for this reassuring sign of female response, but its absence or presence is usually interpreted wrongly—as a sign of "frigidity" on the one hand or readiness for immediate intercourse on the other. Many young men (close to 50 percent of college men we questioned) are confused about the location of the hymen and many aren't at all clear where the vagina itself is located.

Both the male and female must learn to master anxieties about how their own bodies will respond in a sexual encounter. Masturbation can be helpful, but there is still the unknown territory of sex response in the presence of another and in response to another. There is the fear of loss of control. Young men often fear involuntary ejaculation—either coming in their pants, which would be embarrassing or, in intercourse, ejaculating prematurely, which would be humiliating. The female fears loss of control because an out-of-control sexual passion has not been part of our culture's definition of proper female behavior and because she might then lose control over the situation and be "taken advantage of." Beyond this, there is the fear of looking or acting in a way that appears ridiculous, unseemly, vulgar, or ugly. In anticipation of having an orgasm in the presence of another person, either sex may fear complete loss of self, loss of control over the body and its sphincters, loss of consciousness and reality contact. This fear is often greater in those young persons who have not previously experienced orgasm in masturbation. In a situation in which a male or female is unable to let go and experience orgasm with a partner, masturbation to orgasm may help to relieve some of the underlying anxieties.*

There are differences between the sexes in the meanings of sexual mastery and competence. For the male, the emphasis tends to be on satisfying the female and the focus is therefore on technique in petting and on technique plus "staying power" in intercourse. The female's sense of sexual competence is less a matter of technique than an ability to be arousing just by being there as a sexual partner and a sense of security in her own bodily responses. This definition of female sexual competence does seem to be changing. Young women today express more interest in and concern about their active role in providing pleasure for their partner.

The yardstick used to measure one's competence varies; In early and mid-adolescence the yardstick commonly is peers. If one's sexual experiences seem to be roughly similar to those of friends this is some reassurance. Whether a given sexual behavior is pleasing or not to one's partner may be much less important than how a friend reacts when the experience is described.

EXTERIOR: *Amherst campus—night* [7]

Jonathan and Sandy are walking down the street that leads to their dorm. Fall leaves cover the ground.

JONATHAN: And then what?

SANDY: She told me to take my hand off her breast.

JONATHAN: And then what?

SANDY: I said I didn't want to.

---

* In a personal communication John Bancroft, of Edinburgh University, has reported a case of a man in his early 20s who was unable to ejaculate during intercourse. He had never masturbated. Instructed by Dr. Bancroft to attempt masturbation, he was able to stimulate himself to a point close to orgasm but couldn't go any further. In discussing what he felt at this point he expressed a fear of losing control of himself.

JONATHAN: And then what?

SANDY: She said how could it be fun for me when she didn't like it.

JONATHAN: (Disgusted) Jesus!

SANDY: So I said, I thought you liked me.

JONATHAN: Yeah?

SANDY: And she said, I like you for other reasons.

JONATHAN: Other reasons?!

SANDY: So I told her how I really needed this.

JONATHAN: What did you tell her?

SANDY: You know—that it was my first time.

JONATHAN: Your first time what? What did you say exactly?

SANDY: I don't remember exactly—that she's the first girl I ever tried to feel up.

JONATHAN: You told her that?

SANDY: Was it a mistake?

(Jonathan shrugs.)

JONATHAN: I wouldn't.

SANDY: Then she got nicer to me.

JONATHAN: What do you mean, nicer?

SANDY: She put my hand on her breast.

JONATHAN: You mean you put it on and she left it.

SANDY: No, she picked it up and put it on.

JONATHAN: She picked up your hand like this—

(Mimes motion with his own hand.)

JONATHAN: —and put it on like this?

SANDY: That's right. So I didn't know what to think.

(Jonathan leers.)

JONATHAN: You didn't, huh?

SANDY: I mean from just wanting to be friends, she's suddenly getting pretty aggressive.

JONATHAN: And then what?

SANDY: I asked her if she was a virgin.

JONATHAN: (Laughs) You're kidding!

SANDY: Was that a mistake?

(Jonathan shrugs.)

SANDY: Anyhow, she is.

JONATHAN: *She* says. So now you got what? One hand, or two hands, on her tits?

SANDY: By this time she's put the other hand on her other one.

JONATHAN: She put *both* hands on?

(Sandy nods.)

JONATHAN: Two hands?

(Sandy nods.)

SANDY: So I said, what are you gonna do with *your* hands?

JONATHAN: (Laughs) You didn't say that.

SANDY: (Pleased) It just came out!

JONATHAN: Then what?

SANDY: She . . . let me see if I got this right—yeah—she unzipped my fly.

JONATHAN: Bullshit artist!

(He slaps his hands together.)

JONATHAN: And then what?

(A spreading grin from Sandy.)

JONATHAN: *Then what?!*

SANDY: She did it.

JONATHAN: Did *what?*

(Sandy makes a hand motion indicating masturbation.)

JONATHAN: Bullshit artist!

(Sandy shakes his head, grinning.)

JONATHAN: She really did *that?*

(Sandy is virtually jumping up and down in excitement. He and Jonathan begin to giggle. The giggle explodes into a roar.)

JONATHAN: She did *that?!*

Although this play was written in 1970 by an author who probably went through college in the 1940s, the theme of male-male competition in sexual prowess and experience is as alive today as ever. There may be a strong homosexual determinant in much of this verbal intimacy (as Feiffer suggests there is between Sandy and Jonathan). Be that as it may, the sense of competition is all-pervasive. Ironically, almost no one ever feels that he has won this competition. So many young males seem to think that they are the loser—the one with less experience, more anxieties, more failures, and more inept, unsmooth behavior than all the other males around. Even the self-styled "stud" has these concerns, feeling that his experiences were something of a sham, because *he* knows that his partners weren't always satisfied or his penis is too small or he struck out with all the "really" sexy girls—or whatever is the most vulnerable point in his sexual self-confidence.

In the 1950s a college woman kept one eye over her shoulder to be sure she wasn't too far ahead of her friends' sexual experiences. Today many college women are worried about living up to the orgasmic potential they hear other young women talk about. False ideas about what constitutes "normal" female response can destroy what would otherwise be positive sexual learning for a young woman. When an orgasm is experienced less as pleasure than as a disappointment because it is not happening during intercourse or because it is not one of a series of multiple orgasms, a variety of negative learning may take place. The young woman may devalue sex, her partner, male-female relationships in general and/or her self-esteem may suffer.

The Womens Liberation Movement has been extremely helpful in lessening the pressures women feel to live up to a particular, idealized concept of female sexual response. Helping to debunk the myth of the clitoral and vaginal orgasms was a major step—just one part of an overall philosophy which stresses how unique and individual sexual response is. This attitude helps many (young) women to accept their own reactions and sexual idiosyncrasies. Apparently this sisterly support extends beyond the usual institutionalized forms of consciousness-raising groups or a book like *Our Bodies, Ourselves* to a new form of communication through public toilet grafitti. The toilet wall in one campus library contains an initial statement of distress—"I can't seem to come during intercourse" and a series of responses in different handwriting from other women all giving support and advice—none of it competitive!

By late adolescence the yardstick for competence usually shifts in the direction of concern about pleasing one's sexual partner because this is culturally valued and promises to help cement a relationship that one wants to continue. There is also more genuine concern for the pleasure and well-being of the partner.

Giving and Being Given To

When a sexual experience is within one's value framework and the other person is experienced as a person rather than an object, then the sexual experience can truly be an encounter—an exchange—and has the potential to increase the individual's "capacity to unite with another." The Old Testament refers to sexual intercourse as "knowing," and when two people share touch, nakedness, body smells and fluids, and orgasm, they do know each other in a special way.

Edith Weigert has described orgasm as a unique moment:

Time and space seem to be dissolved in the instant of orgasmic encounter. The I and Thou are transparent to each other in a trusting understanding that transcends the words of a rational mastery with which we manipulate the world of I-It contingencies [8].

This description is perhaps over-idealized, but sex does have the potential to be a profound experience of closeness with another. This potential may be heightened in adolescence by the characteristic intensification of experience, particularly "love."

We are in a realm where art is superior to mere description. We do know that sexual acts involve giving and receiving. Whether the giving is active or passive, when the partner responds with pleasure and excitement there is a unique double feedback. The other's pleasure says "You affect me in a way I like. You turn me on. Thank you. You are skillful and sexy." The other line of feedback is the sexual excitement one experiences in response to the partner's increased arousal (Masters and Johnson call this "give-to-get"). Thus "giving" is very powerfully reinforced. Being given to, i.e., experiencing sexual pleasure because of another can also have profound implications. Being touched in ways that please and excite is one of the most basic human needs and, because of infant experiences, is intimately bound up with attachment, warmth, tenderness and love.

Sexual Negotiation

Being sexual partners makes certain demands on a twosome, and the way in which the couple work out the many aspects of their sexual relationship will be crucial to the development of their entire relationship. To begin with, they must negotiate questions of how "far" to go. Although there are some couples whose relationship begins with falling into bed almost immediately, most go through stages of getting to know one another and become sexually involved with some gradation of experience.

Among the student couples who have their first intercourse experience during the college years, there is a great range in the length of time they "date" before having intercourse. We, and others, have noted a trend toward students sleeping together for weeks or perhaps months before deciding to have intercourse. The decision-making process itself can be very important, reflecting the individual personalities and the ability of a particular twosome to negotiate, to talk about feelings and to face their sexual behavior. Across the country, the predominant pattern may be one of not making a conscious, considered decision at all, but just letting it happen. This inability or unwillingness to approach sexual matters in an adult fashion can have very serious implications and consequences, the most obvious of which is an unplanned pregnancy. But allowing oneself to stumble or be bullied into having intercourse can also damage the sexual relationship, the relationship as a whole, and the individuals involved. We very strongly advocate the use of sex education, peer group discussion, and counseling to promote an environment in which individuals (usually as a couple) can approach the question of intercourse thoughtfully, weighing the pros and cons for them. We would agree with Lester Kirkendall's statement that the basis of this decision-making* should be in favor of whatever works to increase trust, confidence, and integrity in the relationship [9].

Once a couple begin to have intercourse on any regular basis, their relationship changes. Petting to mutual orgasm is certainly an important experience between two people, but placing the penis in the vagina, although it may be "only a matter of another inch or two" is realistically and symbolically on another plane. Issues of pregnancy and contraception enter the picture. Feelings about loss of virginity, if this is the first time, may be very complex. And the

---

* In the appendix we have reprinted a set of guidelines for the individual in considering whether or not to have intercourse that was first published in our magazine column in 1973. There have been so many requests for a reprint of this list that we assume it is of some usefulness. The questions are posed for females, but except for some of the wording, they are applicable to both sexes.

sex itself changes, now that intercourse is included. It may change for the better, in the sense of increased erotic pleasure and feelings of closeness or it may change for the worse because of pain, sexual dysfunction, possible decreased responsiveness for the female who was accustomed to responding to oral or manual stimulation, or a generalized pressure to "perform."

Learning to communicate and negotiate about sex is an important developmental step in the growth of intimacy. It is the rare exception when a couple can have mutually satisfying sex immediately. There are matters of style, touch, timing, specific practices, and individual needs that take time to work out. When sex does work well and a couple can talk about their needs openly, sex becomes an important and special part of the bond between them.

It isn't easy for most people to talk about the nitty-gritty aspects of sex. To desire to preserve a valued relationship often provides the first impetus to overcome this reticence. The young woman who fakes pleasure or orgasm with other men, may decide to risk being truthful—because she trusts this man a bit more than she ever trusted a male and because she anticipates a longer term relationship in which faking might prove to be difficult or a dead-end. She may also sense (hope) that he cares enough about her not to reject her because her sexual responses are less than "perfect."

Ironically, the presence of a sexual problem is sometimes a plus. When a young couple confronts a difficulty with sex they are often shocked. They assumed that sex was easy and natural, especially if two people care for one another. If they can talk about and work through a problem, they have grown as individuals and learned an invaluable lesson in intimacy. The ability to work together on a sexual problem can be an important index of the strength of a relationship and, conversely, the inability to problem-solve often highlights important weaknesses in the relationship.

Of course, a serious and unsolved sexual problem in a young couple can be a developmental disaster, undermining many aspects of individual growth and making intimacy appear to be a dangerous venture. This is one reason why we feel so strongly that high quality counselling should be available for any young people who encounter sexual problems. The chapters on counselling will spell out the range of such problems and some approaches to counselling-therapy.

But even a "good" sexual relationship can be detrimental to the process of sexual unfolding and the movement toward intimacy if the timing and the context are wrong. On campuses today it is not unusual to see young men who are bewildered and confused about the meaning of sex in their lives and the nature of their relationships because their early sexual experiences were more or less forced upon them by a more experienced female. They may not suffer from what has been called the "new impotence"; their sexual function may be entirely adequate. But they often feel somewhat overwhelmed by their sexual experiences, a bit fearful of female sexual demands, and unsure as to the male role in a heterosexual couple. A number of these young men have decided to opt out of sex and relationships altogether for months and, in one case, for several years, as if waiting for their own development as persons and their self-confidence to move ahead before venturing again into those murky waters!

Sexual Pressures—The Need for Gradualism

In the best of all possible worlds, the life events which occur during the sexual unfolding process would always be consistent with the emotional maturity, attitudes, values and knowledge of the individual and in the context of a comfortable and empathetic relationship or relationships. For most, this would mean a very gradual experience over many years. Those who have written about the emotional life of college students in the past decade seem to be in substantial agreement on this point. Sanford wrote that "most favorable to personality development, our studies suggest, is a gradual approach to sexuality, one that is accompanied by thoughtfulness, self-discovery, and increasingly differential perceptions of other people" [10].

Richard Hettlinger quotes a study by Freedman and Lozoff who surveyed college seniors and found that those "who seemed to be going a long way in terms of personality development had a history of rather slow and gradual unfolding of sexual interests and behavior" [11].

Chickering uses a lovely passage from *Zorba the Greek* in support of unhurried gradualism:

I remember one morning when I discovered a cocoon in the bark of a tree, just as the butterfly was making a hole in its case and preparing to come out. I waited a while, but it was too long appearing and I was impatient. I bent over it and breathed on it to warm it. I warmed it as quickly as I could and the miracle began to happen before my eyes, faster than life. The case opened, the butterfly started slowly crawling out and I shall never forget my horror when I saw how its wings were folded back and crumpled; the wretched butterfly tried with its whole trembling body to unfold them. Bending over it, I tried to help it with my breath. In vain it needed to be hatched out patiently and the unfolding of the wings would be a gradual process in the sun. Now it was too late. My breath had forced the butterfly to appear all crumpled before its time. It struggled desperately and a few seconds later, died in the palm of my hand [12].

By its very nature, adolescence is a stage of psychosexual development in which self-assertion is difficult, if not impossible, because there is not yet a firm idea of who the self is. Parental and traditional values and attitudes are often dismissed wholesale, although they continue to exert a powerful emotional pull. There is often a kind of vacuum that makes a young person very vulnerable to outside influences. Blos suggests that the danger lies less in the sexual experience itself than in a tendency toward precocious standardized behavior, which is not determined by inner drive but by the need to conform with peer standards [13]. Blos feels that this is particularly true of American young people today.*

The tendency of students toward peer conformity in sexual behavior has been borne out in a study of Teevan at 12 American colleges [14]. The best predictor of a student's sexual attitudes

---

* The psychoanalytic explanation of the need for gradual and sequential sexual unfolding is based upon the idea that personality differentiation is the process by which identity is formed and a premature closure or fixity will interfere with progressive differentiation.

and behavior was found to be the student's perception of the sexual permissiveness of other students (age-mates).

The sexual revolution has ushered in a period in which the average adolescent is subjected to unprecedented pressures to have sexual experience of all kinds. What is particularly new is the extent of this pressure upon young women. Locker-room talk and sexual bragging among males has been with us for a long time, but we will need to find some other term for it because females are doing it almost as much but not usually in a locker room. (Interestingly, there is a trend away from the locker-room talk among college-age males). We are continually seeing instances in which an adolescent girl or young woman has had sexual experiences which, in terms of her readiness and emotional development, were way beyond her depths. Very often the young woman has no understanding of her own motivation, she only knows that something has gone wrong. In the case of Fran, who came to the Sex Counseling Service in her junior year, what had gone wrong was her ability to have intercourse. She had developed fairly severe vaginismus.

Fran described her problem as chiefly pain and difficulty when her boyfriend inserted his penis in her vagina. They had begun to have intercourse the previous spring and continued again in the fall, but this problem had always been present and Fran hadn't really enjoyed their sexual relationship. She had never experienced an orgasm with him although she was orgasmic during masturbation. During intercourse itself she was always very passive. When asked why she persisted with intercourse in spite of pain, she said she felt too guilty to stop.

The story of how and why Fran had begun having intercourse shed light on why she was having trouble. During her sophomore year she had been involved in a consciousness-raising group made up of eight college women. This had an important effect on her ideas about many things. When asked, she recalled that she was the only virgin in the group but claimed she never felt any pressure because of this. In describing her first intercourse experience she mentioned that a funny thing happened; she became dizzy. When else in her life had she ever felt dizzy like that? A long, thoughtful pause and then she had a memory. When she was five or so, she used to swing very, very high, although it made her dizzy, because all the other five-year-olds could swing high and she had thought to herself "I *should* be able to swing like they do without feeling dizzy!"

The meaning of the story was self-evident and Fran was clearly surprised by the insight. She began to talk of her competitiveness and her need to think of herself as perfect. She now saw that she put up with the pain of intercourse because she believed she shouldn't feel it. She thought that, if she did it often enough, she would stretch or somehow magically change, and then she could have intercourse normally, the way she imagined other young women did.

It is important to realize that peer pressure can operate on a pre-conscious level and that making the effects of peer pressure a matter of conscious awareness helps young people to clarify their motivation—to assess what it is they want for themselves. Anything which increases the adolescent's sense of who he or she is as a personality, a sexual being, a body, will promote identity formation. Hopefully, by the latter stages of adolescence, the diverse elements of self-awareness will coalesce into a subjective sense of "this is me."

We must be careful not to forget that learning about who one is can sometimes grow out of an otherwise "negative" experience. Discovering what is *not* me is sometimes painful but it is probably an essential feature of identity formation and, in particular, of sexual unfolding. As with all development, there are often two steps forward and one back. A mid-western girl who attended one of the East Coast's most avant-garde colleges was propelled by peer pressures from naivete and complete lack of sexual experience into intercourse, cunnilingus and fellatio, and finally, late into her freshman year, group sex. After transferring from that school, she continued to have pain with intercourse and little or no sexual pleasure. In talking to us she said, "I've hurt myself pretty badly, but I've learned so much about what messes me up—what isn't for me—and I'm in a much better position now to say what *I* want."

Many young people whose sociosexual experiences lag behind those of their peers are in a particularly difficult situation today because, beyond a certain age (and this would vary from subgroup to subgroup), it is very difficult to find the opportunity for a gradual process of sexual learning. An all-or-nothing ethos seems to prevail. If a junior in college would like to have some sexual intimacy but perhaps not include intercourse or even genital petting, he or she will find this very difficult. In many instances there will be pressure to go on to intercourse from the partner even if the individual is frightened and inexperienced and would really rather take things more slowly. The male may feel under pressure from the still persistent role-stereotype which defines male sexual behavior as necessarily aggressive.

The female can bring her own pressures into the situation. One of the greatest of these is the very widely held myth of the cocktease. This is an expression known to virtually every girl and young woman with whom we have spoken and all fear the label. The term *cock-tease* has no very precise definition. It merely suggests a situation in which a female leads a male on, by way of some sexual interactions, but doesn't "carry through." Two myths about male sexuality are paired with the idea of the cock-tease. The first is the myth of male pain and suffering when he is sexually aroused without orgasm. The most common expression for his supposed agony is *blue balls*. What a graphic and horrible image! Who would ever want to be guilty of inducing such a condition? The second myth is that erection means a male is ready for intercourse, that it is a sign of advanced arousal and signals a great urgency for release of some kind—and fairly soon if he is to avoid "blue balls."

We have been impressed by the degree to which these myths influence the behavior of females, from high-school years on into marriage. We always try, in counseling and education, to dispel these myths with fact. We stress the fact that males have erections during sleep (in the REM phase) and at times during the day, without ejaculating and without discomfort. Erection is, in fact, a very early part of sexual response, occurring in a young man within 15 to 30 seconds of some arousing experience or thought. Males can experience prolonged arousal and erection without any discomfort whatever. *Some* males, particularly adolescents, may sometimes experience testicular aching following prolonged arousal. Masturbation can relieve the aching. Knowing these facts can be helpful in eliminating some unrealistic external pressures in a sexual situation so that the decision about "how far to go" can be more a matter of personal choice appropriate to the persons and the moment.

The young man or woman who is, or feels that he or she is, much less experienced sexually than age mates, often suffers terrible pangs of anxiety in facing a real or imagined sexual situation. The fear of being awkward and displaying ignorance keeps some young people locked into their inexperienced state; they don't dare move out into a risk-taking encounter. There seems to be a socially determined "sensitive period" when it is socially easier to have certain kinds of sociosexual experiences. Beyond this time period there are so many additional obstacles that a successful process of sexual unfolding becomes more and more difficult.

The story of the following 22-year-old graduate student is an example. She had never had a long-term relationship and had very few sexual experiences—no genital petting and no intercourse.

I rarely dated in high school, which was a Catholic school. I'm not "pretty," but I feel attractive in my own way. I'm very independent and care deeply about other people and their way of life. I didn't feel I was with people who shared my outlook on life in high school. I'm sure this came across and possibly alienated people from me. I was always terribly shy—afraid of being ridiculed or embarrassed. It's not that I felt superior to most of those I went to high school with, just different. Now that I am in college, the situation is somewhat reversed—I think the friends I've made appreciate my independence and the things I believe in and I theirs. I've known a few guys in the past couple of years but always ease out of the relationship when it threatens to become a close personal one. I go back to my high school experiences because I think if I had had a "social life" then, it would not be so hard for me to relate sexually now. It's not a case of having sex with someone just for the sake, because I haven't met anyone I feel really close to until now. I usually keep my emotions to myself and because I am so shy, I guess it's the thought of trusting someone with my emotions that frightens me, and now with so much emphasis put on sex in a relationship, I worry that I will be inadequate and seem ridiculous to someone who has much more experience than I do. I realize I cannot go through my life without ever being hurt, but I want to be secure about my total self—and as of now my sexuality has not grown with the other facets of myself.

There is another situation, not uncommon today, in which a sexually inexperienced, virginal female seeks a more experienced male partner but, in this instance, she is not interested in a relationship. She wants to lose her virginity because virginity has come to symbolize, for her, a number of negative attributes. This attitude has become so prevalent among college and graduate students that a phrase has come about describing it: the "virginity-burden" syndrome.

For the female who feels she is virginal beyond the "usual" time, virgin status symbolizes a failure to be appropriately sexual—an uptightness that means she's not "normal" and not as "free" as other young women. Virginity can be a source of embarrassment with female peers and with males she dates. One 18-year-old freshman told us that she wouldn't dream of telling her roommates she was still (!) a virgin.* Others complain that males shun them because they don't want all the "complications" involved in relating to a virgin.

When the virginity-burden syndrome does force a young woman to search, rather cold-bloodedly, for someone who will sleep with her, the results are rather predictable. First intercourse is seldom glorious but, given this situation, it is often disappointing and upsetting. Even though they have approached the project quite matter-of-factly, a surprising number of young women still

---

* There is some evidence that the pressures to have sexual experience are less now, in 1978, than they were in the early 1970s. Freshman women are beginning to describe a milieu in which they feel free to choose the option that seems best for them. They are aware that, among their peers, there are virgins and those with considerable experience.

anticipated sexual pleasure and are disappointed and worried when they feel none. The follow-ups vary considerably but aren't very encouraging. As a general rule, we try to dissuade young women from this approach to ending virginity.

Males, too, feel the pressure to have sexual experience. Our statistics show that close to 70 percent of young men entering college have not had intercourse and of those who are "experienced," many have had intercourse only one to five times. Some have had a traumatic beginning—getting caught by parents while petting or a pregnancy scare—and need a year or so without sexual pressure.

At the graduate and professional student level, virginity poses an even greater problem for men. Unaware that perhaps 30 percent or 40 percent of his male classmates are in the same situation, the older student feels he is something of an odd-ball to be so inexperienced. Sometimes he feels his lack of heterosexual experience is a sign of homosexuality despite the fact there is nothing else about his feelings or experience to confirm a homosexual identity. An older student is in a bind about telling a date or a girlfriend he is a virgin. He may want to preserve an image. One man we saw, a top athlete and scholar, did not tell his girlfriend he was a virgin. She then became his fiancee and then his wife. On his wedding night he felt confused, then scared and did lose his erection. The couple was seen two years later, presenting the problem of an unconsummated marriage. Only in the course of sex therapy did the man reveal that he had not had coital experiences with anyone else.

It is important to add that the young person, male or female, whose sociosexual experiences lag considerably behind his or her peer group may fall anywhere on the continuum of psychological health—from normal to neurotic or psychotic. The lag may be largely a result of life circumstances such as frequent moves or it may reflect intrapsychic and interpersonal difficulties. The healthier individual will be able to cope with the extra problems created by living out of step with peers while the more disturbed individual will obviously have greater difficulty.

In his book about the emergence of psychosis, Bowers cites a case in which a 24-year-old, whose social and sexual experiences had been extremely limited and who was emotionally bound to her mother, becomes psychotic when an older man tries to involve her in a love relationship and wants them to have intercourse. Her diaries show an inability to deal with sex and a relationship in any way except wishful thinking—a naive and vague hope that she can have these experiences. This was, needless to say, accompanied by a great deal of guilt. "She apparently never participated in those myriad incremental steps toward adult sexuality which adolescence demands. This developmental gap which the 'affair' asked her to bridge was simply too wide" [15].

In our counseling and therapy with graduate students, junior faculty and other young adults, we have become aware of how many individuals or couples seek help with these sexual-developmental gaps. At age 23 a female graduate student who had avoided any and all sexual experiences throughout her life came to talk about getting contraception and about her fears of having intercourse. She had, much to her surprise, met a man who was caring, gentle, and patient enough to overcome her massive resistance, antimale prejudices, and fears of touching. She was thinking they might have intercourse but had many questions—very detailed and practical and many emotional. Helping people to bridge the gaps in their sexual unfolding is one of the major roles we find ourselves playing in work with the population we see. We have described this at greater length in the chapter on therapy—in particular, the case example of fifteen-visit therapy which begins on page 206.

Students and Parents

Most adolescents voice some concern over the meaning of their sexual behavior in their parents' eyes. Although more and more young people say that their parents know about and approve of their behaviour or would approve of it if they did know, the majority still believe that their sexual behavior would not meet with parental approval. Often, the student has come to some terms with this discrepancy between his or her behavior and parental expectations by viewing the parents as "from a different generation." They generally do not experience conscious guilt about having intercourse because they feel that, for them, in their current social setting and historical moment, their behavior is entirely moral. They may choose to tell their parents (or one parent) about their sexual behavior, knowing that it will not be condoned, but wanting to stand up for what they believe. In our experience this sort of confrontation of values often leads to a painful kind of interaction between parents and child rather than to mutual understanding and tolerance. The majority of students with "conservative" parents seem to sense that confrontation will not be productive and choose not to tell their parents about having intercourse.

In spite of a prevailing student ethos in which sex before marriage is entirely acceptable, many young people struggle with guilt, and the parents often symbolize and embody moral disapproval. One freshman girl was in a panic about possibly having venereal disease although she had only had intercourse with her boyfriend and was sure he had not slept with anyone else since their relationship started seven months earlier. He had just left on a long trip, and her parents had come to visit for the weekend. They didn't know about her having intercourse, and she felt a sense of strain being with them. It was after they left that she became anxious about having VD and that anxiety grew into a panic.

Families always communicate feelings, attitudes and values whether they mean to or not. Many of these messages are distorted and damaging, passing on the worst aspects of Judeo-Christian and Victorian ideas about sex from generation to generation. A girl might "learn" that men are sexually greedy, no-good creatures, that sex is a distasteful wifely duty—that sex is never to be discussed—that touch is not part of proper human relationships, and so on. Unless she is taught otherwise, by the media, other respected people in her life or her own experiences, she will continue in these beliefs and pass them on to her children. When it comes to the specific questions and dilemmas of adolescent sexual life, all the many questions of "should I? shouldn't I?," the family values are frequently very vague or there is a discrepancy between mother and father (or between the parents and the views of the church they attend).

In the majority of families no direct guidelines or beliefs are articulated. Oblique references are supposed to provide rules and regulations. When Jane mentions that her high school friend might be pregnant, her mother acts shocked and very disapproving. Jane probably concludes that mother believes that sex should wait until marriage, but oblique references often lead to an all-good or all-bad view of sexual behavior. Very little beyond what one can see on TV (a goodnight kiss, for example) is good. The only other reference category is catastrophe, or the unmentionable behavior of "bad" girls. A tremendous number of girls grow up believing that, if they once begin "messing around," they are on the slippery slope toward the "fast and loose." They are either saint or whore.

A young student couple consulted us because, since their marriage seven months earlier, the wife had not had an orgasm. She had been regularly orgasmic with genital petting for one year prior to marriage. They had intercourse several times three months before the wedding, and she did have orgasms then but they had stopped intercourse until the wedding because of her overwhelming guilt. She was not a very religious young woman but she believed she had "sinned in God's eyes." Her mother was liberal, but her father had strict views on "everything." He was hard to please and lost his temper easily. The greatest problem was his inconsistency. Once, when she lost something of value he was very forgiving, but, if she forgot something, he would usually be very angry and say "You meant to forget it." She had actively sought a standard for her own sexual behavior from her parents, her friends, and her church, but never felt she got a clear answer.

Sometimes parents themselves, their mental representations or substitute parent-figures are used in support of impulse-control in very healthy ways. The following is an example of a girl who was caught up in the syndrome of "too-much-too-soon" and used the Sex Counseling Service and her mother in support of a healthy retreat:

Janet, a college sophomore, came in for birth control. When asked, she said no, she and her boyfriend of two months had never had intercourse, but they had been sleeping in the same bed for several weeks. Was she comfortable with what they had been doing? Well, petting was nice, but she became very anxious if he wanted her to take all her clothes off, so they had evolved a pattern of petting while she had on, at very least, underpants and preferably slacks and a top. She hadn't really thought ahead to how they would manage the mechanics of intercourse given her fears of nudity. In the remainder of the interview two important facts emerged: (1) Janet felt ashamed of her body, in particular of labia she thought were unusually large and protuberant, and (2) she felt worried about what her mother, to whom she was very close, would think about her having intercourse. In bed with her boyfriend, she often found herself thinking of her mother. She spontaneously then began to speak of her own ambivalence about having intercourse now. She decided she would wait a while before getting birth control but did proceed to have her first pelvic examination (by P.S.) during which she could see her own genitalia in a mirror and her concerns about labial size could be discussed, the doctor stating (truthfully, of course) that her labia were normal. He mentioned, in passing, that there was an old wives tale about masturbation causing increased labial size but that this was completely untrue. In this way, he could reassure her about possible masturbation anxieties without necessarily having to know whether she did or did not masturbate.

The follow-up a few months later was interesting. When she was at home on vacation she had told her mother that she was "seriously considering having intercourse." Her mother's response was, "You are mature and responsible, and I trust your ability to make the right decision." Janet said, "It's funny but her saying that made it easier for me to know that I really don't want to have intercourse yet." She and her boyfriend continued petting, and Janet said she was becoming more relaxed with nakedness and with her own responses. She added, thoughtfully, "I think the underpants were partly to protect me from getting carried away and having intercourse, but I don't need that artificial barrier anymore."

We know that one of the most difficult emotional tasks of adolescence is the gradual relinquishing of the parents as primary love-objects. Blos [16] and others have written about the mourning process involved in "giving up" one's parents. Another girl in her freshman year couldn't understand why she was having recurrent nightmares about forgetting to take birth-control pills and becoming pregnant. She had had intercourse with two boys prior to her current boyfriend and had always taken pills faithfully. She had never had dreams like this before. What was new in her situation this time was the fact that she had moved away from home to come to college and that now, for the very first time, she felt she was really in love. She came from an exceptionally close-knit family, with fond and tender ties to both parents and a special big-sister, help-mate relationship with her younger brother. She couldn't bring herself to tell her family about her new and very special relationship although they had always known about previous boyfriends. She also realized that she felt guilty about writing and calling home less often because she and her boyfriend spent so much time together. It was interesting that a further detail of her recurrent dream emerged as we talked about her conflict over loving versus leaving her family. The dream often carried through to a scene in which she told her parents about being pregnant and they (as one could easily imagine they would be in real life) were forgiving, loving, and supportive.

Intimate relationships with peers help the adolescent in moving away from his or her family toward independence. The feeling that one is successful at sex-love relationships is, therefore, an important cornerstone for evolving appropriate independence. In terms of counseling or therapy with students, the theme of separating from parents is often the other side of the coin to the theme of trouble in intimate relationships.

References

1. Hettlinger, Richard, *Sex Isn't That Simple*, New York, Seabury Press, 1974.
2. Douvan, Elizabeth and Adelson, Joseph, "American Dating Patterns" in Rogers, Dorothy, (ed.) *Issues in Adolescent Psychology*, New York, Prentice-Hall, 1959, p. 386.
3. Smith, Ernest A., "The Date" in Rogers, Dorothy, (ed.) *Issues in Adolescent Psychology*, New York, Prentice-Hall, 1959, p. 378.
4. Douvan and Adelson, [2], pp. 390-391.
5. Freud, Anna, quoted in Montagu, Ashley, *Touching: The Human Significance of the Skin*, New York, Columbia University Press, 1971, pp. 163-164.
6. Gagnon, John and Simon, William, *Sexual Conduct*, Chicago, Aldine Pub. Co., 1973, p. 26.
7. Feiffer, Jules, *Carnal Knowledge*, New York, Farrar, Strauss & Giroux, 1971, pp. 20-25.
8. Weigert, Edith, *The Courage to Love*, New Haven, Yale University Press, 1970, pp. 32-33.
9. Kirkendall, Lester, *Premarital Intercourse and Interpersonal Relationships*. New York, Julian Press, 1961, quoted in Hettlinger [1], p. 115.
10. Sanford, Nevitt, *Where Colleges Fail—A Study of the Student as a Person*, San Francisco, Jossey-Bass, Inc., 1969, p. 142.
11. Hettlinger, [1], p. 89.
12. Chickering, Arthur W., *Education and Identity*, San Francisco, Jossey-Bass, 1974, p. 307.
13. Blos, Peter, *On Adolescence*, New York, Free Press, 1976, p. 118.
14. Teevan, J. Jr., "Reference Groups and Pre-Marital Sexual Behavior" in *Journal of Marriage and the Family*, Vol. 34, 1972, pp. 283-292.
15. Bowers, Malcolm B. Jr., *Retreat From Sanity*, Baltimore, Penguin Books, Inc., 1974, p. 107.
16. Blos, [13].

3

Sexual Orientation

Nowhere are the complexities of sexual unfolding more obvious than in the area of sexual object choice. Adolescents themselves tend to oversimplify the process in their own minds, putting it in terms of a label. They want to know, "Am I homo, hetero, or bi?" Until recently, the majority of professionals tended to oversimplify in the same way. If we take a closer look, we realize that the gender of the person one has sex with at any given moment in time is not a simple question; it is one bit of behavior determined by many, many variables and with many different possible outcomes or meanings.

It is also important to remember that sexual orientation is not determined *only* by behavior. Particularly in an adolescent group, there will be many whose sexuality has never or rarely been expressed except through masturbation, fantasies, and awareness of erotic and/or loving feelings for others.

Defining some sense of sexual orientation for oneself is always central to the process of sexual unfolding. Some people seem not to struggle very much; they have always felt attracted to the same sex or both sexes and there is little struggle, indecision, or anxiety about it. This pattern is certainly less common for those who feel they are homosexual or bisexual because society labels these sexual orientations as sick, sinful, and illegal. It is much more difficult, in Western society, to experience sexual unfolding in a relatively untroubled way if you are not basically heterosexual in your behavior and self-concept.

Although defining sexual orientation is not a serious problem for everyone, many adolescents do have some concern or questions about their sexual orientation. Not all can articulate or are even aware of a personal concern. The young person who is violently antihomosexual and never for one moment doubts his or her own "normality," is very often defending against such concerns. Most of the adolescent worries about "being homosexual" are transitory and go unexpressed. But a study done in the 1930s showed that, given the opportunity and a climate in which these worries can be shared, 10 percent of the men (at an all male school) who came for counseling presented concerns about homosexuality [1]. A much higher figure is given by a psychiatrist from a California campus. In the past several years, 65 percent of the students who came for counseling expressed some anxiety about being homosexual [2].

In terms of behavior alone, an estimate (derived from Kinsey data) is that 30 percent of college men ever had a homosexual contact with or without orgasm. Only 14 percent of college men had extensive homosexual experiences after age 20. The figures for women suggest that, by age 20, about 10 percent have had some homosexual experience [3].

Obviously, the concern about "being homosexual" does not need an actual experience as a precipitant. For some, the question is simply there along with questions such as : Who am I? Am I bright? Am I attractive? Can I really make it in competitive athletics, as a doctor, as a wife, or husband? Because adolescence is a time of intensely emotional introspection, self-monitoring can be a major preoccupation. One person may focus on physical strength, another on "How crazy am I?"

Internal monitoring with respect to sexual orientation seems to be fairly widespread among males but less so among females. Ovesey used the term *pseudohomosexuality* to describe this phenomenon [4]. He and others have described pseudohomosexuality almost exclusively among males. Our clinical experience corroborates this sex difference. For every female worried about "homosexual tendencies" we see 15 to 20 males.

One can easily see cultural reasons for males to focus anxiously on the question of their own sexual orientation. As early as grade school—even nursery school—boys use terms like *faggot* as an all-purpose insult. Girls don't. The children's name calling mirrors the adult world's uptightness about, and condemnation of, male homosexuality. It also reflects our culture's insistence that males conform more strictly to sex-role stereotypes; females have more leeway. It is permissible for girls to be "tomboys" but not for boys to be "sissies."

Faggot, gay, or *homo* become terms that can mean almost anything that is not "masculine." If a boy or young man doubts himself in anything which the culture defines as male, he almost automatically thinks "homosexual." It may be in the area of sports, strength, height, ability to compete, success in getting dates, competence in driving a car, daringness, beard growth, size of penis, popularity, good looks, etc., etc. Females may have doubts about their feminine adequacy but they are less likely to equate it with homosexuality. Their fear is expressed in terms of being "frigid," unattractive, too fat, having trouble holding onto a male, infertility, or being too aggressive. The fear of success, described by Matina Horner, is one way in which college women channel their concerns about being adequate as a female [5].

Another possible reason for the observed male-female difference in concern about homosexuality is the greater tendency for the adolescent male to focus on genitality. He is more likely than the female to organize his thinking around specifically genital-erotic issues. Until very recently, adolescent males were much more likely than females to have genital sexual experiences with others, experiences which would tend to focus attention on genital responses and raise the issue: with *whom* is one going to have these experiences. It will be interesting to see whether the trend toward elimination of the double standard in sexual behavior will also tend toward equalizing male and female concerns about homosexuality.

The University Environment

The environment one is in can influence behavior as well as one's self-perception, and it has long been appreciated that certain environments can influence sexual object choice. In prison or in the army, many persons who would not ordinarily have homosexual relations will do so, more or less willingly. The one-sex prep school provides an "abnormal" environment at an important moment in sexual unfolding. Gadpaille states that ". . . non-coeducational boarding schools . . . seriously impair the opportunity, and sometimes the capacity, to learn . . . heterosocial and heterosexual interests. Homosexual activity is widespread long past the time when it may be considered phase-appropriate" [6].

College and university campuses today provide their own special milieu. Students on some campuses complain that there is social pressure to experiment with homosexuality. The presence of vocal gay lib organizations can create a false sense of polarity, emphasizing the need to make a conscious, once-and-for-all choice. Occasionally, a student comes out as gay only to realize later that he or she is a "closet" straight.

The atmosphere on many campuses today seems to be an uneasy mixture of blatant hostility toward homosexuality and a newer strain of toleration and liberalism. One student felt tremendous conflict when his roommate came out. He wanted to be liberal and stay friendly with him but thought rooming with a known gay would jeopardize his own reputation.

Another student who was very politically committed to gay rights, but was not gay himself, found that he had developed close friendships with several of the gay men whose rights he was supporting. After a year or so, he began to notice that he was caught up in this sub-group, being influenced by their life style, values, and attitudes. One night, while masturbating, he had a homosexual fantasy. He felt he was becoming very confused about who he was sexually because of his involvement with the gay group on campus.

The politics of feminism, particularly in its more radical forms, has created a new phenomenon, the "political lesbian." No one knows how many young women have become committed to lesbianism in this way or what long term effects this might have. Theoretically, one would speculate that the effects would be similar to those of the one-sex boarding school; the prolonged socialization in relating emotionally and erotically to the same sex may well become the predominant life pattern.

Other aspects of campus life which are not specifically sexual can also be significant. Remember that the majority of entering college students (male and female) are virgins and approximately one fifth will probably *graduate* as virgins. The heterosexual scene can be very frightening. The pressure of school work plus the need to work part-time cause some to choose isolation. Between job and studies, it is easy to use up 18 hours of each week day and most of the weekend. The asocial and sexually inexperienced feel very out of step with their peers. It is not surprising that many, particularly (again) the males, would feel that their difference from the norm may be a sign of *homosexuality* [7].

There is evidence that the atmosphere on some campuses has actually shifted considerably in the direction of viewing homosexuality more positively, as a normal variant of human sexual expression. This can have both good and bad ramifications. For the gay students on such a campus, the college experience may provide an unrealistic idea of the ways in which society reacts to the homosexual. On the plus side (which we feel almost certainly outweighs the minus), students who feel themselves to be homosexual or bisexual will be less traumatized by virtue of their sexual orientation, at least for a few years and the less stigmatized view of homosexuality should ease the anxieties of most students about their own sexual orientation.

Sex Role Stereotypes

Men in college have a culturally determined expectation that tells them they *ought* to have a strong "sex drive." The world is still much more tolerant of a female with little or no sexual interest than of a male. Bright students often know of the findings, by Kinsey and others, which show the "peaking" of male sexuality in adolescence. A senior asked nervously, "If I didn't feel my heterosexual drives at 18 when it was at its peak, there's no hope; I must be homosexual." He had been passively awaiting the onset of these supposed "drives" while holed up in his room for four years, too scared to risk an encounter with a live female. A witty sophomore put it this way: "There's a way I should be / and if that isn't me; If I'm not that way / then I must be gay!"

The sense of being different from peers can originate in childhood, taking on sexual implications in early adolescence. Boys who have been teased for years about being short or weak or poor in sports or "scaredy-cats" are usually called "fag" or "gay" as well. Then they may internalize the label, making it part of their self-image. The boy who is worried about his body, particularly about his genitals, or who develops later than peers, may find confirmation of his worst fears in his own bodily "inadequacy." A black student, Jeffrey, came to the Sex Counseling Service asking about the "funny shape" of his penis. What seemed "funny" to him was the slight curvature which often develops (normally) as the penis erects. When he was reassured about this, his next question was, "Is there such a thing as bisexuality?"

Jeffrey had attended an almost all-white school until the sixth grade. The family moved and during grades seven through nine he went to a tough, inner-city school where 90 percent of the kids were black or Puerto Rican. He found that his speech, his way of walking and eating, everything about him was different from the kids in this new school.

To make matters worse, he was a late developer. He was small, had no body hair and his penis seemed smaller than others during locker-room comparisons. He was teased, taunted and beaten up for three years. He finally did enter puberty and found a niche for himself among the achievers in the school but he continued to doubt his body and his male adequacy. At college he had some sexual experiences short of intercourse but occasional twinges of "feeling" for male friends made him very anxious. He was always monitoring himself to see where he might fit on a continuum from heterosexual to homosexual and had finally decided he must be bisexual. Jeffrey was expending tremendous amounts of psychic energy on his self-monitoring. He, like so many others we have seen, became almost obsessive in his self-observation and constant comparisons with others.

The Heterosexual Scene

Even those young men who are actively heterosexual may feel that the extent and nature of their experience or some preference, attitude or feeling of theirs is peculiar and therefore may be a sign of homosexuality. Young men who reject certain aspects of the prevailing sexual scene such as oral sex, one-night stands, or X-rated films—even young men who just don't masturbate—feel they are less sexually normal than others and then conclude they must be homosexual.

The heterosexual world still puts the male in the role of competitor and initiator. It is still more common for a guy to take the first active step in initiating a relationship and in initiating sexual activity. Young men who are reluctant to compete in general or reluctant to compete with other males for a female may be unable to take even the beginning steps toward a male-female relationship. Something as apparently simple for others as asking a young woman to go for coffee or a drink may create tremendous anxiety if one expects failure, rejection, embarrassment or if one expects a "yes" but is terrified of having to take the further step of doing something sexual. The homosexual world offers an appealing alternative to such young men, because in a single night in a gay bar, they are likely to be propositioned several times or they may seek out the anonymous sort of contact which involves less risk of personal rejection.

The student who has enough self-confidence to seek out a woman, or who finds himself being asked, has further hurdles ahead. He may immediately begin to monitor himself for signs of sexual attraction or arousal. If he doesn't find them he may not think, "Oh, I'm not attracted to her" but rather, "What's wrong with me?" If there is a sexual happening and it doesn't go well, there is obviously a cause to worry, he thinks.

Almost every male student who has consulted with us about a sexual dysfunction has, at some point, expressed the idea that the root cause of his problem might be homosexuality. Many of these young men have never had a homosexual experience nor have they had homosexual fantasies. The presence of a sexual dysfunction threatens masculine self-confidence even if it is transitory, even if it is a single event. The inexperienced young man has little or no backlog of experiences against which to measure the significance of his "failure." And, for all the reasons we have mentioned earlier, he automatically equates sexual problems with male inadequacy with homosexuality.

Particular personality problems that interfere with male-female relationships on a long-term basis may also be interpreted by the individual as a sign of homosexuality. The male whose sexual experiences are all very short-lived, who seems unable to really care about any one woman, may finally wonder about his pattern of relating. This sort of concern does not usually surface until grad school or even later because in high school and college and on into law or medical school, screwing around can be viewed, by self and others, as very macho. At some point in time, however, the cultural expectation changes. Even the most swinging single expects and is expected to "settle down." The inability to relate intimately, to share feelings, to give and be given to, then becomes a handicap. Relating to others as sexual objects is no longer acceptable. As the rationalization for one's "macho" behavior breaks down, some young men become extremely anxious about their sexuality and then begin to wonder about the solidity of their heterosexual identity.

Homosexual Experiences

Particular erotic experiences with others of the same sex are frequently a source of anxiety about "being" homosexual. Most students seem to know and to accept emotionally that some boy-boy fooling around at age 13 or so is alright, but an occasional young man is still very troubled by his one-time experience or by what was an on-going homosexual relationship in early adolescence. Having an erection while taking a shower with a group of friends or while wrestling with a roommate can create such anxieties.

It is fascinating to see how very specific the cultural definitions can be. Each culture and subculture seems to accept certain behaviors which are clearly homosexual in content as permissible. In our society, the circle-jerk (boys masturbating in a group), is permissible, at least up to a certain age. In some cultures (e.g., some Latin American cultures) and some subcultures within the United States only the insertee is viewed as homosexual or feminine while the inserter is not viewed as homosexual [8].

Many of the students who express anxieties about homosexuality have once or twice been approached by another male. They assume that they must have given off some kind of unconscious signal or they would not have been approached. Actually, we know from talking with gay men that they usually need to approach many males before they receive a receptive response. Large numbers of men must therefore have the experience of being invited to participate in homosexual exchange and the invitation does not reflect that they are anymore "latently homosexual" than anyone else.

Homosexual Students in the Gay World

There have been between thirty and thirty-five homosexual students whom we have had an opportunity to know and help deal with sexual issues. All but four have been men. We have also learned about issues in the gay community by attending meetings of the gay alliance and through talking with other professionals and students who are gay and who know the gay community. When working with gay students who are trying to relate in this, the gay world, there are issues which are related to the processes of sexual unfolding.

Gays need to unfold sexually just as any other adolescent young adult does. "Coming out" often means immersion in a world of sexual behavior where too much happens too soon. Some young men are unable to respond to specific kinds of stimulation. They may be unable to ejaculate with oral sex or they may have tenesmus (the anal counterpart of vaginismus), when anal penetration has not been integrated into their sex-value system. What they need in order to unfold sexually, may involve a more gradual process, first becoming comfortable with holding hands or lying next to another man with clothing on. Sometimes a gay man has had essentially no experience of intimate touching with another person. Some men have never, or hardly ever, kissed or held hands or petted in any way with a man or woman. Finally, perhaps in their late teens or early 20s, when they have the courage to "come out," they feel they will be ridiculed if they draw the line in sexual touching at a good-night kiss or at caressing with clothing on. And yet, with respect to their stage of sexual unfolding, such "proceptive" behavior, as John Money puts it [9], would be appropriate. Trying to do too much too soon can lead to sexual dysfunction. Some of the men we have talked to have been impotent when trying oral sex before having experienced less intimate touching. Premature ejaculation (prior to penetration) is not uncommon with first attempts at anal penetration. There have also been four men who have had difficulty ejaculating in early homosexual encounters.

While trying to rush the unfolding process has frequently been a major factor in the development of dysfunction, ignorance of the facts of sexual function has played its role as well. Homosexual men don't understand their bodies any more or any less than heterosexuals. Unfortunately, when normal physiological events occur which are confusing, there has been a tendency for some of the young men to attribute incorrect meanings to the physiology. For example, one man did not know that there is a urethral secretion during the plateau phase. He believed it came as a result of "doing something wrong," in his case, anal intercourse. There was no infection and the secretion was normal but he needed a good deal of reassurance. Another man gave up masturbation when he found a lover. His sexual outlet dropped from almost daily ejaculation to week-end sex with his lover in which he experienced premature ejaculation, a natural consequence of imposed abstinence. When he reinitiated masturbation during the week, the problem disappeared and he was relieved to find it was not a result of his new step into homosexuality as he had feared, but rather of an established sex response pattern.

Whether one is gay, bisexual, heterosexual, or alternates behavior patterns and feelings, the basic developmental tasks of sexual unfolding are the same in one's life, issues of intimacy, commitment and fidelity, sexual function and dysfunction, the sexual style one presents to the world.

Many gay students have sought help with problems of loneliness and isolation in the gay world. The young man who is ready for and wants a one-to-one, trusting relationship with another may often find the homosexual world a difficult place in which to fulfill his need. The gay bar scene doesn't meet this need and some feel turned off by it. In that situation, they feel they are treated as sex objects. Even if they get to know another man a little bit before going to bed, it isn't enough to meet their psychological needs. Conflict over being treated as and treating another as a sex object is so often a cause of sexual dysfunction in the heterosexual world that it is not surprising to find it a factor leading to dysfunction in the homosexual world. For the young man in search of an intimate relationship, the realities of homosexual life in our culture present special problems. How long, realistically, can a couple last? When couples do form, they must deal with the outside world, with families, job opportunities, housing, etc. Although many gay couples do maintain long-term relationships, the students we see have difficulty imagining they could be so fortunate and yet it is their hope and need.

Those who choose to come out as gay or bi do face special problems relating in the gay subculture, to family and to straight friends, getting jobs, and being hassled by the law. These difficulties in the nonsexual areas of life add further complications to the process of sexual unfolding. In today's world, being gay *is* different from not being gay. It is so different that, although the fundamental human issues are the same, this entire book about sexual unfolding probably has only slight relevance to the gay experience. Someone else will have to write that book.

References

1. Arnstein, Robert L., "Homosexual Concerns of College Students" in *Sexual Behavior*, Vol. 1, No. 9, Dec. 1971, p. 26.
2. Personal communication from Sherwin Woods.
3. Gagnon, John H., *Human Sexualities*, Chicago, Scott Foresman and Co., 1977, pp. 253-254.
4. Ovesey, Lionel, *Homosexuality and Pseudohomosexuality*, New York, Science House, 1969.
5. Horner, Matina, "The Motive to Avoid Success and Changing Aspirations of College Women" in *Contemporary Issues in Adolescent Development*, John Janeway Conger (ed.), New York, Harper & Row, 1975.
6. Gadpaille, Warren, *The Cycles of Sex*, New York, Charles Scribner Sons, 1975.
7. Arnstein, Robert L., [1], p. 27.
8. Gadpaille, Warren, Unpublished manuscript for a chapter to be called "Sexual Identity Problems in Children and Adolescents, Including Intersex Conditions," pp. 36-37.
9. Money, John and Ehrhardt, Anke, A., *Man and Woman, Boy and Girl*, Baltimore and London, Johns Hopkins University Press, 1972.

4

Recreational Sex

In this chapter we will talk about the impact on sexual unfolding of campus milieu, prostitute experiences, brief sexual encounters, promiscuity, and peer pressures. We called this chapter "Recreational Sex" because this is an important theme in all the following chapters. From early childhood on, most people learn a great deal about themselves and others as sexual beings through play and recreation—from the doctor games of 5-year-olds or the favorite game of children in Oxford, England aged 7, 8 and 9 "Chase and Kiss," through college "mixers" or a group of guys going together to get laid, to adults at a swinging party.

The form taken by the recreation reflects current norms and values. The "games" can help to legitimate sexual feelings and behavior while at the same time setting limits. The form of the recreation also reflects the developmental needs of the group involved. So, for example, when adolescents "play" with and through sex, their games usually express their need for rebellion, peer conformity, their desire for spontaneity and to appear sophisticated or "cool" as well as their need to learn about and master all things sexual. Finally, the form taken by sexual recreation will reflect current sex role concepts. In the past this has meant quite different forms of recreation for males and females, but the recent trend has been toward integration. In the 1940s and 50s, college men often participated in group viewings of blue movies while very few college women even got a glimpse of anything X-rated. Today they go together to see *Deep Throat* or *The Devil in Miss*

Jones. But not everything in this chapter has become coed or uni-sex. The section on going to a prostitute is still entirely about males buying the sexual favors of females!

So many adolescent pastimes are sexy, or to say it conversely, many adolescent sexual experiences are recreational pastimes. We do not agree with Gagnon and Simon's idea that ". . . learning about sex in our society is learning about guilt" [1]. Guilt is one part of the learning—but certainly not the whole. Learning about sex also includes learning about bodies, tenderness, sensuality, giving and taking, and last but not least, learning how to play with and through one's sexuality.

Having disagreed with Gagnon and Simon's assertion, we will now reverse ourselves halfway to say that play, in our world, is not entirely guilt-free. Antihedonism runs deep in our culture. Working on this book in a rented home in Oxford, we looked up "recreation" in the house's only dictionary: "Blackie's Standard Dictionary" (no date, published in London and Glasgow sometime between the World Wars). The definition given is "Refreshment of the strength and spirits after toil." Play is only allowed *after* work and it must be earned. It can be justified, of course, since it refreshes us for the next round of work! We certainly aren't completely at ease about our times of ease.

But there is fun to be had. The parties, the experimentation, the "X" films can and do lend a zest to life. You can learn valuable lessons about yourself, your erotic responses, what is repellent or provokes anxiety, your tendency to get carried away and whether or not you like that, how you respond to sex plus pot. As one student told us

Early in my freshman year I went to a party where I had a few drinks. I wasn't used to liquor so I really felt it. There was a guy there from my college. We hardly knew each other but we ended up dancing all night. I hadn't ever felt that turned-on before. These marvellous sexy feelings were going all through me. We didn't go to bed or anything. Just danced, *very* close some of the time. In the morning I remembered the feelings: a glow, a kind of recognition that I could feel this sexiness I'd heard about—a great feeling. I wondered if I'd been too obvious and whether the others had noticed. I was afraid to see him again but when I did it was okay.

The Campus Scene

In 1970, we and some students made a short film about sex on campus. The "crew" simply walked around on a warm day in early September, filming and asking random students open-ended questions like, "What is sexuality?" Rock music blared from dozens of windows. Students were strolling, dancing, bicycling, talking in groups and twosomes, playing frisbee, tossing each other into the air on blankets, blowing bubbles, smoking pot, drinking beer. They wore jeans and t-shirts, bathing suits, jeans with bare chests, sheer Indian cotton blouses, no bras. No one was doing anything overtly sexual, not even kissing, so far as the camera could see, and yet it was a marvelously sexy scene, crackling with sexual awareness, alive with sexual play.

The students' responses to the filmmakers ran a representative gamut from one blushing young man who mockingly crossed himself before offering his opinion, to the obviously stoned girl who monologued about men playing with her toes, to the Alice-in-Wonderland, newly-arrived, who thought the men are . . . "like so many cookies in a bakery shop. I don't know which one to eat first. Bye now, I have to go call my parents."

We sometimes forget about the day-to-day, sexually charged life that students (most of us?) lead, quite apart from the "sex experiences" per se that tend to get talked about in counselling and sex education. A campus today is a sexy place. Sex, in one form or another, is happening all the time, much of it public and social. Young people have sex experiences continually at this level: jokes, innuendos and double-entendres, books, films, magazines, parties, dancing apart but with wild abandon, dancing together pelvis to pelvis, rap sessions, music, just being male or female, together and alive, flirting, having fantasies and daydreams.

It is difficult to be a college or university student anywhere in the United States today and not be part of this life. Only the most socially isolated student, living at home, might opt out of this sexual indoctrination, and then not completely. But each student will somehow integrate the mass experience into his or her own personality. Some will remain more or less on the fringes, looking at others' social-sexual experiences with envy or fear or disgust or maybe all three feelings. Others seem to plunge right in and their experience of college life will involve an advanced course in sex— a myriad of sexual experiences that will sometimes be enriching and sometimes hurtful and other times just boring and repetitive.

The Brief Encounter

Sex for the fun of it, light-hearted, noninvolving, friendly, with an emphasis on shared physical pleasure (or at least the relief of mutual horniness) rather than the "meanings" of sex between two people: many students today say they believe in it, if not for themselves, personally, then at least for others. Some feel under pressure to prove to themselves and others that they can enjoy recreational sex because it shows how un-hung up they are.

Females

First, let's talk about females and the brief encounter. We began our work with students in 1969 without any special prejudices on this subject, but our experience has shown us that college women in the early 1970s have had a difficult time with this form of sexual expression. They usually aren't able to walk the fine line between lack of emotional involvement on the one hand and a not very exciting or pleasurable sexual experience on the other. They may go into the experience firmly persuaded that it's just a thing of the moment but find they can't control their feelings. As one woman put it, "When I wake up and see his head next to mine and remember how we spent the night, I just get flooded with all these feelings—tender, loving—even possessive."

On the other hand, a great many women who have tried determinedly to enjoy fun sex find the setting just isn't conducive to sexual response. Gagnon and Simon have written a description of the social awkwardness involved in a typical first sexual experience, when the two people haven't been very intimate with one another before. Its understated humor makes it worth quoting at length:

Coitus involves more extensive commitments of . . . time and energy and learning of etiquette . . . clothing must be taken off and if they are going to be presented to judging others later that night must be arranged in ways that they will not wrinkle. This inhibits the sense of passion. Arousal (an erection and lubrication) must be maintained while disrobing in front of someone who has never seen one undressed before. One begins to expose portions of the anatomy that are commonly only privy to the self and others who may share certain housing or bathroom accommodations. The penis has a size, the breasts look a certain way, one is now being compared with the relatively wide range of others who, at least in fantasy, might be available for sexual contact. There is the arrangement of an unfamiliar body—where are the legs to go? What signals she will make to assure me that I'm doing well? . . . There are unfamiliar odors . . . sheets might be stained by vaginal or seminal fluids.

During the build-up and the physical act itself one may mask worry through excitement. It is when the two actors return to the world of speech that they must now begin to integrate the sexual performance into their other expectations of each other. The first words that they exchange must be assuring of continued pleasure and linked to further desire . . . There are phrases that are routinely used: "That was good," "Hello," or some other re-establishment of conventional realities. There are the other problems of getting up and going to the bathroom after sex, and whether the bathroom door should be open or closed. Should one wash one's genitals? Each of the tiny hurdles must be leaped and done so in silence [2].

It isn't only the social awkwardness of the scenario that inhibits pleasure for the female. Some women find that they need a depth of trust and closeness before they can let go sexually. Then there is the problem of communicating about your sexual likes and dislikes. If she requires some direct clitoral stimulation during intercourse in order to have an orgasm or a certain rhythm or position, she may find it impossible to talk about or show him what she wants. It just isn't worth the possible embarrassment of his potential annoyance. If his style of kissing turns her off, she will probably just put up with it.

A (young) woman needs to have a great deal of sexual self-confidence and self-understanding to integrate sexual experiences that are not so pleasurable. If she has bought into the prevalent myth that a sexually "free" person can always have a wonderful time with any partner, she will experience her own lack of response as a failure on her part and begin to have a lurking fear of sexual inadequacy that could undermine the process of her sexual unfolding.

Some young women do manage to walk the fine line between over-involvement and lack of pleasure and find that sexual encounters, within well-defined friendly limits, are possible and rewarding for them. Perhaps we tend to see somewhat fewer of these female students in the Sex Counseling Service because they feel subjectively satisfied with their sexual lives. We do recall one such young woman who was exuberantly happy about "discovering" sex. She had had intercourse with perhaps half a dozen young men in the past year and felt wonderful about it all. But, just a month or two later, she returned in serious confusion and dejection. Her partners were all from one friendship group, and one of them (not coincidentally from the South where the double standard still holds greatest sway) told her that she was a "slut" and that all the young men were laughing at her behind her back. It devastated her. We have often used her story to illustrate the difficulties of living in a period when rules of conduct are changing very rapidly—when a new set of ideals is proclaimed while the old ones are still operating at the gut level.

When a friendly, but casual sex experience is good, it can be a special sort of moment. A 22-year-old woman told the following story.

She and a girlfriend were bicycling in Vermont. They stopped beside a stream. They took off their clothes and went skinny-dipping. It was cool and sensuous. Lying on the river bank afterwards was relaxing.

A guy came along—with a red beard and an orange knapsack on

his back. The girls started for their clothes but stopped. It was so nice just the way they were and if he was uncomfortable he could leave. "Can I join you?" he asked. Then he stripped and dove in. The girls joined him and they all swam together. Beautiful. Cool. Quiet.

Afterwards, on the river bank, he and one of the girls "made love."

He stayed for two days. The three of them talked, cooked, ate, read and slept. They had intercourse again that night—after the other girl was asleep. The second night they slept together, but didn't have sex.

Then he went his way and the two girls went theirs. The moment was over.

There was no further story. Each of the girls had her own boyfriend to whom she returned afterwards. The girl who had had intercourse told her boyfriend and he didn't have a bad reaction to it. It sounded nice to him.

What role do such experiences play in the sexual unfolding process? One sophomore summarized her feelings about the meaning of casual sex encounters for her.

"I'm 20. I started dating when I was 13. My parents did instruct me well (technically) about sex but I was reasonably prissy because of moral indoctrination. I ended up being referred to as a 'cock tease' because I was flirtatious and affectionate but set boundaries. I had many relationships throughout my teenage years, mostly short ones. However, I went out with one guy (two years older) for two years—never quite felt ready to lose my virginity. After a few months' break I had an affair with a (then) 28-year-old man to whom I decided to lose my virginity. It was not until I came to college that I had anything that could be termed recreational sex. It's no big deal really. I'm neither a nymphomaniac nor a slut. I simply am honest about my basic sexual drive (I am quite frank about most things) and am not totally adverse to the idea of sex for sex's sake, occasionally. I don't think that I could be satisfied with just that, but I don't find it impossible. I think that sex can mean many different things and as long as both partners understand and agree on how they're looking at it, things will be all right. To a greater extent than any women I know, I have been able to enjoy this sort of sexual relationship."

Males

Males also have difficulty not becoming emotionally involved when they have had good sex with a woman. They too can become possessive, have feelings of tenderness and warmth, and suffer loss with separation. However, the single greatest problem for (young) men today, in a casual sex encounter, is performance pressure.

When a man—fairly easily and rapidly—finds himself in bed with a woman, regardless of his age, his natural assumption is that she is sexually experienced. It is not uncommon that he feels that he has to do at least as well, if not better than those before him, nor is it unusual for him to feel that the woman is more experienced than he is. He feels he is expected to do things which he may never have done or about which he is uncomfortable. He also is stereotyped as the one who leads sexually. The stereotype is against his saying that he is uncomfortable or asking for guidance. As one man summed it up: "I wish there was more equality in bed. I feel, horribly, the stigma of being forced to perform or at least to commence and feel that convention at times overcomes emotion." Today the convention is to speed ahead sexually, even when the feelings are to go slow or stop altogether. This is especially true with casual sex. In contrast, couples in a more committed relationship often go slower, letting the sexual behavior unfold at a pace that is mutually comfortable and satisfactory. So, it is not unusual to speak to a male who had intercourse in a one-night stand, who then sleeps with his girlfriend without intercourse until a time when it is mutually desired. In the casual sex scene, however, many men feel they don't have a choice. Rather than a warm coming together of two human beings the scene is one of using and being used.

When sex is a performance—unless one is a professional entertainer—it is often a flop. Students sometimes come to talk with us after such a flop. E.Y. came to the SCS worried about impotence. The problem occurred twice. Both times were with the same girl—the only sexual experiences he had with her. He was seen just two days after the second experience. The details were clear in his mind. A Saturday night, a college dance, a girl he'd never seen before. He had heard she was experienced. He had enough to drink to get up the nerve to go to her. After a few dances they went to a friend's dorm room. He still was having thoughts of his ex-girl-friend. These thoughts made him have fears of not being able to respond sexually. If he'd been a better lover (the girlfriend hadn't been orgasmic with intercourse), maybe he'd still be with her. He experienced a bit of shyness with this new girl, Fran. He recalled some fumbling in the dark, complicated by a need no urinate. Fran seemed irritated at his not knowing just what to do. He'd never really been sure about how to insert his penis. And then he started to get soft. Fran sucked him to get him hard again. He felt a little revolted by the whole scene. She became angry and said "Let's go to sleep." The next morning, he remembered his need to urinate; where do you go in a girl's dorm? How do you say to her you have to go, especially when there's some erection and she's starting to get turned on. He became soft again. On Tuesday night they were together again. This time he felt he had to prove he could do it. Nothing worked. She became very angry. Then he tried to masturbate and that didn't work. That's when he called for an emergency visit.

E.Y. and I (P.S.) talked for a few hours. At first I wanted to hear about what had just happened and what it meant to him. Most of the thoughts and feelings described above only came out in our discussion. At the time that things were happening there was little or no awareness of the interweaving themes of loss of the girlfriend or of the pressure to perform in this girl's presence—a girl whom he knew was experienced. The sense of outrage, the hostility en-countered, the absence of feeling for the sexual partner—if any-thing, a feeling of revulsion, these feeling-facts only came out with the opportunity to step back from the scene.

After our first discussions, it turned out that E.Y. still wanted to see Fran. He felt that since their first experiences they had become better friends. Even though it hadn't worked out in bed, he thought the relationship had a future.

At the next visit, he seemed happier. He wasn't seeing Fran any longer. The discussion focused on leaving the past and making plans for the future. From a sexual viewpoint, we talked about what had happened as a particular moment in time. It all seemed to make sense given the circumstances. Fran needed help. So did he, but maybe not so much as he thought. Masturbation was working okay. He was sleeping okay. School work was going well.

Follow up: It worked out. Two girlfriends and two years later, E.Y. wrote saying that he was engaged. He had no problems sexually. He was in love with a girl he met since leaving college, and feeling good about himself and the future.

Casual sex is risky. But, it can be worth the risk. Risky or not, it happens a lot. People can grow emotionally as a result. When it is natural and easy, it can be a good time. It can also be a time of feeling used and losing self-esteem. It can be a set-up for failure.

Promiscuity

When does recreational sex become promiscuity? The definition of the term *promiscuous* is difficult because it is often a matter of the eyes of the beholder or, as one humorous definition puts it, "A person is promiscuous if they're getting more than you are." The best definition we have seen is in one of Richard Hettlinger's books (borrowed by him from a book on male homosexuality). Promiscuity is ". . . the indiscriminate compulsive seeking of a series of transient sexual encounters based neither on love nor on friendship but merely on the relief of sexual tensions, in which little or no significance is attached to the nonsexual attributes of the partners" [3].

The words *indiscriminate* and *compulsive* are key words which can help to distinguish between promiscuity and a more normal period of adolescent development in which there are a series of casual sexual encounters. A year or so of "sleeping around" is becoming more common among young people. It is important, therefore, to be able to overcome a tendency to equate numbers and promiscuity. Every year we see several new freshman girls who are worried about what has happened since they arrived at college. They've never done anything like this before but lately they have had intercourse with three or four different men and wonder about the change in their behavior. They are having trouble setting limits. Obviously the freedom, the presence of hundreds of eager males, the availability of privacy and the distance from parents all play some part. With such students it is usually not difficult to clarify the ways in which they are using sex to meet nonsexual needs—to assuage loneliness, for instant popularity, to spite rigid parents who had kept a close watch at home, etc.

We think it is not a useless semantic argument to differentiate recreational sex from promiscuity because, in our experience, the truly promiscuous person, the person driven to find one sex partner after another, often without knowing anything at all about the other person, is someone with a personality disturbance. When this kind of promiscuity is seen in a student, we do not feel that sex counseling is appropriate. The treatment recommended is psychotherapy.

In some cases it is difficult to decide about the severity of the problem. One freshman presented with a story very much like others but with the important difference that she was pregnant. After her abortion she accepted the suggestion that she enter psychotherapy but, one year later, she again became pregnant. In thinking about her, retrospectively, we realized that her story had some special features which should serve as a warning signal to those who do counseling. She had described a particularly intense and compelling need for being held, cuddled, and fondled. It was for the gratification of these needs primarily that she had intercourse. The psychiatric literature does tell us that such intense need for bodily contact may lead a female into multiple sexual encounters as an indirect way of meeting those needs. Malmquist and others reported that out of 20 women who had three or more illegitimate pregnancies, eight reported a conscious awareness that sex was just a way to get cuddling [4].

It may be that the continuum between recreational sex and promiscuity will become more blurred and confused as time goes on. In a few decades the word *promiscuous* may well sound antique. Professionals who need to make diagnostic distinctions as a guide to who should have therapy and what kind of therapy may find that there are no longer any objective criteria for diagnosing promiscuity; in which case the determining factor will be the individual's degree of discomfort with his or her life—the same criteria, really, that we all use in practice.

The tenor of our times makes sexual activity a likely avenue for expressing a variety of adolescent conflicts. It is quite probable that there will be an increase in the numbers of young people who seek professional help because they have been bewildered, traumatized and confused by their own multiple sex experiences. If a girl is emotionally vulnerable because, for example, her parents are divorced, her father has been distant, and she feels unattractive, it would be a very easy "solution" for her to find confirmation of her sexual attractiveness and fill a need for attention (love?) by having intercourse with many partners. This essentially nonsatisfying behavior may bring peer approval and she may not feel at all uncomfortable about it for quite some time. One student with such a history became aware that her sex life might be problematic when she came to college from a particularly liberal and sexually free high school environment. Meeting large numbers of 18-year-old virgins in her dorm was a revelation! She started to ask herself why she had intercourse so casually, why she didn't enjoy it more, why she didn't maintain a long-term relationship. This is when she came to talk about her "sleeping around."

We are aware that all of our comments on promiscuity have been about females. This is not as sex-role stereotyped as it may appear. The definition of promiscuous we have used, which emphasizes the compulsive and indiscriminate nature of sexual behavior, applies exactly as well to males as to females. Certainly there are males whose behavior, by this definition, is promiscuous. The so-called Don Juan syndrome is an example. However, we have had little clinical experience with men, college age or otherwise, who were actively promiscuous, and we felt that we should not write about something in the abstract with which we had so little clinical experience. The fact that males do not come in to talk about promiscuous sexual behavior tells us something about the cultural attitudes which still support a double standard in this regard. The man who is hopping from partner to partner (whether heterosexual, homosexual, or bisexual) may have a nagging anxiety about the meaning of his behavior but there is enough support in the culture for his sexual life style that he can easily rationalize his experiences as normal or even super-normal. Certainly some amount of "sleeping around" is a part of normal sexual unfolding for many men. It becomes a problem only when the man feels that he is out of control or when he is unable to relate to a sexual partner in any mode other than a fleeting contact.

Prostitute Experiences

In the mid-1950s, in the Northeast, an educated guess would be that close to 50 percent of college men had a prostitute experience by the time they graduated. What that experience consisted of will never be known. There is reason to think, from sex histories 20 to 40 years later, that it was a double-edged sword. True, an initiation rite may have been passed but for many there was humiliation and failure. As noted by Kinsey, and Masters and Johnson, these early prostitute experiences often played a major part in causing subsequent sexual dysfunction. Prostitutes often earned (and still do) by the ejaculate—not by the hour. The quicker the man came, the quicker he was out the door. For others, anxiety, guilt or repugnance might lead to impotence or inability to ejaculate.

For some, it was a good experience. Certainly, the claim of some prostitutes that they play an important service role for humanity should not go completely unheeded. One professor, in his 60s, described his positive experience: "When I was 17 my father took me to a woman who serviced only the better families in town. He explained what she would do. He would come back later to pick me up. She was wonderful. She knew just how to ease my nervousness—through warmth and holding and gently guiding. I have to smile now, when I think that she also showed me how to move —I didn't know about that. I asked her lots of questions about women, and she let me look at her genitals—that was another first. She was clean and I liked the smell. She also told me what I would have to do with a 'proper lady' for example, to protect her virginity and not let her get carried away but to wait for our wedding night, to be gentle, and to pleasure her. As I think about it—she was also saying that pleasure for me in sex was what she was for."

Among males in our sex courses in northeastern schools (12 different schools surveyed over a five year period: 1970-74), only 2 percent indicated on the anonymous questionnaire that they had had prostitute experience. Even in the control group of randomly selected men not taking the sex course the figure was less than 5 percent. There may be some regional differences within the United States. For example, 18 percent of students in a large southern university claimed prostitute experience. Data from the Midwest and Northwest were essentially the same as the Northeast.

A dozen or so male students have told us about their prostitute experiences. Most have been during the summer while traveling in Europe: Amsterdam, Rotterdam, Hamburg. It should be remembered that these scenes have been described by men coming to see us for help. The situations have been overdetermined. Many times the set purpose for visiting the prostitutes is to overcome virginity. But, there are problems of a foreign environment, not speaking the same language, being in the seedy part of town, etc., and so there has almost always been sexual inadequacy, a sense of humiliation not infrequently compounded by the reactions of the women involved. It seems there aren't many of the good old "social worker"-type prostitutes around anymore!

Even when the scene is plush and closer to home it may be psychologically foreign and therefore hurtful: "I didn't expect it. A friend of my father's sent me on some pretext or other, to this woman. When I came in she was dressed only in a night gown. I was a little bit mesmerized so I don't know how it all happened, but I do remember she was naked and had me undressed, and then I just couldn't get an erection. The phone rang while I was there. I figured out it was my father's partner calling to find out how I'd done. I got out of there fast. Now that I think about it, I'm pretty angry about the whole thing—I think I was angry even then, but I didn't know it."

For him, it was a first experience. He didn't want it. He was hurt by it. He felt manipulated and dehumanized. He didn't initiate contact with any girls for almost 6 months after this experience and came to the Sex Counseling Service (SCS) to talk about his fears.

Another student presented a different problem. He had had intercourse with half a dozen or more prostitutes over a period of almost four years, since age 15. There had never been a problem. His impression, perhaps somewhat naive, was that he and the women had always been satisfied. Now he had a girlfriend and he was impotent. His conclusion was that he had been affected by the early experiences in such a way that he could never be good for the girl he loved. Fortunately, we had the time and the two of them had the motivation to do sex therapy and it worked out well. There were things she was doing that were leading to his impotence. She also had never been orgasmic which was a constant worry to him and in turn a worry to her. There was a premature ejaculation pattern to reverse. In their case the therapy was done early in the relationship, and before the impotence was an entrenched pattern. But, we have seen others in their 30s, 40s, and older who had similar experiences in college who then stopped relating to others—frozen by their fear of inadequacy.

Literature is replete with examples of young men's earliest sexual encounters with paid prostitutes or older women who help to initiate them. These descriptions often capture the youth's anguished conflict over the experience. In one of Colette's novels, young Phil, who is in love with Vanca, goes to the home of an experienced widow for his first sexual experience. Afterward, in an act of revulsion against the experience, he tries to scour away all traces of it with water [5].

Blos uses a literary example (James Joyce's *Portrait of the Artist as a Young Man*) in discussing the adolescent encounter with a prostitute [6]. Blos says that for Stephan Daedalus, as for most young men, this experience may affirm masculine sexuality but it does not influence personality development with respect to love objects, i.e., does not help the young man in loosening libidinal ties to his family nor help him on the road toward establishing adult intimacy (see Chapter 5 for a definition of intimacy).

Both Phil and Stephan Daedalus managed to have a sexual experience but, because of guilt and the dehumanized quality of the experience, they were not enriched by the experience even in the sense that their lust could become something to celebrate.

Conclusions

In the case material we have cited in this section on recreational sex there emerge several identifiable themes which we recognize as playing an important role in determining the quality and the *meaning* of a recreational sex experience for the individual in the process of sexual unfolding; these are: (1) guilt; (2) the extent to which the other person is viewed as an object or is stereotyped; (3) performance pressures; and (4) the perceived consequences of the experience.

Guilt. When there is *intense* guilt, as in the case of Stephan Daedalus, for example, the aftermath may be an intensification of guilt or the strengthening of some defense against sexual feeling such as disgust, sublimation, scrupulous religiosity, intellectualization, etc. Guilt and defenses are frequently adaptive responses which help to allay a flooding of the ego with too much sexual excitement. Guilt can help a person to realize that they have perhaps, gone "too far." Students are often astonished by their own guilt responses. After having intercourse with an old friend because they were together and a little drunk, one student said, "I thought I was completely free of those religious hang-ups and my parents' ideas of morals, but I guess that was only intellectual. Those old feelings are still in me somewhere." This kind of learning about aspects of one's self and the recognition of internal conflict is an important step on the road to identity formation vis-a-vis parents and moral values.

Sometimes the guilt over a one-night stand or some "far out" sex experience leads to a new seriousness about sex. By and large, we have seen this to be a healthy trend, away from the false notion of sex as a toy that can be played with anywhere, anytime. Some recognition that feelings about sex tend to run fairly deep is probably a sign of maturing. This trend can be carried too far, however, toward the idea that sex should never be silly, impulsive, novel, under the influence of pot or *just* lustful. Guilt about the recreational aspects of sex can then produce a routinized rather sterile approach to sex.

Sexual objectism. Going to a prostitute is usually the epitome of using another person as a dehumanized sexual object, but sex encounters where no one is paid can also be very impersonal. Viewing a sex partner as an object can serve a defensive function. The young man who is a scared novice can avoid having to deal with a whole series of complications that would enter the scene should this female be thought a *person.* He doesn't have to deal with her feelings or needs—perhaps not even her sexual needs and he doesn't have to worry quite so keenly what she might think of him. The same can hold true for a young woman who views her sexual partner as an object—whether the object is sex or status.

A sexual partner can also be turned into an object by being strictly stereotyped. E.Y., for example, stereotyped Vicky as "an easy lay" and "experienced." He responded to her in terms of these stereotypes and this contributed to his anxiety in bed with her and thus his sexual dysfunction.

Performance pressures. The presence of performance pressure or expectation weighs heavily on both male and female. When sex cannot be relaxed and easy, there is likely to be a problem. In the context of a brief encounter or with a prostitute, dysfunction is so often a reaction to situational stresses that it is certainly no measure of the individual's potential for sexual function in other contexts, but the adolescent hasn't enough perspective or even knowledge to understand this and is often unnerved, even shattered, by an instance of sexual "failure."

Perhaps one of the bonuses in certain recreational sex experiences is the possibility of responding sexually without the need for it to go anywhere. Sexy dancing and talking or an X-rated film can often be enjoyed for themselves, unless, of course, one anticipates that they must or should be a prelude to intercourse. The ability to enjoy sexual play without the necessity of going on to intercourse is something that we believe is of lifelong value. Couples with a sexual problem usually do not have this ability (and one of the goals of sex therapy is to develop this ability).

Consequences. When playing with sex leads to VD, pregnancy, a pregnancy scare, abortion, strong parental disapproval, or peer disapproval or is followed by rejection or intensified inner conflict, it is easy to see that sexual unfolding may be set back in minor or significant ways. Luckily, we are all able to reason as well as to rationalize and forget, so we can learn to be more careful the next time!

Negative consequences, like guilt, can be useful or they can lead to an over reaction against the experience or some part of the experience (e.g., the pleasure, the person it was shared with, or the emotions involved).

These conclusions sound a bit gloomy and negative but, in fact, we believe that recreational sex is an important, perhaps indispensable part of human experience. So let us end this section on a more positive note.

Every sexual experience, including the recreational, has the potential to enhance sexual unfolding. Positive "recreational" experiences are particularly valuable in increasing the capacity for playful, nonguilty erotic pleasure, but they can influence other aspects of sexual unfolding as well. When a person approaches another, even when the stated aim is "just for sex," there can be pleasant surprises. Besides being a shared moment of erotic pleasure, the experience can turn out to be one of special meaning: closeness, empathy, a mutual influence. The personality may be subtly or profoundly affected. Something the other does may change one's perceptions of oneself or one's feelings about sex. The "after" feeling can be a glow, a sense of having learned something, an expanded awareness and an eager anticipation of more.

References

1. Gagnon, John and Simon, William. *Sexual Conduct*, Chicago, Aldine Pub. Co., 1973, p. 42.
2. Gagnon and Simon, [1], p. 79.
3. Hettlinger, Richard, *Sex Isn't That Simple*, New York, Seabury Press, 1974, p. 84.
4. Malmquist, C. P., Kiresuk, T. J. and Spano, R. M. "Personality Characteristics of Women with Repeated Illegitimate Pregnancies: Descriptive Aspects" in *American Journal of Orthopsychiatry*, Vol. 36, 1966, pp. 476-484.
5. Colette, *The Ripening Seed*, New York, Farrar, Straus and Giroux, 1955.
6. Blos, Peter, *On Adolescence*, New York, Free Press, 1962, pp. 112-114.

5

Intimacy, Commitment, Fidelity

Intimacy

One of the central processes in sexual unfolding is the gradual evolution of the capacity for intimacy which includes eroticism, emotional closeness, mutual caring and trust. Erikson believed that the adolescent could not achieve the capacity for intimacy until he or she had a firm sense of ego identity [1]. His view of these adolescent tasks evoked a step-ladder image. Lidz, in contrast, sees these two processes as closely interrelated, moving upward like intertwined spirals [2]. We would tend to favor Lidz's description which stresses the role of bonding in the formation of identity. For most adolescents, sexual experiences and caring relationships are crucial to their evolving sense of identity. We have seen, however, that there is individual variation. Some young people do seem to follow a more stepwise course, needing to resolve conflicts with their family or settle into a career before they can enter a significant sexual/love relationship. But the majority of adolescents show a gradual movement toward intimacy, an increasing fusion of erotic and tender feelings, and a growing ability to share their evolving sense of uniqueness with another.

For many years, sociologists described a pattern of learning about male/female relationships in adolescence in which boys started out as sexually motivated, slowly learning about love while girls were preoccupied with love and only gradually integrated sex into their concept of male/female relations. Starting from opposite ends of the spectrum, boys and girls mutually influenced one another over a period of years and finally ended up, more or less together, in the middle—enjoying sex and able to love.

For the male, there was a gradual evolution from sexual objectism (experiencing females primarily as objects with which he could have sexual experiences) toward more awareness of females as unique and valued persons who stirred feelings of love and protectiveness. The first case in this chapter (Alan and Betsy) is an example of this process. The female half of this courtship pattern was a romantically oriented young girl who was only dimly aware of her sexuality until she was taught to value it because of (for the sake of) young men. Given this kind of structure for male/female relationships in adolescence, it is not surprising that Kinsey and other researchers found what they imagined to be a biological difference between male and female patterns of "sex drive," with males having their peak in adolescence while females only came to life sexually after many years of experience, not until their late 20s, 30s or even 40s. Today, as females are increasingly encouraged to be sexual, we are beginning to realize that previous assumptions about "natural" male/female differences need to be questioned.

The courtship pattern described above depends upon quite specific and distinct roles for young males and females. The boy or young man is cast as sexually needy and aggressive, while the female can only be coaxed or seduced or pushed into sexual behavior. His role is to try to get as much as possible; hers is to set limits but gradually "give in."

Psychoanalysts have a concept that sheds some light on this division of roles—the concept of "the splitting of ambivalence." When individuals split their ambivalence, they may take one half of a mixed feeling (love/hate, for example) and project it into the outside world, feeling only the acceptable feeling as their own. The unacceptable feeling belongs to the other person or persons. In the traditional division of male/female roles in adolescent sexual behavior we see one way of handling the powerful conflicting feelings generated when boys and girls must learn to relate in new, adult ways. He charges boldly ahead, barely noticing that he's scared, not sure what to do and maybe he'd rather be playing basketball. As long as he can rely upon the female to play her part— to be scared, shy and set some limits, he doesn't need to ask himself what he really feels, what he really wants. The other side of the coin, her role as "no"-sayer, allows her to experience sex without admitting that she's doing it because *she* wants to. Her upbringing has made it too difficult for her to admit to sexual desires. She would feel too guilty and unfeminine.

If this pattern sounds slightly out-of-date, it is. These rigid distinctions have never been absolute and recently they have been losing ground very quickly. Sexual roles are changing, becoming blurred and fluid. The impact of these changes is apparent in the area of sexual behavior between young people. More and more young females are aware of and value their own sexual feelings. The change in reported incidence of masturbation among college women is one striking index of this change. As recently as 1970 our figures showed that about one-third of college women masturbated. By 1976-1977 the figure had soared to (approximately) three-fourths. Young (college) women are more often taking an aggressive role in initiating relationships, touching, and getting into bed. They may carry a diaphragm around with them. For their part, the young males we are familiar with are less oriented toward "scoring" and more likely than in the past to be sensitive to the emotional aspects of relationships.

The movement away from well-delineated roles for young men and women is changing the process of learning about intimate male/female relationships. The old model of male teaching female about sex while she teaches him about love is becoming less valid with each passing year. What is taking the place of this model is not as easy to describe because there seems to be more individual variation. When there are no prescriptions for behavior, each couple has to improvise. Certainly we are hearing daily, in our work with students, about kinds of interactions that would have sounded very peculiar 10 years ago. Young men are saying: "No thanks, I don't want to sleep with you" or "I want to have more of a relationship before we get sexually involved" or "I think we started to sleep together too soon and I'd like to de-escalate the sexual side of our relationship" or "I just don't think I'm ready to have intercourse with anyone yet." And we aren't hearing about these interactions from the young men. They aren't coming for professional help, asking "What's wrong with me that I feel this way?" They seem to accept their own feelings. Most of these stories are coming to us by way of the young women who feel confused and sometimes rejected.

The breakdown in sex-role stereotypes is making it necessary for young men and women to talk to each other about their feelings more than they needed to when they knew what sort of behavior was expected. Each individual is having to confront his or her ambivalent feelings about sex and about love, trying to find or to mold a relationship to meet his or her needs. There is a lot of trial and error, emotional investment in relationships that go awry, and a great deal of time and energy invested in the business of "relating." Potentially, having to face up to one's ambivalence, identify and communicate one's feelings to another person, and hear someone else's feelings is very good training for a long term relationship which emphasizes intimacy, i.e., for modern marriage or cohabitation.

We feel we can go only so far with generalized descriptions of this process. The case histories that follow are an attempt at presenting *some* of the issues involved in learning about intimacy.

Alan

The dialogue which follows is a transcript of a tape of an actual office visit. Alan had been seen briefly (15 minutes) one month earlier at which time his problem was the inability to have an erection with Betsy, his girlfriend. He had been able to have intercourse with a previous girlfriend. The only suggestions made at the first appointment were that he and Betsy limit their sexual relations to activities that were relaxed and comfortable for both of them and that Alan return for a longer appointment (an hour) at which P.S. could gain a better understanding of the situation in which he was impotent. The following material is reconstructed from notes of that interview.

P.S.: We can pick up anywhere you'd like.

ALAN: In the past month things have changed and since right after I saw you the last time, Betsy and I tried to make love again and it was OK.

P.S.: You didn't lose your erection?

ALAN: It wasn't like, uh, as good an erection as it could have been but since then it has been. But I figured—I don't know—There's another problem for Betsy now in that she's been finding it very, very painful and very unenjoyable.

P.S.: OK. Well, now, let's see if we can go back in time and—what I'd like to hear then is about you and Betsy and how things were from the beginning of your relationship.

ALAN: OK.

P.S.: OK. Now that starts when?—last summer?

ALAN: Last summer—in the middle of the summer.

P.S.: How did you meet her?

ALAN: We both worked at the same summer job.

P.S.: How long did you know each other before you became a couple?

ALAN: Well, I guess about four to five weeks.

P.S.: How did she come across to you before you really got to know her? Can you describe how she appeared from a distance?

ALAN: She was—I thought that she was very attractive and she seemed like the type of girl who was asked out a lot. I have always been very shy. That was one of the reasons it took me so long to ask her out. I asked her out after about three weeks knowing her and she seemed very, very worldly and experienced, not only, I don't mean in a sexual sense—in everything else.

P.S.: Can you tell me something about her personality?

ALAN: My first impressions?

P.S.: Or your early impressions.

ALAN: I thought she was very vivacious and unlike any other girl I ever went out with. She really was very, um—I'm trying to think of a word—she knew what she wanted—she had like her own mind, so to speak—do you know what I mean? She just wasn't like—girls —Yeh, right, she doesn't let people walk over her.

P.S.: Can you give me an example?

ALAN: OK. It's like just silly things—like whenever I'm with a girl —you might say even if we're in a store—uh, and you wanna ask a question about where something is—or something, any other girl I was with—they were always embarrassed and they made me do it. You know, I didn't care—that's just like a silly example that comes to mind. Betsy—she would do it or I would do it—it didn't matter, you know, things like that—she would just stand up for herself.

P.S.: That was attractive to you.

ALAN: Right, if she heard me say this she'd disagree with this.

P.S.: What would she say?

ALAN: She would like to be like that but she doesn't think she is. After a few weeks of going out, we just started talking about what we thought of each other before we started going out and she couldn't believe that I thought that she went out a lot, 'cause, I mean—she went out but like not anywhere near as much as I had imagined—because she was very beautiful to me and she couldn't believe that I was scared to ask her out because she wanted me to ask her out sooner.

P.S.: But what about these qualities of being—assertive—of being clear in her mind of what she likes and so on? Would she agree with that?

ALAN: She would want people to think that—in other words she wants to think it *of herself* but she doubts it in some ways.

P.S.: What was her impression of you?

ALAN: She thought I was cute and funny. She just wished that I asked her out sooner because she liked me.

P.S.: Well, how do you like to think of yourself? You know, do you like the idea of being funny?

ALAN: Yeh. You know, like, whenever I'm nervous or something, I always act the clown.

P.S.: The times when you're a comedian, are times when you are anxious?

ALAN: Definitely. I noticed that about myself in the last two years.

P.S.: Well, has Betsy seen you be serious?

ALAN: Of course! Once we started going out—this is the first girl I really feel myself with—who I don't have to put up any kind of acts at all.

P.S.: So your other relationship really was sort of like the first?

ALAN: Yeh. Even though it wasn't like the breaking in, it was really the first.

P.S.: This relationship really goes a lot deeper.

ALAN: Yeh.

P.S.: How far did the sex go the first time you were together. Remember?

ALAN: Yeh. The first time—our first date—all that we did was kiss. I was too nervous and she was too nervous and she thought she acted stupid—I thought I acted stupid.

P.S.: And that was your first date.

ALAN: Then the second date—it was again just kissing and petting —I guess—with all our clothes on.

P.S.: Did you feel she had much sexual experience? What had you thought?

ALAN: I thought that she had—a lot. I didn't know if she was a virgin or not. It didn't make *much* of a difference to me. Just curiosity.

P.S.: Although it didn't matter whether she'd had intercourse or not—your impression was that she might very well have.

ALAN: Yeh.

P.S.: So, were you also wondering what she would think of you?

ALAN: Yeh.

P.S.: So on that second date, you did extend your touching to petting, touching breasts but keeping clothes on.

ALAN: Yes.

P.S.: Did she touch you outside your clothes?

ALAN: Uh. I don't think so. No.

P.S.: Then how did things unfold?

ALAN: OK. It was only about five weeks after we first started going out that we had to come back to school. About a week before we came back to school it developed into a relationship with complete petting—without clothes.

P.S.: Were you seeing each other each day?

ALAN: Yeh—because of work.

P.S.: So you were really getting to know each other—in action. Learning a lot about each other's ways of dealing with issues— working together.

ALAN: Right.

P.S.: You started—you extended to nudity and genital touching before she left for school. How did you feel with that? Were you comfortable?

ALAN: Oh yeah, completely.

P.S.: Were you feeling any demand to respond in any particular way? How were you feeling about having an erection in her presence or coming in her presence?

ALAN: Very good about it.

P.S.: That was nice. Did she seem comfortable?

ALAN: Yeh.

P.S.: By this time did you know whether or not she was a virgin?

ALAN: Yes.

P.S.: When did you ask her? Or what did she tell you?

ALAN: Well, I'm trying to think. Oh, no—I'm sorry, I didn't—I didn't—OK. She left for school and I didn't want to ask her 'cause if she was a virgin I didn't want to seem at all—pushy or something, 'cause I was curious but it didn't really matter to me.

P.S.: Well, how comfortable was she with genital touching? Your touching her.

ALAN: She was very comfortable.

P.S.: So, that seemed natural—

ALAN: Right.

P.S.: Would she show you what she liked?—Would she guide your hand—Would she let you put your fingers in the vagina?

ALAN: Uh-huh.

P.S.: So, in all of these things—the two of you could be very open with each other.

ALAN: Yes.

P.S.: She didn't pull back.

ALAN: No. No. Not at all. Like that was one thing that surprised me —cause well like any other girl who I've had that with—I was the first guy.

P.S.: And would they be somewhat tentative?

ALAN: Yeh. But all this I liked—I really did, you know. And I still do—her freeness.

P.S.: But it was still an unknown whether she had had intercourse?

ALAN: Right, right.

P.S.: For all you knew she had had genital touching before—she might not have, but the likelihood was that she had.

ALAN: Right.

P.S.: Did she experience an orgasm in the touching?

ALAN: No.

P.S.: Did you?

ALAN: Yeah.

P.S.: Was she comfortable when you came?

ALAN: Yeah.

P.S.: So that wasn't something that you hid from her?

ALAN: Oh no.

P.S.: Did she seem to like that?

ALAN: I think so. I don't know if she liked it—she liked it *for me.* I don't know if she liked it for herself. But she definitely didn't make me feel uncomfortable about it. She was very nice.

P.S.: How many times did you pet this way?

ALAN: Maybe three times.

P.S.: Then she went off to school?

ALAN: She went off to school and we started writing each other every day and then she sent me a letter telling me that she was a virgin and that I'm the first guy who she feels that she would like to make love with and everything—which also surprised me again 'cause for the same reason like—she—had enough in her to even be able to say that.

P.S.: How did you feel about that? Her doing that.

ALAN: Very good.

P.S.: You were glad to see her do that?

ALAN: Oh yeah. Definitely. If anything I guess I was sick and tired of whenever a girl wasn't like that.

P.S.: Did you write back saying that you had had intercourse? Did she know that you had had intercourse?

ALAN: No. The day I got the letter I was going to see her—like within a day. I went down to see her—We discussed it and I told her my experiences and everything. We discussed past experiences a little see—and she said that although she wants to make love she's not really sure yet 'cause it's very special to her—. Which really didn't bother me that much—I don't think it bothered me at all. And then eventually she said that she decided to make love. We discussed it again and she said she wanted to. I didn't want to pressure her at all—I didn't think it was fair. And since then—like after we decided, it was three weeks before we had a chance to because we kept on going home. I would feel funny and she would feel funny having intercourse in her home with her parents there.

P.S.: This was in November?

ALAN: So the first time was like the end of November—when we first tried it.

P.S.: Where was that?

ALAN: Here at school—in my room.

P.S.: Really then there was an understanding between you that in your parents' home the thing you could be comfortable with was petting?

ALAN: You know it's a very strange thing because with this girl I was going out with before Betsy it was so different. If the house was empty for two hours or something we would go. With Betsy I didn't want to—which surprised me 'cause I was just the opposite before.

P.S.: Well, it's obvious there was something much more meaningful about this relationship.

ALAN: Yeah. OK. And—so we decided that we wanted to make love and we tried and I tried—we tried—and I couldn't get an erection. I didn't think I was scared at all but I guess I was.

P.S.: There had been the whole build-up—from the letter—from the going home and several times when you sort of said no, not now—not here and so that weekend was built into *The Weekend*, like this is the weekend we're going to have intercourse.

ALAN: Probably—yeah—not probably—it did. That's right.

P.S.: So that was the setting where in trying to have intercourse there was no erection?

ALAN: And then—that was a Thursday night—and the next—

P.S.: What was the reaction to that?

ALAN: Well—looking back on it—I can't believe how I reacted but at the time it was like the most traumatic thing that ever happened to me.

P.S.: What was the feeling you felt?

ALAN: Well, I felt like I was very worthless and I guess in some ways I was also scared about what she would think. But I knew, even without asking her, she saw how upset I was and—she tried to comfort me and everything. She was very nice.

P.S.: So she responded warmly to you?

ALAN: Definitely.

P.S.: Do you have some insight as to why on that night you didn't have an erection?

ALAN: I really don't know—Betsy and I discussed it. I guess it could range from anything like a common thing to—to being some kind of psychological block—. I guess it always is a psychological block.

P.S.: What feeling towards Betsy did you have in your mind?

ALAN: I felt that possibly one of the reasons behind my problem was that it meant so much to her. —A lot of the time that we were together went into discussing whether she was sure and the position I took was not convincing her—just asking her—talking about it in general. So I felt that maybe I thought I knew how important it was and maybe I was just scared to hurt her.

P.S.: You felt this meant some kind of emotional commitment to the relationship on her part?

ALAN: I guess I did—yeah.

P.S.: And did you feel ready to make that kind of commitment?

ALAN: I thought I did.

P.S.: So you think Betsy was saying this as well?

ALAN: She's not the type of girl who would say, "Well, this is the guy I'm going to marry." Our relationship always was and is something. It's fantastic now.

P.S.: So you're saying intercourse did not mean permanence but a special level of commitment of two people sharing?

ALAN: Right.

P.S.: You knew it was very important to her. Were you also concerned about hurting her physically?

ALAN: Hurting her physically? I guess I was concerned but I wasn't scared.

P.S.: The other girl you had intercourse with—she had never had intercourse before?

ALAN: Right.

P.S.: What happened the first time you had intercourse with her?

ALAN: There was no problem at all. In fact, there wasn't any pain.

P.S.: Do you remember your reaction to that?

ALAN: I was very surprised.

P.S.: You were expecting her to have pain?

ALAN: Yeah.

P.S.: Were you expecting her to bleed?

ALAN: I was expecting her to have pain or bleeding.

P.S.: And when she didn't—how did you feel about it?

ALAN: I don't really think I thought about—I guess I was glad she didn't.

P.S.: In that first time—did you come?

ALAN: Yeah.

P.S.: How did you feel about the timing?

ALAN: (Answers sheepishly) It was too short.

P.S.: Too short for what?

ALAN: For her to feel anything.

P.S.: What was her reaction?

ALAN: I felt bad but I knew that it was normal—well, not normal but I knew that it was common.

P.S.: To come fast the first time?

ALAN: Yeah. Or for the girl not to come. And she knew that too —she felt bad, I think. I think she felt there was something wrong with her, that she didn't come. She had come with petting. A very strange thing is that Betsy still has never come even with petting. She said actually she never has.

P.S.: Has she ever come masturbating?

ALAN: I asked her that—no she hasn't. I do find that still now I do come too quickly. I feel that it's too soon—maybe about 10-15 strokes.

P.S.: That's not so fast, you can move—you don't come as you're trying to enter her?

ALAN: That's the way it was at first.

P.S.: Well, now the first time ended with her comforting you. You were very upset by it—

ALAN: The next few times it repeated—once the same weekend—just as bad. But then the next time things got better so that I was able to keep the erection and put on a prophylactic. Just before I entered her I came.

P.S.: It's almost as though you're evolving—

ALAN: Right. But then, she's been very very tight. She's had unbelievable pain.

P.S.: Can you put two fingers in her vagina?

ALAN: Not easily. It feels tight. Always does—always has—which was another thing I was comparing in my mind. With my first girlfriend it wasn't at all a problem.

P.S.: You knew about the tightness of Betsy's vagina from the summer—before the first attempt at intercourse.

ALAN: Yeah. That might have been on my mind. The time we had our first intercourse I got in before I was completely hard.

P.S.: Did you come that time?

ALAN: Yeah.

P.S.: So you came without the fullness of erection?

ALAN: Right. She didn't feel anything and I didn't expect her to, especially since my erection wasn't that large. So the next time we tried it I felt I had a stronger erection which gave me more confidence in itself—whether it means anything physically or not—psychologically to me it did and I went ahead and it hurt her a lot.

P.S.: Did she say where it hurt?

ALAN: She said that she liked having me in her but that sensually I guess she didn't really feel any kind of special pleasure right off and that it was a little painful. Since then it's hurt her on the outside.

P.S.: Since you've started having intercourse have you had a time when you agreed ahead of time, because of the pain, not to have intercourse?

ALAN: Yes, once—when she was very upset about school, she asked that we not make love.

P.S.: How was that?

ALAN: Fine.

P.S.: Has she seen a gynecologist? It sounds like she might have vaginitis—it's a pretty common problem among the students we see.

ALAN: I never knew that it was that common. She also urinates a lot. Does that mean anything?

In the remaining minutes of the interview arrangements were made for Alan to return with his girlfriend. Although she had told him that she was reluctant to see the gynecologist at her own school—mainly out of fear that the examination would be painful —she had welcomed his suggestion that he go with her to the doctor and that he would try to arrange for her to be seen by us. Such arrangements were made. At the examination she had severe vulvo-vaginitis with a vaginismus reaction to vulvar touching. Fortunately, response to treatment was successful. The couple have continued the relationship. When last seen, two years after the initial contact, they were not having any sexual difficulties.

Alan's story is one of moving from one stage in sexual unfolding —an intermediate level of personal involvement where there is liking for the other but not intense caring or love—to the threshold of an intimate relationship, his first. His powerful feelings for Betsy make him very sensitive to her feelings. He is reassured by her "freeness" about sex, her ability to take care of and represent herself and her frankness in saying "I want to have intercourse with you." On the other hand, he gets to know her well enough to see past his early impressions of her. At first he thought she was worldly, experienced, vivacious, knew her own mind, and perhaps (probably) was not a virgin. Later she tells him about her insecurities, her *wish* to be an assertive person, the fact that she is a virgin, and has some ambivalence about intercourse.

He then begins to be ambivalent about having intercourse with Betsy. Perhaps he didn't fully experience his own doubts and hesitations but his words in telling the story and his actions—going home several weekends in a row so that they have no opportunity for intercourse—speak his mixed feelings. He is worried because it means so much to her. He is afraid to hurt her emotionally and physically. He can't ignore her feelings and "push on" because he cares too much. Loving makes him vulnerable and sensitive. This is, at least in part, the reason why he loses his erection and it is not at all uncommon. One might consider this sort of impotence as a normal, developmental phenomenon. (See discussion of transitory impotence, pp. 155 ff, below.)

Of course there were important physical factors—Betsy's pain and tightness. He knew from petting that her vagina was rather tight. She was communicating her ambivalence and fear of pain through her body and it seems clear that Alan picked up these nonverbal cues which fueled his worries about hurting her.

Their relationship was strong enough for him to seek counseling. Through counseling, he gained insight into what had happened and Betsy's problems were able to be treated.

Ellen

Ellen presented with a problem of pain during intercourse. She was found to have severe monilial vaginitis and vaginismus. She was in her sophomore year and had been dating one young man (Zeek) steadily for the past seven months. Prior to this relationship she had had intercourse with a number of different boys and men since she was a high-school senior. Sometimes intercourse was in the context of a "relationship," but more often it was with casual friends or acquaintances.

In Ellen's history of sexual unfolding there was a recurrent theme—the fear of being "used." It may have been present as early as age 5 when a little boy asked Ellen and two girlfriends to take off their pants. The other girls ran away but Ellen stayed and complied. Later, she told her mother, who was very angry and said, "Never let boys do things like that to you." Ellen also remembers her mother's telling her to close her curtains when she undressed because boys liked to peep. In ninth grade, in a new school, a boy took her out and was very interested in "making out," but Ellen thought that he disowned and ignored her at school. "I felt he was interested in me for purely sexual reasons. He dropped me. Then I dated his best friend and worried about the same thing with him."

There was usually not much sexual pleasure for Ellen in her making out sessions during junior-high years and into high-school. She said, "Somewhere along the line, in spite of my parents' efforts to be liberal, I got the idea that sex was nasty." At 16 Ellen "went steady" for a time with a boy a few years older. For the first time in her life she felt a boy was interested in her as a person and she was interested in him. "I remember one incident when I first let him touch my breasts and take off my shirt. I was very upset afterwards and cried and worried about being used. He seemed to regard it as natural and was sorry I was upset. He didn't see sex as dirty at all, unlike others, and he was so patient with me." Ellen and this boyfriend did not have intercourse. Her first intercourse experience was in the context of a short-term relationship while she was traveling with a group. After this she entered a period of casual sexual encounters. "I even made love with one boy though I wasn't particularly attracted to him—it just seemed expected of me and even then I felt it was a spineless thing to do."

In her freshman year Ellen had a relationship that lasted a few weeks until he ended it. "I got very depressed and started thinking over my sexual history and felt there were too many bad patterns." A month later she had intercourse with someone else. "I thought I would really like him, but after I got to know him I saw he wasn't my type. Though he was very good sexually, the sex didn't excite me because I didn't like him alot."

"This year, when I met Zeek, I held off going to bed with him for over a month, trying to see what sort of relationship I wanted to have. I was getting tired of this merry-go-round."

When Ellen was diagnosed as having severe vaginitis and vaginismus, the theme of "being used" emerged clearly. She was very reluctant to ask Zeek to help in any way. She feared that the temporary prohibition on intercourse that is part of the treatment would anger him and he would quit the relationship. Having an adequate history, it was not difficult to see and then point out to Ellen her very persistent pattern in relating to men. We encouraged her to try talking to Zeek.

Much to Ellen's surprise (and our relief) Zeek was very concerned and co-operative. He came in to the office to talk about the problem and was willing—even happy—to help in the treatment.

In a final session with Ellen, we suggested that her tendency to feel used by men and her inability to feel cared for and valuable as a person might not just evaporate because of her present experience.

Ellen's early experiences with males and sex reinforced her idea that males used females for sex and didn't care about them as whole persons. At 16, in going steady, she had her first experience in a relationship in which she felt her boyfriend was "interested" in her and she in him. His patience with her, his ability to accept that she felt used and his positive attitude toward sex as natural were all very helpful to her, beginning to challenge some of her previous assumptions.

For a while she tried turning the tables on men, "using" them as sex objects without caring about them as persons. With Zeek she made a conscious effort to try to fuse caring and sex. She was tired of the merry-go-round that wasn't so merry. As in the case of Alan and Betsy, her coming for help with a sexual problem and her involving Zeek in this were very positive steps, a measure of a new (for her) trust.

Sarah

Sarah's story is used to illustrate a pattern which is more in line with Erikson's model in which there is no real capacity for intimacy until crucial issues relative to identity formation can be worked through. The process of sexual unfolding in her case could never get past square one until she was in her early 20s.

Sarah's story is important because it makes the point that sexual experience and sexual unfolding are not one and the same. Merely having lots of sexual experience will not necessarily promote growth or even generate much learning. The individual must be free enough to learn from what he or she is experiencing before growth can take place. Almost everyone has some experiences with sex that seem to be nonevents; the personality remains untouched in any way. For some young people, the entirety of their sexual experience seems to leave them unchanged. At 20 or 27 they need to *start* the process of sexual unfolding and, in particular, the merging of sex and love.

How is it possible for repeated sexual experiences to be simply that—repeated experiences? When the sexual behavior is generated out of severe conflict or distortion, and is used as a way of trying to resolve that conflict or clear up that distortion, then little or no real learning can take place. When sexual behavior is used almost entirely for extra-sexual purposes, rather than for the pleasure and closeness, or uniqueness of the experience itself, there will usually be hollow repetition.

Sarah, a young woman in her mid-20s, came for therapy with her fiancé. This was the first time in her life that she was in a serious or close relationship, although she had been having intercourse since age 15 with many sexual partners. She never experienced orgasm in any way and was anxious in all sexual situations. The most significant factor in her life experience was her conflict with her mother, a large, physically powerful woman, who had regularly beat her in order to keep her in line. She was never allowed to express her own feelings or opinions. Self-assertion only led to more beatings. Her father was a kindly, passive man who was never present when his wife administered the beatings. At 15, Sarah had intercourse. When her mother "found out" she said to Sarah, "Well, at least now you know it's not all it's cracked up to be." Sarah tried to persuade her mother that she had enjoyed her sexual experiences, although in fact they were painful, upsetting and nonpleasurable. Even at 15 and 16 Sarah was aware that she was using sex to get back at her mother and to become independent of her.

At college her working class origins made her feel inferior. She rejected the life style she associated with her mother, her cousins and her home town peers—a life of marriage, having children, being "traditional, old-fashioned and up-tight about sex." She felt that being "cool and cosmopolitan" would help her to gain the approval of peers at college and help to separate her from identification with and dependence upon her mother. She pretended to be casual and flip in talking about sex, although just hearing a sexy joke made her anxious. Her strong career ambitions were another facet of her intense need to break away.

Sarah's feelings about sex were also influenced by three attempted assaults in early adolescence. In all three she escaped without anything much happening, but she was terrified and felt that her family didn't protect her as well as they might have.

Her sexual pattern was one of inviting males to be sexual without "knowing" she was doing this and then feeling trapped into continuing in order to maintain her self-image as someone who enjoyed sex, was cool, and not hung-up. She felt unable to assert her own needs or protect herself. In the guise of meeting the man's needs, she inwardly felt a rage about being used or forced. During these unpleasant sexual encounters she would often fantasy that the man loved her and imagine being married to him and having children. But she never allowed herself to feel any tender feelings or to admit that she had needs, either emotional or sexual.

The pattern of her sexual experiences remained essentially unchanged for eight years. During this time, by finding a beginning sense of herself through career goals, making new friends, and gaining some independence from her family, she began to be dissatisfied with her nonrelationships with men. The death of a close relative put her suddenly in touch with her need for love and affirmed the value of family ties and some aspects of tradition. She then had a successful experience in brief individual psychotherapy in which she focused on her relationships with men and talked about her parents. At this point she felt ready for a deeper kind of relationship. Soon afterward she met her fiancé.

We have certainly not covered all facets of Sarah's sexual behavior nor the life experiences that influenced it (the role of her relationship with her father, for example, is also important). We wanted simply to convey some ways in which sexual unfolding can be arrested, permanently or temporarily, not only by conflict which is directly sexual but by other developmental struggles which are played out in and through sexual behavior.

Commitment

Whether an individual's sexual experiences are in the context of just a few relationships or encompass a great deal of experimentation, the general trend among students is towards pairing that involves greater and greater emotional intimacy. Along with greater depth and intimacy there is usually a parallel growth in commitment. By commitment we do not necessarily mean an agreed upon sexual fidelity or a move toward permanence. What we mean is, ". . . a willingness to stay through friction, to work on problems when they occur, to be a little stuck with each other." Very often issues of commitment, intimacy, and sexual function are inextricably bound together. These issues may be worked out simply or may call for considerable professional help.

Linda, a sophomore woman, came to the SCS to talk about a medical concern but also mentioned that she was not having orgasms with her boyfriend (Fred) although she could come easily during masturbation. She thought that his premature ejaculation was part of the problem. He was in the waiting room and they had talked in advance about their being seen together so we asked her to invite him to join us. He did.

He immediately focused on his worry about premature ejaculation. Questioned more closely it turned out that Linda and Fred only saw one another on weekends. He "lasted" about 30 seconds on Friday night, two minutes on Saturday and four to five minutes on Sunday but they had never really made the connection between abstinence and his coming quickly.

Linda spoke about her sheltered upbringing and the lack of previous sexual experience. Fred was her first real boyfriend and they had only been together for three months. Within three weeks of knowing one another they had begun to have intercourse without any gradual sharing of physical intimacy. They used condoms and foam at first but now she was on the pill.

At a follow-up interview two weeks later, Linda and Fred said the premature ejaculation problem seemed to be gone now that they were seeing each other some during the week. Linda still hadn't experienced orgasm with Fred but they weren't feeling too uptight about that. "We think it'll probably happen."

They had attended a lecture (given by us) on sexuality and intimacy that was very meaningful to them. After the lecture they had spent hours talking. Fred had never been able to tell Linda or anyone else about his deep feelings, but he was spurred on by our discussion of honest and open communication to tell her some of his worries. He said he was afraid his moodiness was driving her away, but he didn't want the relationship to end. She confessed her fears of losing him if she was her "real" self, expressing her ideas and wishes openly. They realized, with surprise, that her urging him to attend our lecture was the first time she had ever asked him to do anything she wanted to do.

Linda said she guessed she was afraid of risking rejection because she had always had such a low opinion of herself but she was starting to feel better about the person she was and about her own physical attractiveness so maybe she could be more assertive. Fred said, "Well, look what happened when you stood up for yourself. We went to the lecture and it really was great for both of us."

Linda then told us about a dream in which she was saying goodbye to Fred. She asked for his address, but he wouldn't or couldn't tell her and she felt panicked. Her dream opened a discussion of his plans after graduation, the extent of their commitment to one another, and their ambivalence about getting close. Linda said to Fred, "I think I've always felt that our relationship was temporary, that you might call it off any moment, but the other night, when we talked and you were able to tell me things like you did, I felt that if you trusted me enough to tell me those things our relationship was pretty solid. I think my not having an orgasm with you is somehow connected with some insecurity I had about our relationship not continuing. Maybe that's why I think it's going to work out OK."

In late adolescent and young adult couples, sexual problems are often a matter of developmental processes rather than a genuine dysfunction although, out of early difficulties, an entrenched problem can easily emerge. Fred and Linda's case presents the usual sort of mix—some specifically sexual issue that is relatively superficial (such as Fred's premature ejaculation) that yields to reassurance and education plus some underlying struggles with being emotionally intimate and committed. With Fred and Linda the deeper level of communication was sparked by a lecture. They were obviously ready for a new stage of intimacy and commitment and only needed some gentle encouragement. They themselves sensed that the issues in their sexual relationship were part of larger issues between them.

The next story, that of Kathy and Peter, is an example of a young unmarried couple dealing with problems of intimacy, commitment, and sexual dysfunction over a period of several years. They were able to work toward a deepening relationship but were stymied by the sexual problem.

Kathy

Kathy came to the SCS during her senior year, complaining of pain during intercourse and lack of sexual response. She and Peter had been going together since their last year in high school. He was at school in another city. They had been having intercourse for over a year but it was always painful for Kathy. Before Peter, Kathy had a boyfriend with whom there was some light petting through clothing. She hadn't felt sexually aroused but the experiences were reasonably comfortable.

Kathy was a petite, attractive, and stylishly groomed brunette. She was very engaging and articulate. As she began to speak about her problem she tended to define it as entirely her own. She came alone and focused all "blame" on herself. One of the important facets of the interviews was helping her to see the problem as both hers and Peter's and to express the anger at Peter that she had been denying.

What follows is a reconstructed verbatim report from the initial interview between Kathy and L.S.

KATHY: I don't think I was really eager. It *wasn't* like I didn't want it and he was pushing me. Pause. But I certainly wasn't relaxed. In fact, I was uneasy. I didn't have moral misgivings; I just didn't enjoy it.

L.S.: Peter was more eager?—(K. nods "yes"). It sounds like a difficult scene for you.

KATHY: Peter was always ahead of me. He's always *pushing* (some anger in this word) me to the first steps . . . I never felt comfortable. I always felt like it was something new and I wouldn't be doing it if he wasn't . . . uh . . . encouraging me.

L.S.: Did he usually know how you were feeling?

KATHY: (tearful), He once said he didn't care that it hurt me. That annoyed me.

L.S.: You were angry?

KATHY: My feelings were hurt and yet—I guess I had a right to be angry. In my mind I was doing this for his pleasure anyway.

L.S.: Why do you think you have continued having intercourse even though it hurts?

KATHY: I just keep hoping it will stop hurting—and it does hurt less now than it used to—and I know Peter gets pleasure (long pause). You know he really has changed a lot. Now he *does* care that it hurts me and he wants to help me. He's much more open and warm. I really believe he cares about me. He said he'd take a day or two off from school and come in here with me to talk to you. He's not generally a compassionate person but he really wants to help me with this.

L.S.: Tell me a little about the changes in Peter and in your relationship.

KATHY: Well—I don't think of myself as acting upon him but I suppose I'm the main factor in his changing. Three years ago he wasn't warm and understanding—but gradually, between the two of us . . . It's been a really painful and traumatic process of breaking up and coming back together, many times. But each time we got closer. About a year ago we had a "final" breakup which was very painful for him—the first time he ever missed anyone—and since then, just having someone who really cares about *him* more than anyone else. . . . He was always sort of repressed—not outspoken. He was popular but never had a real friend. After our "final" break-up, I couldn't believe it—he actually sought out a friend to talk to—a real first for him. And he's different with me now. It used to be he couldn't—or wouldn't—tell me his thoughts even about a play we'd just seen. I never knew what he was thinking. He's so much better now about saying what he thinks and feels.

[At this point we would like to add a few words of Peter's from a subsequent interview with Dr. Sarrel. This was our only contact with Peter.]

PETER: In the first two years of the relationship I put in very little effort. She wanted close communication all the time and I just wasn't up to that. The big difference is now we talk about things where before we'd just chalk up differences and disagreements as "That's another reason I don't want to marry you." Another important factor was that it took me years to get comfortable with how bright and ambitious Kathy is. She'll be an equal—a professional. In my family my father dominates. For a long time I kept up an interest in this other girl who's much more, well, submissive. But now I've really decided on Kathy.

[Returning again to Kathy, another important theme emerges—the positive changes in her and, in particular, the positives in their sexual relationship. It was important to elicit and support these positive elements.]

L.S.: How have you changed?

KATHY: I've changed a tremendous amount in these years. I'm not very close to my family anymore but I guess I'd say the main change is—I've come to feel so close to Peter. And sexually, I *have* changed. He was always pushing me and that had a bad side but it was good too, because each time we'd go on to the next step, I'd be comfortable with the last one.

L.S.: There were things you enjoyed.

KATHY: Mmm—the holding and when he kissed me.

L.S.: How do you feel about kissing now?

KATHY: (laughs), I love it.

L.S.: So, you really like kissing. Would you say its erotic?

KATHY: I'd say kissing is *the most* erotic. Pause. There *are* things that excite me—when he puts pressure between my legs and rubs—like with his leg or something—I guess that rubs my cl . . . cli . . . clitoris.

L.S.: Your clitoris and labia—the whole area.

KATHY: Yeah. (Then, with emphasis) I think *that* is probably the most erotic thing.

L.S.: So—you are aware of erotic response in yourself.

KATHY: (very exuberantly) Yeah, I know what there must be; I just want more.

L.S.: And you feel good when you have those kinds of feelings? (She nods yes) You like that.

KATHY: Yes.

[The next portion of this interview focuses on sexual communication. Two important points emerge: (1) that Kathy's ambivalence about her sexual feelings and her own general reticence with feelings is interfering with needed communication; and (2) that she does not protect herself. These became focal points in subsequent counseling.]

L.S.: Do you let him know what feels good?

KATHY: No, I haven't.

L.S.: Embarrassed?

KATHY: I guess it would be a form of embarrassment. I just wouldn't know what to say. I suppose I could say "that feels good." Pause . . . I'm very verbally uncommunicative as far as sex goes. It's very hard for me. I don't think I've ever asked him to do something for me.

L.S.: Do you know why?

KATHY: I have trouble explaining something to him. There's a hangover from the past—which is—I don't think he cares to hear about it. It's also just hard to get the words out about sex or if we have a disagreement—I feel locked up physically. That's from my family. They can't yell at one another, never, never, never. My father's never expressed any feeling about anything—no, that's an exaggeration but he gets mad and holds it all in. I've been trying to get over that—to be able to express my feelings but it's hard.

L.S.: In the sexual area—Have you ever told him, for example, how you like to kiss?

KATHY: No. He does say—"Please tell me what you like"—but I just can't answer.

L.S.: If he were touching you in some way and asked if you liked it—could you answer?

KATHY: I'd just say "yes." I always say "yes" even if I don't mean it.

L.S.: He has no way of tuning in to you. Does he ever show or tell you what he likes?

KATHY: Yes, he's had to learn to do it—but he does. And I'm glad when he does. And I always do what he asks.

L.S.: Even if it's not something you enjoy?

KATHY: He never asked me to do anything I dislike. At the worst, I'm indifferent.

L.S.: Do you feel OK to touch his penis?

KATHY: Sure—yes.

L.S.: Do you stimulate his penis with your mouth?

KATHY: Yes.

L.S.: Are you comfortable with that?

KATHY: Yes—well—uh—I suppose I really didn't—don't (pause) I guess I don't say no even though I *don't* like that. I just do it.

L.S.: You should protect yourself. [She nods in agreement.] *He* needs you to as well as for your own sake. If you want open communication, you've got to say what you do and don't want.

The total treatment in this case, consisted of five appointments for Kathy with L.S., one hour between Peter and P.S., plus several gynecologic examinations for the treatment of vaginismus.*

* Kathy did have a hymeneal septum which contributed to her pain and difficulty with intercourse. See page 260.

The vaginismus was cured and Kathy's sexual responsiveness and her pleasure in her responses increased greatly.

Kathy and Peter illustrate the unfolding of sexual response and sexual exchange in a growing and changing relationship. They evolved, over three years or so, from noncommunication toward an ability to share feelings, from little commitment toward serious commitment, and from an inability to problem solve to taking on and sharing in the resolution of their sexual problem.

A sexual problem or the sex therapy process itself may serve as a defense against commitment. Most of the unmarried couples who seek help with a sexual problem have a strong commitment to continuing the relationship and most think they will probably marry but they are worried about the outcome of sex therapy and its implications for their future. The remnants of their ambivalence about marriage tend to become focused on the question of solving or not solving the sex problem.

We have always brought these issues out into the open, not once in the course of therapy but repeatedly, to make sure that ambivalence about commitment isn't sabotaging the therapy and to try to separate the issues of sexual function from the issue of commitment. Couples have used the therapy as an opportunity to work out both of these issues and, interestingly, several couples have become engaged (and one couple even married) in the middle of sex therapy.

One young man, midway through therapy, put it this way: "At first I thought if the therapy failed and she couldn't have an orgasm, I'd have second thoughts about marriage. But the more I think about it the more I think it doesn't matter. We've covered so much basic ground now, gotten to know each other at a new level and we both like what we see. I think we'll probably get married no matter how the therapy turns out."

Working with young married couples has often involved similar issues of commitment. In the first years of marriage, before they've had any children, these couples have often kept open an emotional escape clause; they haven't really decided to stay married. One such couple, married for two years, presented with a problem of little or no interest in sex on the part of the wife. In the initial interview she presented a very negative view of the marriage, saying she had married too young, for the wrong reasons, and had been unhappy ever since. She felt her husband had trapped her, under false pretenses.

L.S. asked to see her twice alone, in order to discuss the question of commitment to the marriage. She was both relieved and frightened to talk about it. I pointed out that she seemed to need to see herself as trapped in the marriage, with no way out. She said that although she had been miserable, she had never allowed herself to even imagine leaving. She realized how utterly dependent and fearful she felt. The idea of managing realities like an automobile or buying anything more major than groceries on her own was terrifying. Her life had always conformed to her parents' and her community's expectations. She was *always* a good girl. She did admit to being attracted to another man, but these feelings made her anxious and guilty, so she worked very hard at suppressing them. She had never "confessed" her feelings to anyone before.

In the week between the two individual interviews she was in turmoil, allowing herself to fantasize, for the first time, what it would be like to get a divorce and live on her own. She began to think she could manage it and survive but she also began to feel that she didn't really want to leave, that she did love her husband. When she returned to see L.S., she felt she was really ready to go ahead with sex therapy, not because she was trapped into it but because she wanted to try to work out her marriage. This was the first time she had referred to it as *her* marriage!

Fidelity

Serious relationships in college or graduate school present dilemmas of fidelity which would tax a Solomon (and his partner?). It isn't easy for the couple to work out the details of such a relationship because there is often a tremendous emotional investment and yet a need to keep things open. This can become quite a balancing act. One couple who were having difficulties finding their balance said despairingly, "Do you know *any* couples who are sleeping together and really care about each other and who are happy?"

This particular couple, like many couples these days, was trying to maintain a serious relationship while allowing each other the freedom to have sex with others. She wasn't really interested in using this option but he was. In exercising his "rights," he was hurting her terribly—and this hurt him. But he felt he was too young to be "monogamous." Even when both partners are seemingly comfortable with the idea of occasional sex with someone else, they have trouble with the nitty-gritty realities. "How can I leave her alone on a Saturday night while I go out to a mixer?" The cult of honesty so prevalent among students makes covert sex outside of the pair almost impossible but dealing honestly with this issue is never easy and is often incredibly painful.

When couples come to us to talk about this problem we try, first of all, to help them clarify what each feels. It is interesting to see, among students, a tendency to think that jealous feelings are wrong. You *shouldn't* feel jealous and if you do you should learn to suppress it. This belief sometimes causes one partner to grin and bear his or her jealous agony in silence, only to retaliate in some way later on. The many struggles and dilemmas presented when a couple tries to be committed and intimate but not "monogamous" have been discussed very humanly in Carl Rogers' book *Becoming Partners* [3]. We usually acknowledge that these are existential matters for which there are no simple answers and suggest that the couple read Rogers' book.

Another book which students have found helpful in clarifying issues about sexual fidelity is Robert and Anna Francoeur's book *Hot and Cool Sex* [4]. This book expresses the belief that a couple can relate sexually with others and still maintain a continuing bond *if* they have a strong, healthy primary bond and *if* they have had several years of "monogamy" in which they have forged these primary bonds. Obviously most couples in college and graduate school have just not had the time to work out their own relationship. Relating to others at too early a stage is quite likely to threaten their relationship. This, in fact, is what we have seen—the couples in trouble. Of course we wouldn't be likely to see the couples who *do* work it out successfully.

We don't want to give the impression that college students are not sexually faithful within their relationships. Most are. Many of these relationships resemble traditional marriages (although traditional sex-roles, such as male-earns-the-living, female-keeps-house, are seldom observed) in their degree of caring for and commitment to the other person.

This leads to problems of another sort. Many couples complain that because of the time spent together they have little time left for friends, extracurricular activities and solo recreation. Some feel a unique opportunity to experience life's many facets is being sacrificed and will never come again. Sometimes dramatic splits and reunions occur because of the intense ambivalence. These splits occasionally result in an "unwanted" pregnancy. The young woman stops taking her pill because they have stopped seeing each other. In an unanticipated moment of passionate reunion they have intercourse without contraception. The pregnancy and probable abortion then serve to end the unbearable ambivalence. They become a more solidly committed couple with all the sacrifices that entails or they break up permanently.

More and more young couples are having the experience of prolonged geographic separation while each pursues a career. During prolonged separation issues of fidelity are inevitably present, if only as an unspoken possibility. Such separations are extremely difficult to negotiate successfully. We see couples who have developed a sexual problem in anticipation of, during, or following prolonged periods of living apart. At least in part because of real or fantasized sex outside of the relationship, times of reunion are sexually pressured; there's a need to make up for the time apart and prove that this relationship is still good. This is more of a burden than sex can easily sustain.

The themes of intimacy, commitment, and fidelity are everpresent in young couples (for that matter, in all couples). Sexual exchange influences feelings about the other person; closeness and the ability to be oneself with another person influences sexual function. Anyone who counsels or treats couples understands these interconnections, but sometimes professionals tend to lose sight of the person behind the problem or the total context of a dysfunction. In the chapters on counseling and therapy, we hope to emphasize the need to understand the person, the couple, and their stage of sexual unfolding in the process of helping with a sexual problem.

References

1. Erikson, Erik, "The Problem of Ego Identity" in *Journal of the American Psychoanalytic Association*, Vol. 4, 1956, pp. 56-121.
2. Lidz, Theodore, *The Person* (revised edition), New York, Basic Books, Inc., 1976, pp. 368-371.
3. Rogers, Carl R., *Becoming Partners: Marriage and Its Alternatives*, New York, Delacorte Press, 1972.
4. Francoeur, Robert and Francoeur, Anna, *Hot and Cool Sex*, New York, Harcourt-Brace-Jovanovich, Inc., 1974.

Part II

SEX COUNSELING AND THERAPY IN THE UNIVERSITY SETTING

6

Sex Counseling

Sex Counseling in the University Setting

The Sex Counseling Service (SCS) began in the fall of 1969, when Yale College became co-educational, admitting enough females that year to create a 6 to 1 ratio of male to female undergraduates.* The SCS was started because those responsible for student health anticipated pregnancies, venereal disease, and a need for contraception among the entering young women. Luckily, they were not entirely correct. There have been few pregnancies and almost no VD. But there has been a great need for the prescription of contraception and an even greater need for advice, counseling and therapy—not just for the female undergraduates but for the entire university community.

From the beginning the SCS was staffed by a team, i.e., both of us. There is an office and a regular gynecologic examining room set in the middle of a large and flourishing student mental health service.

Since 1969 approximately 2500 female and 500 male students have used the Sex Counseling Service—voluntarily of course. Approximately 30 percent of students come in as a couple; 55 percent are women by themselves and 15 percent are men by themselves. Reasons for their coming to the SCS include (all approximate figures) 35 percent for contraception, 15 percent for contracep-

* At present, there is a sex balanced admissions policy and close to equal numbers of males and female students.

143

tion plus a concern about sex, 40 percent for sex counseling or therapy, 10 percent for miscellaneous problems.

As part of an overall health service which provides total medical care the SCS is one option available to students.† They may choose to get medical or gynecologic care from an internist or the gynecology service or to talk about sexual matters with other members of the mental health staff, other doctors or a nurse.

We originally decided to place the SCS in the Mental Hygiene Division for two reasons. This excellent division of the health services at Yale has a good reputation among students for quality and confidentiality. The second reason was our desire to emphasize the counseling and therapy aspect of the service. We knew that students would make use of the medical care offered—contraception, pregnancy-diagnosis, VD diagnosis, abortion (which is provided for under the Yale Health Plan) but we also knew that many students would need and welcome a chance to talk about sexual decisions, worries, the meaning of relationships, sexual function and dysfunction, or feelings about a pregnancy.

Over the years, we have seen many hundreds of young men and women, either alone or as a couple, who have been struggling with sexual problems. The availability of a counseling service which students trust and will use when a sexual problem arises undoubtedly plays an important preventive role. Many of the sexual problems in the university age group are normal, developmental hurdles or setbacks which can be helped through a brief counseling process. Other problems are more severe and require therapy or referral.

Sex counseling is usually short term (one to three visits), predominantly educative, does not require comprehensive history-taking and tends to focus entirely on the presenting sexual concerns. Where sex counseling is done in a medical setting, it may include a physical examination and medical treatment or prescrip-

---

† Yale University has a prepaid health insurance plan for all students. Most faculty also belong to the health plan. Sex counseling and therapy are free for students. Faculty and employees are entitled to "consultation"—approximately 4 hours of professional time. Beyond that they must pay a standard fee for psychotherapy—the payments going to the university.

tion. A prototype of sex counseling in a medical setting is the way in which we handle requests for contraception in the SCS (see Chapter 9 on contraception). Other examples of sex counseling are: talking to a male student for an hour or two after he has had a single experience of impotence, medically treating a vaginal infection and discussing the effects of painful intercourse on a sexual relationship, talking with a student couple who are worried about her not having orgasms one month after they began having intercourse.

Sex therapy is usually longer term (from four to 15 visits) and involves a comprehensive sexual history which places the sexual problem in the context of personality and relationships. Although education is part of the process, it is by no means the main ingredient. The opportunity to practice new sexual behaviors as prescribed by the therapists is usually a feature of sex therapy. As we will describe later on, we use several formats for sex therapy, up to and including fairly "orthodox" Masters and Johnson therapy.

Female Problems

We see several female students daily who are worried about some aspect of their sexual response, many complaining that they are not sexually satisfied. Sometimes these young women could appropriately be called nonorgasmic and some form of treatment such as Masters and Johnson sex therapy or a group such as that described by Barbach is called for [1]. However, the majority of women students concerned about their sexual response can be helped, most appropriately, through short-term counseling.

Sometimes the "problem" is only a phantom. We have found that at least half a dozen students a year, who are not certain whether their sexual response included orgasm are, in fact, having orgasms. Their confusion can usually be traced to a mistaken concept or fantasy about orgasm. One young woman who had "studied" (she said) Masters and Johnson's writings was convinced that she couldn't be having orgasms, because she never had a "sex flush." Obviously, she hadn't studied too carefully because Masters and Johnson make it clear that not all people experience a sex flush and those who do show this vascular change don't do so every time. More commonly, the mistaken idea about orgasm involves an over-idealization and exaggeration borrowed from literature or film: "the earth and stars will move," "there will be waves crashing over me," "I will faint or afterwards I will feel totally exhausted and satisfied." One student had a mental image of the postorgasmic state taken from the film, "Room at the Top"—languorously smoking in bed. Since she felt rather peppy and exhilarated after sex, she thought she must not be having "real" orgasms.

A graduate student came to talk about her problem with non-orgasmic response. She and her lover were very disturbed by the problem which had persisted for over a year. He was a somewhat older man who had been married before. She entered this relationship with very little sexual experience. The goal of their sexual relations was her orgasm. Although she experienced prolonged and intense pleasure he told her that she wasn't having an orgasm. As we talked, it became apparent that she was indeed having an orgasm—many orgasms each time. Her multiple-orgasm pattern wasn't familiar to him (because his wife's pattern had been different) and she had accepted his definition of female response.

So many of the women who come to the SCS saying they are dissatisfied sexually are dissatisfied because their sexual response does not measure up to their expectation of what they *ought* to experience. In moving away from the old tyranny of thou-shalt-nots, we are rapidly succumbing to a new tyranny of thou-shalts that can cause just as much human misery and harm as sexual repression. When a young woman and her partner approach sex in this way, they will tend to have a strong goal orientation. A goal orientation in sex stresses the end result rather than the pleasure of getting there. For the female today there is a hierarchy of goals to be "achieved": These goals are usually thought of as "shoulds" and so a list might read as follows:

1. I should have intercourse.
2. I should enjoy intercourse.
3. I should have an orgasm.

4. I should have an orgasm during intercourse with no clitoral touching.
5. I should have multiple orgasms.
6. I should have my orgasm when he has his.
7. I should want sex all or most of the time.
8. I should enjoy oral sex.

Masters and Johnson (and Kinsey before them) stressed the fact that sex response cannot be willed. The harder one tries to make something happen, the greater the anxiety about producing a result, the more one simply disrupts the natural sequence of sexual response. One becomes a tense observer, removed from real participation in the feelings of the moment, what Masters and Johnson called being a "spectator." And so, paradoxically, the focus in recent decades on female sexual function has, for many women, created a new stumbling block to sexual fulfillment—a quest that leads instead to spectatoring, a sense of failure and then a near panic about not being "normal."

In the college milieu there is already a tendency toward an achievement-oriented outlook. Many students are accustomed to solving problems by reading, studying, and working hard. When they try to apply this problem-solving approach to sex, things usually go away.

The students we see have a fairly sophisticated level of understanding about *some* aspects of sex. For example, most of the females don't expect to have an orgasm the first time they have intercourse. This is very realistic since only a tiny percentage of the women we have seen did have an orgasm with first intercourse (approximately 8 out of 2,000). They usually expect that they will have to "get used to it" a bit before having an orgasm. But they are often unrealistically impatient about how long it should take. It isn't unusual for us to see a couple who has had intercourse only 10 or 20 times concerned about the fact that she hasn't *yet* had an orgasm. One young woman in her junior year, who was extremely upset by her lack of orgasm, said that she had had a relationship in her freshman year in which she didn't have orgasms either, "But then I didn't know how things were supposed to be, so everything was very nice."

The majority of female students who come to the SCS concerned about lack of orgasm come in with their boyfriends. Not uncommonly, he is more worried than she is. It is very helpful to be able to see both partners in this situation because the problem often has important interactional dimensions. Frequently, the young man is worried about his sexual adequacy. He may ask her every time they have intercourse, "How was that? Did you come this time?" Or he may communicate his anxiety in more subtle ways through a look, a sigh, a sultry mood after intercourse, or simply by *trying* so very hard to make it happen.

Almost invariably, in talking with such a couple, we can help the young woman to say how all of this makes her feel and, almost invariably, she feels under tremendous pressure to have an orgasm at least partly to relieve *his* anxieties! His efforts to "give her" an orgasm often make her tremendously self-conscious. She watches him watching her and tries to reward his efforts with some increased level of response. It is amazing, given all of these pressures as well as her own concerns about adequacy—how she compares with other females, will he still want her, etc.—that so few young women we see fall into the trap of faking orgasms. They are trapped, though, in a vicious cycle of worry, leading to more pressure, leading to more worry. When something happens, coincidentally, such as a doctor's prohibiting intercourse due to vaginitis, and the test-and-failure situation is temporarily eliminated, they often rediscover the pleasure they used to have before the vicious cycle began. There aren't nearly as many "shoulds" and "oughts" in petting. You can just relax and enjoy the feelings.

We have never spoken with a female who wasn't delighted at the prospect of her partner's touching her for the pleasure *he* found in her body rather than having him "work on her." Sexual abandon is contagious and his letting-go is actually a much more effective trigger for her sexual responses than any special "erogenous zone."

Another goal of sexual performance still sought by many couples is the so-called vaginal orgasm. In spite of the evidence of Masters and Johnson that vaginal, clitoral and labial stimulation all contribute to the orgasms a female has during intercourse, the myth of the vaginal orgasm persists in the minds of many people. We are not saying that there is now conclusive proof that there are no subjective (and perhaps even physiologic) differences between orgasms obtained through different modes of stimulation. What we do argue against, very strongly, are the remnants of the Freudian idea that there is one "mature" way for women to have an orgasm and that must be purely vaginal.

Belief in the existence of a vaginal orgasm as something different from and superior to other orgasms can be incredibly destructive. The letter below from a graduate student is a poignant example of this:

My husband and I have just separated and the problem was sex. I know that our problem was common for I have read many books that deal with such occurrences. But I could not find a straight answer to the nagging question that basically separated us. Why couldn't I achieve vaginal orgasm? I have read enough to suspect that it is possible for most women to have vaginal orgasms. Is this true? You see, for my husband and for most men, vaginal climaxes would be preferred. After all that's the way we are biologically constructed. And equal sex response has got to be one of the most important components in a relationship.

During our courtship I *never had a vaginal orgasm but was very happy to reach orgasms with manual manipulations.* However, I suspected that my husband-to-be was not totally satisfied. But I rationalized that after we were married we would work it out together. When it didn't, I blamed him for not being more affectionate and for not taking more time to make love and for achieving orgasm too soon. I tried to talk with him but he wouldn't really talk about it. As my unresponsiveness continued he grew internally more upset with his inability to help me. All the time I was asking for love making and open discussion and more consideration he was feeling uncertain about his manhood, insecure and alienated. Therefore, his silence.

We're going to a marriage counselor now, but he hasn't answered my big question of obtaining vaginal orgasms. I want to know if it really involves deep emotional commitment or whether I can just achieve it with someone I like. Somehow I feel that knowing about it and practice with it makes it attainable. Would this be true? And if there is a way to practice it, I want to try it. I guess the emotional involvement of love just heightens orgasms, or vice versa. But how can you have love if you can't have good sex. The love just dies.

When the problem of nonsatisfying response has persisted for awhile, the counselor or therapist is faced with a difficult question: What sort of help is appropriate for this person (couple)? The initial contact helps in answering the question, but there are no precise criteria that one can easily use. If we have the feeling that this person might respond well to brief one-to-one counseling we will often start with that approach—moving on to a greater depth or complexity (e.g., involving the partner taking a fuller history, etc.) only if the first approach is not helpful. The following is an example of brief counseling which focused largely on sex education and communication issues while implicitly and explicitly giving permission to experiment and to have sexual feelings.

Barbara, a graduate student, sought help for "frigidity." She had been seriously involved with a young man in another city for the past two years. He didn't know the extent of her dissatisfaction, assuming that she was having orgasms. She didn't want to tell him of her frustration for fear of ending the relationship. At this point, a counselor could insist that she be honest with her partner and involve him in the counseling. L.S. chose to start with this student where she was at the moment, in part because she seemed so shy, reticent, and apprehensive that any insistence might have driven her away. In asking about her past, it became clear that her very religious upbringing, in a family in which sex was a totally taboo subject, plus her lack of knowledge and prior experience were all contributing to the problem and to her inability to talk about it with her partner. She was unable to talk about sex with him or to show him anything about her own preferences.

In spite of her early reticence on sexual matters, Barbara responded very well to reading that L.S. suggested and purposely let her boyfriend, Sam, see the book "accidentally" as a way of opening up discussion between them. The counseling process was quite short, only four half-hour sessions. The main goals were education about sex, helping Barbara to value her own sexual responses and overcome her shyness about showing Sam what pleased her. She was able to make good use of the sessions and in a very short time reported a marked increase in her sexual pleasure.

One final word on counseling young women who have a problem of sexual response. In many instances we have found medical conditions associated with sex problems. Vaginitis, cystitis, estrogen deficiency, hymeneal septa, and so on, are part of a long list of conditions which we have had to deal with in our sex counseling. In these cases, treatment has meant both medical treatment as well as sex counseling. This is a point we have made more fully in other sections of this book, but it should be reiterated here in the context of our everyday sex counseling.

Male Problems

The concerns and problems presented by male students which are amenable to short term counseling cover a wide spectrum of presenting complaints. We will focus here on the problems of premature ejaculation and impotence.

PREMATURE EJACULATION. We have learned from our work in the SCS, the feedback from students in our human sexuality course, and data we have collected from other schools, that premature ejaculation is an extremely common phenomenon, affecting over 90 percent of male students at least some of the time. This is not surprising when one considers the Kinsey finding that the median length of time to ejaculation in adolescent males was 1.91 minutes [2] and the fact that, given a period of abstinence, most men will ejaculate faster than they normally do. Students generally have an irregular pattern of sexual relating, often abstaining during the week. In our lectures in human sexuality we refer to Friday night as "premature ejaculation night" on campuses across the country.

The fact that premature ejaculation, or at least rapid ejaculation, is so common does not keep young men from worrying, even panicking, about it. Some of the men have not thought of themselves as having a problem until reading about sex in one or more of the popular sex books of recent years. One widely read book led to dozens of men seeking counseling. It placed dysfunction in a hierarchy from not-so-bad to terrible. This book suggested that if you're going to have a problem, ejaculatory incompetence is the best one because you simply last a long time giving your partner orgasm after orgasm. And, after all, isn't that what sex is all about anyway? Impotence isn't so terrible since you don't get your partner all turned on and leave her frustrated. But premature ejaculation is the worst problem since you leave your partner hanging and never give her the orgasm she wants so much.

One student who read this book became convinced that his coming quickly must be a terrible frustration for his girlfriend although she insisted she really enjoyed their love-making, despite the fact she didn't have an orgasm during intercourse (she did from oral stimulation). He asked her to come with him to the SCS because he couldn't believe she was telling him the truth; the book said otherwise. In the office she tried to explain her feelings. She said not only was she sexually satisfied, but she considered his rapid response a compliment. It showed how sexy she was and how much he was turned on by her. We urged this young man to derive his idea of what is sexually satisfying from his own and his girlfriend's experience—not from someone else's stereotype.

Students can be very creative in getting around the problem of rapid ejaculation. They learn, through experience, that the first time of intercourse after several days of abstinence there will be rapid ejaculation but if they have intercourse again, within a few hours, or four to five times in one weekend there will be little or no problem. Certainly sex counselors should support the idea that such variations on a theme are entirely normal. As long as a young man can stay relaxed about such a pattern, he will probably not develop a problem.

For others the trick of having intercourse several times in close succession doesn't work. One man actually tested the system and found that, even on the fifth time in one night, he still came quickly. About the only change he noticed was that the ejaculate gradually decreased so that by the fourth and fifth orgasm there was *no* ejaculate. That concerned him greatly and led to his seeking help. (This case actually required more help than just counseling.)

Another variation of normal sexual response which some young men worry about is a pattern of very rapid ejaculation in one or two intercourse positions but not in others. Most commonly the position which triggers premature ejaculation is the male-above, "missionary" position. It is probably the overall muscle tension which contributes to rapid response. A position in which the male's muscles can be more relaxed, and there is a general sense of leisurely pace (such as the lateral position described in *Human Sexual Inadequacy*) is usually helpful [3].

Since the ejaculatory reflex can be triggered with or without erection or with a partial erection (on the way up or on the way down), some young men may experience occasional rapid ejaculation without erection. Most have never heard that this can happen. Whether it occurs in masturbation, petting, or intercourse, even one such experience can be frightening and confusing. Unless this is the *usual* pattern of sex response, coming without erection is not a problem. This reassurance can be enormously relieving and can help to prevent sex response from becoming the focus of anxiety.

Some men manage to worry about their sexual response if it is less than at ideal. Perhaps the most extreme was the man who complained that he and his girlfriend experienced simultaneous orgasms only 70% of the time! One should understand that they were both perfectionists, had maintained straight A averages and this, indeed, was the only thing they didn't "perform perfectly" at least as far as could be determined.

It was a bit hard to take him seriously and yet, to him, it was serious. This was the first relationship in which he was having intercourse. Believing that simultaneous orgasm was supposed to happen all the time, he blamed himself for not lasting long enough. He considered himself a premature ejaculator although intercourse lasted 15 minutes or more. He feared that she would be frustrated and angry and would break up the relationship. This perfectionistic, slightly scared young man did not change his ideas about normal sex response that easily. He was referred to selected reading. That helped some. P.S., who was seeing him alone, had a creative idea. He played an audio tape for him of an off-the-cuff-discussion between five "jocks"—all stars in their respective sports. On the subject of intercourse, all five admitted to anxieties and occasional impotence. It seemed none of them had ever experienced simultaneous orgasm with a partner during intercourse. They concluded that it must be impossible! Or perhaps, they thought, it was some secret that older couples knew about. The student did gradually come to accept his experience as satisfying and special.

It may be the female partner who complains about premature ejaculation. Her feelings should be carefully elicited. She may complain of extreme frustration, of being left hanging all the time. This degree of frustration almost always reflects emotional rather than physical factors. Yes, there can be a real element of physical arousal which may contribute to her feelings but women who are orgasmic with some regularity do not report this sort of intense frustration. The woman who cries, who berates and criticizes her partner each time, is acting out more than physiological frustration; she is expressing worry about her lack of response and sexual adequacy, and her frustration about having a sexual problem.

Women whose partners are ejaculating quickly tend to believe that he is having a wonderful time getting it off while she suffers. One of the more helpful things a counselor can do is give the male the opportunity to say how he feels when he ejaculates prematurely. Almost without fail the man will describe displeasure rather than bliss. He usually focuses his energy on trying not to come. Then, realizing it's too late, he gives in to defeat and mentally says, "Oh, shit" (or something like that). Understanding his feelings, some of her anger is usually dispelled.

Up to this point the examples we have given show us playing a reassuring role, often helping young men and couples to see that what they thought was a problem was not. Almost as frequently we are in the opposite role—helping a young man to recognize that he does have a problem related to "premature ejaculation"; not that he comes in less than X seconds or his partner orgasms during intercourse in fewer than X percent of tries but that *he always worries about coming too soon.* His mental processes and behavior in bed are those of a premature ejaculator. He is inhibiting and distracting himself, conjuring math problems, football plays, or, as they say in the British Isles, he is "thinking of England," fearing to do anything "too exciting." He may ejaculate quickly or may actually last a long time and feel proud of his performance, but he hasn't really participated in the sexual experience. This may leave him dissatisfied. Partners often sense the holding back and are confused about what is going on. The absence of his erotic enthusiasm removes an important stimulus for her, and she may then wind up having problems responding sexually. So many men who have this premature ejaculation psychology find that if they risk letting go, allowing the control to come from within, they do not ejaculate "too quickly" and actually have a good time in bed for the first time in their lives.

TRANSITORY IMPOTENCE IN YOUNG MEN. The experience of being unable to have or maintain an erection can become a problem, even when the situational circumstances clearly explain why and how it happened. Some men feel embarrassed and humiliated. Others get depressed. Some panic that the experience is the harbinger of future failures. Others conclude they are unable to love or to be heterosexual. Rarely is the experience felt as a normal human reaction given the factors involved. Self-analysis is blurred by the feelings. It can become a problem especially if the scene is duplicated, the failure recurs, and spectatoring sets in. For many reasons, this is an ideal kind of sex problem for the sex counselor who is able to work with the men soon after the experience has occurred. Then there is the opportunity to help the individual step back from the situation and more clearly see and understand the factors which determined his impotence. Once aware of the issues involved, the men become able to avoid such situations or deal with these situations in a different way. Almost invariably their erectile difficulty is resolved. Some of the more common situations in which young men have been impotent include:

(1) Situations in which sexual demand is implict and, although the men may feel ambivalent or conflicted or fearful, they nevertheless feel there is no choice but to go ahead with intercourse: This happens in one-night stands. Some of the men didn't even know the name of the woman they had been impotent with. It often happens when young men go to prostitutes—scenes that are not only blatant performance scenes but frightening as well. It happens when men are set up on a date with a "hot chick." Sometimes men are set up on such dates by friends or relations (in one case, a father, in another an uncle) without realizing until it starts to get hot and heavy that that's what the date was all about. Reactions can range from surprise to shock to panic. Later the men become self-deprecatory, feeling they have not been able to do what a normal male is supposed to be always ready, willing, and able to do. The myth dies hard! Another kind of situation is when a man knows he is with a sexually experienced woman which to him means that anything short of intercourse would be viewed as kid's stuff. And so, he feels he has to have intercourse even though for him, it might be a first time or it might be something he only feels comfortable doing when he has an established relationship.

(2) Situations in which biophysical factors prove an impediment: Alcohol, drugs, and fatigue have made men impotent. Usually there is a combination of a little psychological conflict and a good deal of biophysical compromise. In one case mentioned elsewhere (pp. 95-96) we described the impotence problem of a man with a full bladder. What usually happens is that the initial impotence is shrugged off as due to the drinking or the fatigue but there is a lingering self-doubt. The next time the man—and often both partners—set out to prove there is no problem and that is when spontaneity disappears and spectatoring sets in.

(3) Lack of privacy: many men simply cannot respond sexually

if there is the possibility of being discovered by others or if others are within sight or hearing distance. Impotence has occurred when a roommate has been in the next room or when a parent lurks at the top of the stairs. Making love in the back seat of a car or in the open spaces is too much vulnerability for some men who don't realize they are fearful of exposure until this happens. A further complicating factor in such scenes are the uptight reactions of the women—the body tension, the vaginismus, the general nervousness—that further compounds the main anxiety. We have heard so many "after the prom out on the lawn" impotence stories!

(4) Transitory impotence in a relationship: A man can go through a period of impotence when first developing a relationship. It can be part of worrying about hurting the partner. It may be fear of pregnancy before contraception is established. It can simply be as one man said, "a slow start at something new." This discomfort with new surroundings, with a new relationship, with first times, seems to be very common.

Another time when relationship impotence occurs is when intercourse represents escalation of commitment. This was discussed in one of our case presentations ("Alan"). (See p. 111 ff.)

Sometimes the male partner's impotence reflects a female condition—vaginitis, vaginismus, aversion.

Men have been impotent when their girlfriends have had another sexual partner. The impotence may reflect hurt or anger or, sometimes, fear of venereal disease; most often, however, the man has a need to "do better than the other guy." Sex becomes an arena for competition, the price being the girl and one's sense of manhood.

(5) Moving from homosexuality to heterosexuality: Many men (Kinsey indicated about 40 percent) have homosexual experiences when they are adolescents. The typical man then begins to have heterosexual experiences which subsequently become his primary sources of sexual outlet [4]. For many of the men we have seen there has been a transitional period during which they still have homosexual attachments but are beginning to relate heterosexually. The carry-over of the earlier experience can influence their early

heterosexuality. Some men experience homosexual fantasies during sex with a girl. Others feel impelled to prove to themselves, in intercourse, that they are not homosexual. In several instances, men with previous homosexual experience found they monitored their erections as a measure of their heterosexuality. For many, the need to have heterosexual experience is urgent. As a result, they do not give themselves the opportunity to gradually unfold heterosexually and try to start with intercourse. Men with any of these feelings and approaches are vulnerable to impotence and, unfortunately, when they are impotent, they feel their worst fears have been corroborated.

Most of the time when a young man gives this sort of sexual history we consider the issues more appropriate for therapy than for counseling. However, it has been impressive to see the effects of just listening and sharing the Kinsey data as well as some of our own feelings about the normality of homosexual relating. With their "secret" out and their sexuality understood and accepted, quite a number of men have been able to relate heterosexually without difficulty. When they have returned for their "series" of scheduled appointments they are no longer troubled by impotence and further sex therapy has not been necessary.

(6) Impotence after there has been ejaculatory difficulty: As indicated in earlier discussions, men with premature ejaculation or ejaculatory incompetence can become so anxious over sex that they become unable to respond at all. Such cases are not really counseling cases but require more therapy to deal with both the impotence as well as the earlier problem.

Sharing basic information about sex response has been an important part of our sex counseling work with all men and, in particular, with men who have had impotence experiences. Because an erection or lack of it is so obvious to all involved, men are in a particularly vulnerable position with regard to the normal changes of sex response. For example, Masters and Johnson observed that during sexual relating, it is normal for the fullness of an erection to come and go. However, when a man or his partner is anxious about their sexual exchange, then even the slight outflow of blood from the penis which happens normally can raise anxiety levels which then inhibit further response. In actuality, the physiological events which make up the sex response cycle present a long list of possible "traps" for people who are watching at every moment to be sure everything is working well. Some of the more common "normal" changes which men have been confused about and made anxious by include:

1. That erection comes and goes during sexual arousal;
2. That secretion appears at the tip of the penis during the plateau phase (in some men this can be a considerable amount and they become confused about whether or not they are ejaculating).
3. That orgasm has two phases: (1) deposition of the seminal fluid at the base of the penis, and (2) release of the ejaculate. Some men try to hold back when they feel phase one, are unable to since the orgasm has already been triggered and then with ejaculation feel they lack the control which a man should normally have. After ejaculating, it is not unusual for a man to feel disappointed or dejected or even depressed, and occasionally, as some have said, to have a "feeling of worthlessness."
4. That after orgasm there is a brief time, the refractory period, during which many men feel uncomfortably sensitive to penile stimulation. This is usually a short time—less than a minute. The common notion, however, is that once a man ejaculates, that's it. As a result, he tries his best to satisfy the woman before ejaculating and not infrequently, tries to keep himself from being aroused too quickly.
5. That after orgasm, erection remains and there is the potential for further sexual relating. Unfortunately, many men and women don't realize this potential. If they did, there wouldn't be so much focusing on performance the first time around and the incidence of male and female dysfunction would probably be lessened considerably.

There is also a list of female sex response changes which affect males and their spontaneity in relating sexually: breasts and nipples can become uncomfortably sensitive to touch at different times of the menstrual cycle and at different points of vascular congestion during sex response; the clitoris retracts with greater states of arousal and also can become a source of discomfort when touched; vaginal lubrication occurs inside the vagina so that a woman can be very "turned on" and not show any external lubrication; a facial grimace or eyes tearing or a verbal outcry can be a mark of increased pleasure but perceived as pain by the male partner. These natural body changes have been disconcerting to some of the men who have talked to us.

Sex counseling serves a very important function in the university population. So many individuals and couples are in the process of unfolding sexually and trying to integrate new experiences. With appropriate education and medical care, a chance to talk about experiences that have been confusing or upsetting and gain some perspective, a great many young people can be helped. Sexual problems can be prevented or easily reversed before dysfunction becomes an established pattern.

Other problems are not as easily handled. These call for education, medical care *and* a therapy process. While there is a continuum between counseling and therapy, it is helpful to draw distinctions. In our view, sex therapy is a more complex process which requires diagnostic skills, an understanding of individual and interpersonal dynamics, and specific therapeutic skills. The following chapter will discuss the sexual therapy techniques we use in our work with university students. We have called the section "Sex Therapies," plural, because a variety of approaches is discussed.

References

1. Barbach, Lonnie Garfield, *For Yourself—The Fulfillment of Female Sexuality*, New York, Anchor-Books-Doubleday, 1976, pp. xi-xviii.

2. Kinsey, Alfred C., Pomeroy, Wardell B., and Martin, Clyde E., *Sexual Behavior in the Human Male*, Philadelphia, W. B. Saunders Co., 1948, p. 178.
3. Masters, William H. and Johnson, Virginia E., *Human Sexual Inadequacy*, Boston, Little Brown Co., 1970, pp. 311-312.
4. Kinsey, [2], p. 652.

7

Sex Therapies in the University Setting

Our original training in sex therapy came from Masters and Johnson at The Reproductive Biology Research Foundation in St. Louis. We have continued to use their therapeutic approach* with some student couples but we have also evolved some modifications to suit our own setting. We now have three categories of therapy for working with couples: (1) symptom-focused therapy; (2) a seven-visit format; (3) a fifteen-visit format.

Our philosophy of treatment is pragmatic. We try to do the least possible therapy required in each case. This apparently simple formula, which is probably followed by most therapists, is actually quite complex and varies from therapist to therapist. So many value judgments are implicit in this decision. Is it always "enough" therapy when sexual dysfunction is reversed? If not, what other goals can be used? Our exposure to a wide range of psychotherapy techniques suggests that each school has a set of assumptions or biases about how much therapy is enough. When a psychotherapist moves into the new field of sex therapy he or she often brings along these biases.

The behavior therapist may tend to focus on behavior—the symptom—and to define therapy and its outcome in these terms alone while someone from a psychoanalytic or gestalt therapy background may want to do more therapy. This generalization has ob-

---

* In recent years, we seldom use the two-week format, preferring a more spaced out schedule of appointments.

vious exceptions. Helen Kaplan is one. She is a psychoanalyst whose therapy focuses rather strictly on the dysfunction, and she only interprets intrapsychic or interpersonal defenses when they are blocking progress in reversing dysfunction.

In answering the question of how much counseling or therapy to do, it is helpful to use a therapy contract which is negotiated at the start and may be renegotiated at any point along the way. The therapy contract should specify the goals of therapy. Clients sometimes have inappropriate or grandiose expectations which should be dealt with (for the first time if not definitively) before therapy begins. The client's goals may be different from those the therapist would set and this needs to be discussed openly. The therapy contract should also specify other aspects of the working agreement such as payment, length of the therapy, follow-up, participation in research (if any) during the therapy, confidentiality, taping and avenues through which clients may register a complaint.

Symptom-Focused Therapy in Vaginismus and in Premature Ejaculation

All therapy for sexual dysfunction is, to some extent, symptom-focused. The individual or couple almost always present the problem in terms of a sexual symptom. They are seeking professional help to reverse a symptom or symptoms. We have separated out one kind of therapy and given it the label "symptom-focused" because there are two sexual dysfunctions—vaginismus and premature ejaculation—which can very often be treated with simple behavior modification techniques alone. Masters and Johnson do not make distinctions regarding treatment modalities. They use essentially the same format regardless of the severity of the presenting symptom (although some couples do finish therapy before the full two weeks are over). We have found that approximately 90 percent of vaginismus problems and approximately 70 percent of premature ejaculation problems can be resolved through a process which focuses almost entirely on the teaching of a behavior modification technique (plus some education in normal sexual response). We have treated several hundred cases of vaginismus using this approach. After an initial consultation, the office visits usually last 15 to 30 minutes as progress is made reversing the symptom. The therapist's total time input may be under three or four hours. In premature ejaculation there might be three one-hour visits.

When do we *not* use the symptom-focused format for vaginismus or premature ejaculation? The following criteria would lead us to consider a lengthier, more complex therapy.

1. If the individual or partner is too psychologically disturbed to participate in the behavior modification—e.g., one graduate student was too paranoid to tolerate the start-stop technique for premature ejaculation.
2. If the couple is not feeling good enough about one another or the therapy process to follow suggestions.
3. If the problem has existed for a long time and/or has had significant spin-off effect on the entire relationship or the partner's sexual function.
4. If the individual or couple runs into insurmountable and unexpected hurdles, such as extreme anxiety, when trying to carry out the behavior tasks.
5. If the problem is of a very severe nature. In vaginismus, this would mean total inability to penetrate the vagina and marked fear of approach to the vulva. In premature ejaculation, this would mean ejaculation prior to penetration or without a full erection.

Symptom-Focused Therapy in Vaginismus
(And the Vaginitis-Vaginismus Syndrome)

Vaginismus is usually considered an uncommon sexual dysfunction. It is defined as involuntary contractions of the levator muscles around the opening of the vagina, making insertion of the penis *impossible*. Our working definition is slightly different and, because of this, we find vaginismus to be quite common. We consider that vaginismus also includes cases in which insertion of the penis is *difficult* and *uncomfortable* due to involuntary levator muscle contractions.

The diagnosis of this milder form of vaginismus is made through history plus physical examination. The history almost invariably includes a characteristic description (which the professional involved may need to elicit through careful questioning)—difficulty in managing penile insertion, pain or discomfort (often said to be a burning sensation) as the penis penetrates the orifice, and then, about 30 seconds to a minute after insertion, a cessation of pain or discomfort. On physical examination, the muscle contraction is usually elicited by the examiner's approaching the patient and placing his or her hand on the inner aspect of the patient's thigh or by touching anywhere in the genital area. The patient herself is often completely unaware that this contraction is taking place but she can see it for herself in a hand-held mirror.

Our understanding of vaginismus is that it represents a rejection of penetration which is generalized, i.e., the woman usually rejects penetration by a penis, speculum, cotton applicator, tampon, or even her own finger. Sometimes, however, a woman can accept some forms of penetration while rejecting others. The feeling state in almost every case is fear or apprehension and often it is quite specifically the expectation of being hurt or being made to feel physically uncomfortable.

In Chapter 1 on unfolding we discussed the theory that there is a strong predisposition toward vaginismus in all women due to some "instinctive" or early-learned fear of penetration. Life experiences will tend to exacerbate or allay anxiety about vaginal penetration. Experiences which associate the genital area with pain or discomfort, e.g., an injury or infection in that area or great difficulty with tampon insertion, tend to exacerbate penetration anxiety. Actual experiences of insertion which are comfortable, or anything which familiarizes a woman with her vagina and dispels fantasy will reduce the anxiety.

The following is part of a verbatim record of an interview which elicited a history of vaginismus from a woman who had no idea what her problem was. The presenting complaint was, using her word, "frigidity." As is so often true, her vaginismus seems to have had its origin in multiple causes.

L.S.: The pain or discomfort you have experienced with intercourse, does it tend to be at the time of entry?

ANNE: Yes. It's not so bad once it gets going—after a minute or so.

L.S.: Is there burning or irritation after intercourse?

ANNE: Not usually—only when I've had a flare up of my cyst. I've had a problem with a Bartholin's gland cyst on and off in the last few years. It's been a real nuisance. I first got it about four years ago. The doctor said he couldn't remove it at the time he operated because it was infected, so he just drained it. It recurred three years ago and again he gave me penicillin. It drained so much then that he couldn't operate—so I still have it, I guess.

L.S.: Is there pain at that side?

ANNE: No. But I wasn't sure. Someone told me that the Bartholin's gland generates lubrication.

L.S.: The Bartholin's glands actually play a very minor part in vaginal lubrication. I suspect that your pain comes from what is called "vaginismus"—an involuntary spasm of the muscles around the opening of the vagina. Do you find that after intercourse has begun, and there's been some movement of the penis in and out, that there is adequate lubrication?

ANNE: I don't really know. He says it's dry and I don't *feel* wetness.

L.S.: Are you aware of being wet after intercourse?

ANNE: No.

L.S.: The muscle contraction can tend to keep the lubrication, which is produced within the vagina [using model here to illustrate], inside so the opening doesn't feel moist enough for penetration.

ANNE: You know—there is a drainage afterwards but I thought that was the semen.

L.S.: Is it just a little bit?

ANNE: No. It's a lot. It can go on all day after we have intercourse in the morning. I can't really say how much there is.

L.S.: In a man's ejaculate there's only one-half to three-fourths of a teaspoon of liquid. It sounds as though you are describing more than that.

ANNE: Yes.

L.S.: You probably are lubricating. Many women feel that they are not lubricating when it's just that it's all staying within the vagina. The angle of the vagina is downward and then as you respond sexually, the inner two-thirds of the vagina balloons. It's easy for fluid to tend to collect inside—especially if the opening is narrowed. You may need to insert a finger—yours or his—before inserting the penis and bring some lubrication to the opening.

ANNE: But what about this involuntary muscle contraction? Is it psychological? Is it physical?

L.S.: Both. The origin of it may have been psychological—stemming from the feelings you had when you and he started having intercourse—a lot of ambivalence—perhaps some fear of an expectation of pain the first time. And then it did hurt a lot. You don't need much more than that to cause involuntary muscle spasm. It's kind of like a flinch or a blink—an unconscious self-protective mechanism.

ANNE: I do see a gynecologist regularly. Wouldn't he have diagnosed it?

L.S.: He might easily have missed it if he wasn't looking for the involuntary muscle tension. It is possible to examine a woman in spite of moderate tension but it usually hurts.

ANNE: Oh, my gynecological exams have always hurt—a lot. I

thought that was par for the course. You mean it doesn't have to hurt when he puts in his fingers or that instrument?

L.S.: No, it doesn't have to hurt. It shouldn't. I'm sure that your painful examinations have also played a part in making you tense up at the thought of vaginal penetration.

ANNE: Mmm. I can see what you mean. I never thought of it before.

L.S.: Can you insert tampons?

ANNE: Not very easily. When I was 16, my best friend tried to coach me, but I never got it right so I usually don't use them.

The causal factors we identified in this case are common in the etiology of vaginismus—difficulty with tampons, painful cysts or injuries in the genital region (or even inner thigh near the genitals), painful pelvic examinations, ambivalence about intercourse (past and/or present) and a variety of confused ideas about female anatomy, physiology and sexual function.

The single most common cause for vaginismus, in our experience, has been vaginitis. This is so widespread that we will discuss it separately.

Approximately one-fifth of the 450 or so female patients seen each year by us have some degrees of vaginismus. This figure probably sounds very high, but it reflects the presence of a common syndrome which we call the "vaginitis-vaginismus" syndrome. Vaginitis is a very common problem in the population we see. In one sample of 205 women seen over a four-year period, 195 were found to have vaginitis on at least one occasion and many had it two, three, or more times in four years. Most of these cases were of monilial vaginitis.

In many instances, the girl or woman who has vaginitis is not aware of symptoms in the early stages or indeed at any point. If she is sexually active, she is likely to continue having intercourse. It is in the sexual situation that she may begin to note some symptoms but she usually does not understand them. She may feel that she is dry and tender, that penile thrusting creates a scraping sensation or simply that intercourse is much less pleasurable than usual. If accustomed to having an orgasm, she may suddenly find it doesn't happen or that it is difficult to experience from vaginal stimulation. She may find that she is sore after intercourse and, if she urinates afterwards, that she feels a marked burning sensation. Some women notice that their vaginal secretions have a foul, unpleasant odor. A surprising number of women put up with a variety of symptoms—including pain—over weeks, months and years! Intercourse is thus repeatedly paired with pain or other negative experiences.

It is not at all surprising then, given our understanding of learning theory, to find that many women who have vaginitis develop vaginismus. They have, consciously or unconsciously, come to anticipate that intercourse will be, in part or in total, unpleasant or painful. They may eventually manage to avoid the situation entirely by saying "no" and perhaps finally seeking medical advice, but if they continue trying to have intercourse, the vaginal muscles will, so to speak, say "no" for them or at least try to protect the vulnerable vagina.

Even when a woman does seek medical help and the vaginitis is properly diagnosed and treated, she may continue to complain of some pain or discomfort with intercourse. This often baffles the woman, her sexual partner, and the doctor. In fact, she may be cured of the vaginitis but the vaginismus may persist. The pain caused by the involuntary muscle contractions can become self-perpetuating. The muscles tense involuntarily in anticipation of entry, entry is then difficult and uncomfortable, once more providing a negative conditioning experience. Many women with moderate vaginismus complain of dryness. This is caused by the trapping of vaginal secretions behind the tensed orifice. Once the penis (or a finger) has penetrated the orifice, lubrication is usually normal within the vaginal barrel.

The apparent lack of lubrication and the problems associated with penetration are often very confusing and distressing to the woman and her partner. In the vaginitis-vaginismus syndrome, the woman often has a previously well-established pattern of comfortable, satisfying sexual response. The symptoms of vaginismus are perplexing because she feels aroused and "wants" to have intercourse but her body seems to contradict her feelings. Her partner is also dismayed by the apparently contradictory messages and frequently feels personally rejected or to blame. Both may come to feel that the woman's genitals are, as one couple put it, "a disaster area."

How is vaginismus treated? An important first step involves the demonstration of vaginismus to the woman and her partner as the doctor approaches the pelvic region in the examining situation. The muscle tension can usually be seen quite easily. We believe that it is very important for both members of the couple to see and understand the phenomenon. For the partner, seeing the vaginismus response elicited by the doctor's approach helps to allay his feelings of personal rejection. In cases where there is pronounced vaginitis he is often amazed to see the extent of reddening and obvious soreness and this too, is helpful. From a vague and amorphous problem which has often been interpreted as "psychological" or interpersonal, the difficulty can be seen as having a genuine physical basis, albeit with important psychological and interpersonal ramifications.

When all pelvic disease or pathology has been adequately treated, the couple can begin to treat the vaginismus. Masters and Johnson, Helen Kaplan, and others have described the behavioral treatment in detail and we see no need to recapitulate here, but in our experience, many doctors and even sex therapists need to be reminded of some cardinal principles, principles that we always spell out for our patients. Whether using her own fingers or dilators, the female is not trying to stretch her vaginal opening, she is trying to learn that the vagina can be entered without discomfort. If she pushes on bravely, in the face of pain or discomfort, she is making things worse. The cardinal rule is *not* to permit anything uncomfortable. The partner must also understand this so that he can cooperate patiently. His support is vital. If he tries to rush or pressure her or if he forces penetration, this will seriously set back the treatment. Because of the importance of the partner, especially when the time comes for the female to attempt inserting the penis in her vagina, we always try to work with the couple. Our patients have had a 100 percent success record using this approach.

While on the subject of partners, we feel it is worth noting that, sometimes, vaginismus causes premature ejaculation in the male. Treating the vaginismus may be sufficient therapy for the premature ejaculation.

Symptom-Focused Therapy in Premature Ejaculation

We have already mentioned in the section on counseling that premature ejaculation is not always easy to define and that a strictly behavioral definition leaves out the central issue of the individual's or couple's degree of anxiety about premature ejaculation. When education and reassurance are not sufficient help for a young man or couple to overcome the problem, and they do not present any of the special contraindications to symptom-focused therapy, we will usually attempt to treat the problem through instruction in the start-stop technique, taking the couple through the stages of therapy in only two or three visits.

The start-stop technique which we use (originally developed by Dr. James Semans, a urologist) is described in detail by Helen Kaplan in *The New Sex Therapy* [1]. It is a technique which requires a couple to work together in the early stages using noncoital stimulative techniques. The noncoital stage proceeds in this way. The couple may begin kissing or caressing as usual. When they wish to move on to genital touching, the males lies on his back with his head toward the foot of the bed while his partner sits against the headboard with her legs spread open. He moves his bottom as close to her as he can (between her legs) with his legs flexed and placed over hers. This is a very physically and psychologically vulnerable position for a man. He must trust his partner in order to be relaxed in this position. She must be fairly comfortable with the idea of touching his penis, looking at it and having him ejaculate outside the vagina. If either partner cannot be relaxed with these procedural tasks, a lengthier therapy is needed in which there will be time to explore attitudes and feelings more fully. On the other hand, some anxious people have found that going through these procedures has allowed them to become vastly more comfortable with many aspects of genital touching.

In the above described position the woman* stimulates the penis manually. The man is asked to concentrate on his own physical sensations. He must be able to assume that the woman is enjoying herself or is at least comfortable with what she is doing. If he cannot keep from worrying about her the technique will not be as successful. The penile stimulation should continue until the man feels that he is close to coming but *not* to the point where orgasm has actually begun. The male therapist must educate him about the point of inevitability (stage one of the male orgasm), where ejaculation will occur no matter how he tries to stop it. When the man signals that he is close to orgasm the woman immediately stops genital stimulation for 15 to 30 seconds. She then resumes stimulation and once more brings her partner close to orgasm. Again he signals her to stop. The procedure is repeated a third time. When stimulation is resumed after the third stop, it is continued to the point of orgasm.

If a couple can complete this sequence several times they tend to feel very encouraged and are ready for the intermediate step which is exactly the same as the initial procedure except that wetness is introduced. There may be manual stimulation using a lubricant and/or oral stimulation. Oral stimulation is awkward in the position described for the initial steps and the couple may use any position for fellatio which they like except the "69" or mutual oral-genital position. Again the male is told to concentrate on his own erotic sensations.

The third phase involves coital stimulation. With the woman straddling the man, she inserts the penis. She moves until he feels close to orgasm, at which point he signals her to stop. This is re-

---

* The partner could theoretically be a male, although no male homosexual has ever come to us complaining of premature ejaculation.

peated twice more. Finally, coital movements are continued to the point of his ejaculation. Later variations on the theme will involve other positions and more active thrusting on his part.

We have a bias in favor of using symptom-focused therapy in a college population where the couple's commitment to their relationship is an open question. We feel concerned about the impact of a therapy process upon a forming relationship. Therapy could cause a premature closure or commitment. On the other hand, it is certainly wrong to deny therapy simply because there is no marriage license or a "permanent" partner. We prefer to deal with the sexual dysfunction in the simplest way possible, but, with some dysfunctions or with some particular couples, focusing on the symptom is not adequate. The next level of therapy we use is a "seven-visit" format and, beyond that, a "fifteen-visit" format.

Seven-Visit and Fifteen-Visit Formats for Couples' Sex Therapy

It may be surprising to some people that we speak of seven-visit and fifteen-visit therapy rather than using more indefinite categories such as "short term" and "long term." We specify the exact number of visits because of our belief in a carefully prestructured therapy contract. (It so happens that it is easier to teach and communicate about therapy of a precise length but that is not our reason for specifying numbers of visits.) Masters and Johnson evolved a time-structured therapy out of practical necessity, but that necessity did give birth to a valuable invention. With the overwhelming majority of their patients coming from out of town, leaving work and children behind while paying for accommodation in St. Louis it was vital to do the therapy as quickly as possible and to know in advance how long one would be in St. Louis.

When we were training at the Reproductive Biology Research Foundation, Masters and Johnson asked us to promise that we would do sex therapy exactly as they taught it for at least one full year before we introduced our own innovations. We honored that commitment and for two years we saw couples every day for 14 days in a row (only one of us worked on Sunday—the same practice used by Masters and Johnson). This was a valuable experience but personally very demanding. Other sex therapists were, by this time, using Masters-Johnson techniques on a once-a-week basis. We decided to try some kind of extended therapy format and arrived at a compromise between every day and once a week that compressed 14 visits plus one follow-up into a period of about two months (see section on fifteen-visit therapy pp. 206-221). Since 1972 we have used this fifteen-visit format for the most difficult cases of therapy with a couple with a problem of sexual dysfunction.

We don't believe there is anything critical to successful therapy in the particular arrangement of visits we devised but we do believe that some tight structure *is* an essential feature of sex therapy. We have become increasingly convinced of the importance of structure through our experiences supervising therapists who have not used any structure; they have used the open-ended approach that is typical of most psychotherapy, particularly psychoanalytic therapy. Over and over again we saw therapists who seemed to be doing good therapy in most respects flounder completely midway in sex therapy. We believe that a prearranged format serves several important functions and greatly enhances the chance for sex therapy to be successful.

A prearranged format orients the couple to their therapy contract, defining their commitment and giving them a sense of the rhythm of therapy—its beginning, middle, and end. A format helps to orient the therapists to the couple's progress as compared with other couples'. It is an aid in diagnosing resistance and in planning the pacing of sexual "tasks." Therapists can, in some instances, extend beyond the original contract so that structure does not become a self-defeating straight jacket.

Before describing examples of seven- and fifteen-visit therapy we want to describe in detail specific aspects of sex therapy which are common to both formats. This material is, in many ways, a restatement of Masters and Johnson concepts, but we felt that the concepts are so important and so often misunderstood, even by practicing sex therapists, that they should be spelled out.

Consultation

The couple is seen together by a co-therapy team (male and female) for about 15 minutes, after which the foursome usually splits into two groups—the female therapist and patient together—male therapist with male patient.* They are immediately told that they may tell the therapist anything they wish. If it is something they don't want shared with their spouse or partner, the therapist will not divulge secrets without the individual's consent. For the last 10 minutes of the consultation hour, the foursome regroups to discuss referral or treatment plans.

This first contact is important in determining what sort of treatment is appropriate: referral, medical treatment, two sessions of counseling, seven-visit therapy, or fifteen-visit therapy. The individual or couple needs to participate in this decision, thus establishing a therapy contract.

In deciding on seven- versus fifteen-visit therapy, one is really estimating how much therapist input will be needed in order for this couple to progress through sex therapy. The variables which influence this are individual psychopathology, quality of the couple's communication, the nature, severity and duration of the sexual problem(s), and the couple's willingness and availability.

The history-taking process will begin in the consultation as does the relationship between therapist(s) and patient(s). We believe that this relationship is a very important factor in sex therapy, as it is in all therapies. In sex therapy the professional role is somewhat specialized. People expect sex therapists to be particularly knowledgeable about sex and to have "heard everything" so that nothing will shock or outrage them. This expectation (and its fulfillment by the therapist who *should be* knowledgeable and unflappable) permits a person to plunge quickly into the details of sexual experiences that may have been deeply disturbing.

---

* Masters and Johnson do not describe consultation because their out-of-town couples rarely have a consultation visit [3].

For many people, coming to a sex counseling or therapy program means the first reaching out to another person to share a part of themselves that, for one reason or another, embarrassment, guilt, shame, or fear, they have hidden. Much of their psychic energy has been bound up by their feeling of being sexually handicapped and unable to move from such a position. The first interview is, therefore, an important moment, a moment of attentive listening, of acceptance, of careful inquiry about the problem, its origins, and its meaning to the couple.

Autobiographical Statements
If we are planning to do sex therapy with a couple (or individual) we ask for a sex-focused autobiographical statement describing the attitudes, experiences and feelings which they believe have contributed to their sexuality. This is to be submitted before the next visit. We explain that the autobiography is to help us focus on what the individual regards as most important. We ask that autobiographies be limited to 10 pages.

Sexual History
Many sex therapists, researchers, and other professionals have written about the importance of the sexual history. Masters and Johnson devoted a chapter to the subject in *Human Sexual Inadequacy*, detailing the kind of information it may be important to elicit when a couple are being treated for sexual dysfunction. One therapist we know, who is experienced in individual and family therapy but not in sex therapy, decided that it was appropriate for her to take the sexual history of a woman client she was seeing. She followed the outline in *Human Sexual Inadequacy* to the letter and found it required five hours to complete! Kinsey and his research workers spent two or three hours per person obtaining their carefully structured histories.

In the ordinary course of work, a therapist usually has one or even more consultation visits with an individual or couple before proceeding with sex therapy. The therapist already knows what the problem is, knows something about its origins, and has a feel for the person or couple, their motivation, style, degree of distress, etc. Some therapists do not take any sexual history beyond this, but most do.

The way in which they proceed with a more detailed sex history will vary greatly from therapist to therapist. We have our own way of approaching a sexual history which reflects our philosophy of therapy. We would like to say something about this, but more particularly, we want to focus on taking a sexual history from clients or patients who are late adolescents or young adults. The nature of the history will vary from therapist to therapist and even from case to case. Our format for gathering history in cases where we are planning to do co-therapy, using a seven-visit or fifteen-visit schedule, involves interviews of between one and two hours duration with the therapist of the same sex and interviews of approximately 45 minutes, male therapist with female client, female therapist with male client.

In co-therapy the "cross-sex" history-taking is *not* a repeat of the same-sex history-taking. This second history-taking session is focused on the spouse. Thus, if P.S. is meeting with client, Mrs. X, he will ask her to talk about her husband as she sees him and perhaps how significant other family members see him and interact with him. This is a continuation of the basic co-therapy model in which the male therapist focuses on understanding, representing, and treating the male, while the female therapist focuses on understanding, representing, and treating the female. Therapists working alone usually modify the structure of history taking, seeing each person once for their entire history taking.

The goals of history-taking fall into three areas, data-gathering, establishing a working client-therapist relationship and formulating some ideas about how one will work with this person or couple.

In a young population, such as we see in the Sex Counseling Service, the data-gathering can be intensive rather than extensive, since there is simply less life-experience to be covered. The data must also be evaluated somewhat differently in this age group. Sexual experiences and the person's feelings about them must always be viewed in a developmental context because many college and graduate students are still in the process of working out late adolescent issues.* For example, a 24-year-old law student may be having sexual difficulties in his first close relationship because he is in the early stages of learning to be close to a female. His previous sexual experiences may have been emotionally uninvolving. Graduate school can easily prolong this phase. Now, when he wants something more meaningful, he finds he is impotent. Another developmental issue which is commonly associated with sexual problems in this age group, including young married couples, is an incomplete separation from family which creates a deep ambivalence about commitment to a sexual partner. Actually, any of the issues and concerns discussed in the first half of the book may create a development impasse which manifests itself as a sexual problem.

The sexual history, then, is a history of the individual's sexual unfolding process in some detail. There are certain questions that must always be asked—the standard questions which elicit information about family attitudes toward sex, childhood experiences, puberty, first menses or ejaculation, previous sexual experiences including problems, the current relationship, etc. Rather than attempt a listing of such questions we would like to emphasize the importance of eliciting information in five areas.

Sexual experiences, including the problem, should be the first point of concern. A definition of the sexual problem is not as easily arrived at as one might think. Words such as "impotence" or "frigidity" obscure rather than clarify. A therapist must always get a detailed *operational* definition of the problem, i.e., a careful description of exactly what happens and/or happened in the past. A surprising number of men are confused about erection and ejaculation and may use these words as if they were synonyms. No definition of the problem is complete without knowing what the problem means to the person, how it has affected his or her self-concept, interpersonal relations, moods, etc. Other sexual experi-

---

* In light of the recent emphasis on life-long psychological changes, one could easily argue that all sexual problems should be seen in their developmental context.

ences should be discussed sequentially to help the therapist and client to see them as a process. All *first* experiences with any sexual behavior should be understood in detail—the events and the feelings about those events. If there is any sexual relationship in the present, knowing exactly what happens can help to pinpoint significant causes of the difficulty.

The therapist must also know the client's current state of health, drug usage, method of contraception. The therapist must have a sense of how the person feels about his or her body—its appearance, size, function and odors. Experiences from the past such as illness, doctors, injury or obesity or extreme weight loss can be very important. Experiences with and feelings about genitals are obviously relevant.

Socio-cultural and religious influences ought to be delved into. What is the value system the person grew up with? What values are held now? What conflict or guilt stems from a difference between old and present values or between values and behavior? Are there specific beliefs, prohibitions, unrecognized assumptions which were or are determined by these influences? What is the impact of peer culture? Has the person tried to integrate two or more sets of values—e.g., moving from Mexico to the northeastern United States at age 12 or having parents from widely disparate backgrounds? Are the client's current values and attitudes different from the partner's? We have found that over 80 percent of the couples with whom we have done sex therapy came from different *major* religions.

Knowledge of interpersonal relationships is important in the therapy. What were family relationships during childhood and adolescence? Were there important losses through death, illness or divorce? How did people in the family communicate feelings? How are feelings communicated with the sexual partner? How does the client give to other people? Can other people give to him or her?

Finally, the therapist should inquire into the patient's feelings about him or herself. This is the most difficult area because the data-gathering is more indirect. The therapist observes verbal and nonverbal communication, notes the impact of the person on the therapist's feelings, and tries to see common threads. Psychiatric diagnosis may be important. Psychosis or depression may be contradictions for sex therapy. That sexuality is a dimension of personality is a truism but a useful one. Sometimes an individual who is very guarded and cannot or will not talk directly about sex can easily talk about something else that is an important part of his life—work, playing a musical instrument, participating in a sport. The way in which a person goes about life out of bed can speak volumes about his sexuality.

History-taking by way of a questionnaire might be more accurate in terms of the facts elicited than a face-to-face interview but this would negate one role of the history-taking—the therapist's establishing a relationship with the person. Much has been written on the subject of therapist-client relationships and there is no point in trying to summarize that literature here. We would simply like to stress the importance of this rather intangible commodity, the relationship. In taking a sex history it is possible to be so fact-oriented that little or no feeling is allowed to enter the room. We believe this is a mistake. Some human acknowledgment of the client's anxiety, anger, sadness or hope is an essential ingredient of a good history-taking hour. The client and therapist need to feel engaged with one another in a mutual enterprise.

Some sex therapists have stressed the role of the therapist as "authority." The word has a pejorative connotation to many people, perhaps because it is associated with authoritarian rather than authoritative. We believe that a sex therapist should be an authority in the area of human sexuality or the offer to do sex therapy is fraudulent. In taking a sex history the therapist's knowledge of and comfort with the subject of sex will show. This is as much authority as is needed to establish credibility and a willingness to trust without making the client unduly dependent. People who come for sex therapy do not leave their autonomy in the waiting room.

The decision to proceed with sex therapy, made after initial consultation, may be the wrong decision and this may only become evident as the fuller history-taking process is underway or completed. The couple can then be advised to seek other forms of help. Doing sex therapy on a campus, we see many unmarried couples with sexual problems. The issues of commitment and the meaning of sex therapy for their relationship are usually very important (see chapter 5 on Intimacy, Commitment & Fidelity). The history-taking must focus in part on these issues and sometimes it becomes clear that sex therapy is not advisable, at least not at that time.

Sex therapy has a definite format and yet it is individualized. During the history-taking, one begins to see the ways in which these individuals and this couple are unique and the implications of this for therapeutic strategies. For example, in a case in which the husband is suspicious and argumentative with the male therapist during the history-taking and medical examinations, one might opt to have the male therapist spend an extra hour or so with the husband trying to talk about it. Or, if there is a co-therapy team, the therapists may try to use the female therapist to defuse any conflicts which the husband enters into with the male therapist. Another example would be the decision to extend the sensate-focus phase of therapy due to a woman client's previous experiences of always being rushed and pushed sexually in spite of her own fears. The list could be quite lengthy. We do want to stress the fact that strategies derived from the history-taking phase must be flexible because new data continue to surface via the on-going therapy process.

Before ending this section on the sexual history we would like to comment on something which we have found to be of particular value in listening to histories, and that is words, the words the person uses which seem to reflect central issues or emotional states. Virginia Johnson makes a special point of paying attention to language and we have found her guidance in this (and much else) to be extremely helpful.

The words we are referring to tend to be repeated several times as the person talks about himself or herself. They are words like *vulnerable, seriously hurt, humiliated, impotent* (in its several meanings), *dead*, or words that encapsulate the culturally given meaning of sex for this person such as *animalistic, gross, divine, decorum.* The therapist should always ask the client to say what he or she means when using such words. The therapist can then use the client's own words with some security that they are speaking the same language.

Draw-A-Person Test

We usually ask for a Draw-A-Person Test immediately after taking the sexual history.* The patient is given two pieces of paper, and the instructions are simply, "Draw a picture of a whole person on this piece of paper and a picture of a whole person of the other sex on this piece." We have found this to be a helpful diagnostic tool. We also use it as a barometer of progress by getting drawings during and after therapy [2].

Medical History and Physical Exam

We always take at least one hour to obtain each medical history and to do the physical examination. In the next chapter we detail the physical exam as we do it. In a couple's sex therapy we frequently, but not always, do the physical exam with both partners present in the examining room. Since it is the male (P.S.) in our team who is the physician, he performs the examination procedures. The female therapist (L.S.) is present while the female is being examined.

Not all couples in sex therapy are ready to share an experience as intimate as a physical exam. Sometimes they have never really seen one another's bodies. In other instances there may be so much anger and emotional distance that one or both cannot be so open and vulnerable in the other's presence. When a couple is not psychologically ready to share the examination at this early stage of therapy, we usually find that their attitude changes partway through the therapy. We may then suggest that a portion of a

---

* This is not used by Masters and Johnson.

therapy hour be set aside for them to share the educational aspect of the physical exam. (See the following chapter.)

Roundtable

The roundtable discussion includes both therapists and the couple. The format we use for this session is essentially the format we learned from Masters and Johnson. There are four parts to this session.

One part of the session involves giving feedback to the couple. This is done by turns. The male therapist summarizes the most important themes in the male's history which have contributed to and perpetuate dysfunction. The female therapist does the same for the female. There is a need to present some positive as well as negative feedback. The therapists are not trying to offer a complete explanation of the sexual problem in this part of the roundtable. The goal is to help clarify some aspects of causality. They show ways in which personality, body events (such as illness, chronic vaginitis, or a specific handicap), and the interactions of two persons' values and backgrounds have not allowed sexual function to flourish. It is always valuable to use quite specific examples from the individuals' histories and even to use some of their exact words for events and feelings.

This part of the roundtable discussion may include disclosures of previously unknown material, perhaps an affair or the ongoing homosexual behavior of one of the partners. Like Masters and Johnson, we never disclose secrets without permission of the individual involved. When there is a very serious disclosure to be made we plan on extra time (possibly two full hours) for the roundtable. In general we would use the fifteen-visit format in any case where such a major "secret" was to be disclosed.

We usually attempt to cover the basic concepts of sexual function as follows.

The couple needs to believe that change is possible—that they can move away from the painful and destructive patterns they have lived with or that they can learn to relate in a satisfying way even if they have never had such an experience. The therapists' statement of a need to close the door on past patterns and pessimism seems to be very meaningful. The couple must be warned not to lock one another into the past by assuming they know exactly what the other thinks, feels or will do in any given situation.

We stress that sex is a natural function. This is obvious and yet so many people with a sexual problem have thought they could learn some way to force their sexual response. We stress that the (healthy) body will take care of itself when the couple are able to open up to one another, accept their own and their partner's eroticism and share pleasure. We usually mention the periodic nature of erection and vaginal lubrication in infancy and during the REM (rapid-eye-movement) phases of sleep to underscore the naturalness of bodily responses.

We underscore the fact that there is no such thing as an uninvolved partner. This point has usually been made in the first part of the roundtable by demonstrating the interactional nature of a dysfunction, how it resulted from and/or is perpetuated by the couple. In some cases it is necessary to underline this point because the couple has evolved the myth that one of them has the problem and the other is an innocent "victim." The pattern of blame and recrimination leading to guilt and counter-attack must be interrupted or sex therapy cannot be successful.

We discuss "spectatoring." If this concept has not been elaborated in part one of the roundtable it is described now. As defined by Masters and Johnson, spectatoring is the *immediate* cause of most sexual dysfunction. Essentially it is the anxious watching of sexual performance—one's own or one's partner. Watching oneself per se is not the problem. It is the anxiety that interrupts the natural flow of sexual feelings, distorts behavior and causes dysfunction. Telling oneself to "relax and enjoy it" does not usually work. The step-wise program of sex therapy is designed specifically to eliminate spectatoring, and as the couple progresses in the therapy, instances of spectatoring will be discussed and the therapists will make suggestions that are in line with the person's attitudes and values about sex. It is stressed that sex is not like many other endeavors; it will not yield to a goal orientation. Working harder at trying to *make* a sexual response will undermine rather than enhance sexual response.

We point out that sex is a way of being intimate, a part of the total relationship. Intimacy is a matter of giving and letting oneself be given to, both in and out of bed. We often find that one member of the couple (usually the male) has assumed a stance as invulnerable, strong, the provider and protector while the other has become dependent and feels angry about being controlled. The "strong" partner may have trouble allowing the other to see any "weakness," which in our culture may mean that one simply does not display emotions. In bed there may be no appropriate selfishness, no ability to identify one's own needs.

We also attempt to establish communication guidelines in the roundtable discussion. Young people today place a high value on open and honest communication. They tend to talk a lot—intensely and with almost scrupulous honesty—but this is not synonymous with clear, effective, nondefensive communication. There generally is a commitment, at least intellectually, to the idea that a couple should share feelings and attitudes. They are usually eager to learn about ways of communicating.

When a young couple has a sexual problem, they usually talk about it as a couple and perhaps with a close friend. They less often do what so many older couples do—i.e., pretend that everything is all right while secretly and silently nursing anger and frustration. The generation in college now is definitely freer in talking about sex and confronting problems when they exist. They generally feel comfortable with and understand words such as *penis, vagina, intercourse, condoms,* IUD, and *orgasm.* They also know the names of common sexual dysfunctions such as premature ejaculation and impotence. They have often read one or more books on the subject of sex and sexual problems before coming for help. It isn't unusual to learn that a young couple has read the condensed version of *Human Sexual Inadequacy* and tried to follow the instructions for sensate focus or the squeeze technique. The lines of communication about sex are open even if some crucial messages never seem to be sent or received.

The guidelines we give in the area of communication apply equally well in bed or out of bed. The two basic principles are self-assertion and self-protection. By self-assertion we mean representing your own needs, wishes, feelings, and attitudes. For example, self-assertion calls for saying, "I'd like to go to the party," instead of assuming that your partner should know what your wishes are and rather than second guessing what your partner wants to do. In bed, self-assertion means saying or showing what pleases you. Self-protection means not allowing yourself to be bullied, railroaded, or otherwise dominated or repeatedly hurt by your partner. It also means that you *must* tell your partner if and when you are hurt or overlooked, rather than allowing these injuries to accumulate until the feelings burst forth in anger and accusation. In bed, self-protection calls for saying "ouch" when something hurts, not allowing a psychologically or physically painful situation to continue or to be repeated.

Behind these rules lie several basic assumptions which we articulate. The relationship between a couple is potentially special, a place where each can be most truly his or herself, sharing joys, hopes, doubts, fears, and self-criticisms without being judged or rejected. There must be an implicit or explicit understanding that each will listen to and accept the other's feelings with some sympathy, not analyzing, labelling, or blaming. Masters and Johnson use the shorthand phrase, "Feelings are facts"—facts which are neither good nor bad, superior nor inferior. When this understanding exists in some unit (a couple, a patient and therapist, an encounter group), it opens the way for honest, emotionally felt, communication. In the absence of such communication people often misjudge one another, impute false motives, feel defensive and, because they don't understand the other, inflict more hurt than they intend or realize. In the sexual area there are often dramatic examples of this sort of poor communication. For example, Mrs. A. thinks her husband rejects her sexual feelings because whenever she becomes passionate, Mr. A. loses his erection. What she doesn't know, because he is too "manly" to tell her, is that her sexual arousal makes him want and need to "perform" so very much that he becomes anxious and that this anxiety stems, at least in part, from experiences of impotence with other women before marriage. Another quite common example of pain inflicted through lack of communication is the woman who does not tell her partner when intercourse hurts. Unknowingly, he is inflicting pain, reinforcing her negative attitude toward intercourse. Ultimately this situation is very damaging to their relationship.

If a couple is to establish a pattern of effective and nondefensive communication, they must not assume responsibility for the other's feelings. A spouse or partner can easily assume that they have caused sad, angry, or frustrated feelings in the other when the real cause is outside of the twosome. If Fred feels like a bad husband or poor lover whenever Sandra cries or doesn't have an orgasm, he will react to such events by sulking, withdrawing, becoming defensive or angry. She will soon learn to hide her real feelings. It also doesn't help to take responsibility for changing another's feelings by being artificially cheerful or making "helpful suggestions." The most truly helpful stance is simply listening and being available.

If the above communication guidelines are followed, there will be few, if any, angry scenes because the sorts of hurts and slights that normally lead to anger will be talked about. The "I" mode of communication is particularly important here. There is an obvious difference between, "You always leave me out of things— I suppose I embarrass you in public," and "I felt very hurt and left out when you didn't ask me to come along. It made me wonder whether my behavior is somehow wrong in your eyes." A "You always" statement usually leads to defensiveness, anger, or retaliative accusation.

In the sexual area there is an obvious and crucial difference between these modes of communication: "You're frigid just like your mother. You should see a shrink" versus, "I'm very upset about our sex life. I don't get any feedback that it's pleasurable for you and that makes it awful for me. I'd like to get some help with this problem." We have somewhat overloaded these examples, but even subtle differences in wording can be effective in promoting communication.

The fourth component of the roundtable discussion centers on the sensate-focus instructions. These are instructions for touching that are given as the first step in sex therapy. They are called "sensate-focus" (Masters and Johnson's term) because the couple is asked to focus on their own sensations when they touch. The therapist can bridge from a discussion of the general principles of communication into sensate-focus instructions by pointing out that there can be no distinction between in-bed and out-of-bed patterns of communication so that the two fundamental principles for verbal exchange, self-assertion and self-protection, will also apply to in-bed exchange. As the touching instructions are given, the ways in which these principles are to be applied becomes clear.

One therapist begins by telling one member of the couple to initiate. Whether it is male or female, who initiates first is not usually important. If there has been a chronic struggle over initiation, however, the therapists would need to take this into consideration in choosing who should initiate first. In any case, following the same-sex principle of co-therapy, if the female is to initiate, the female therapist gives these instructions; if the male, the male therapist instructs. Let us assume the male is to initiate the first touching.

He is told to issue a clear verbal invitation, starting his invitation with the word, "I." It is to be a statement, not a question. He is not to second guess whether she is in a receptive mood but is to invite when *he* wants to. He is being asked to go out on a limb and risk rejection so that these feelings can be discussed with the therapist. If the partner feels neutral or positive she will accept; if not, she *must* decline.

The couple is told to touch without clothing on. They may not have intercourse, and breasts and genitals are strictly off-limits. The woman should lie down in a comfortable position. The man should then touch her in a way that he would like *in order to please himself*—not to turn her on or produce any particular reaction in her. He can be silly, serious, tender, loving, rough, or express any mood or combination of moods he feels. He may touch briefly or at length. He is being asked to assert himself through touch.

The female therapist tells the woman that no particular response is expected of her. She might fall asleep and that would be okay. She has only one responsibility and that is to protect herself (and thereby the relationship) by telling her partner if anything feels bad—either physically or psychologically. She need not explain why. He must stop doing whatever makes her uncomfortable, although he is free to touch in that way later on (because what one feels at one moment may not be felt at another moment).

When the man says he has finished his touching, the woman has her turn. The instructions are the same. She is to touch for her pleasure. He is to let her know if anything is uncomfortable. She need not match him in style, tempo, or duration of touch. When she is finished they have completed one session of sensate-focus.

Before the next visit with the therapists, the couple is told to have a second sensate-focus time. The instructions are the same except that she is to initiate verbally, when she wants to, and she is to touch first.

Educational Component

Sex education is an essential component of sex therapy. Although education in the facts of human sexual response is carried on throughout the therapy process, from initial history-taking onward, and particularly during the physical exam, there is a need for an *organized* presentation of facts sometime between the roundtable and the point when a couple moves on from sensate-focus to genital touching.

The reason for presenting accurate information about the physiology of sex response before the couple extend their touching to include genital touching is that the normal genital changes are often a course of confusion and anxiety for couples who have a sex problem. If they understand the normal sequence of excitement,

plateau, orgasm, and resolution phenomena, many of the sources
of anxiety are eliminated before they have had an opportunity to
disrupt the progress of the therapy. At this point in therapy, couples are still quite vulnerable. True, it is a point when they have
been using the communication guidelines, have established something of a state of neutrality with regard to the past, and have become increasingly vulnerable and trusting with each other. But
they can easily fall back into spectatoring and the goal orientation
which played so much of a role in the development of their sexual
difficulties in the first place. Providing this information at this
point is another way of maintaining a sound, structured approach
to building a foundation for dealing with sex. It is not surprising
that when we turn the hour to teaching facts about sex, couples
immediately focus on what is being said and often stop us at points
in the description where they recognize how they themselves had
been confused by normal events. It has been particularly interesting for us to see how often professional people—many of them
physicians—have been just as in the dark as anyone else. One physician, a university professor, commented after the male and female
response cycles were described, "You've just clarified at least 22
different things I never understood."

In presenting this material we do not try to individualize the
information, based on our understanding of the individual's sexual
history, although we will be sure to clarify those aspects of sexual
function the couple has misunderstood. Of course, there is indi-
vidualization with regard to the vocabulary we use so that we can
be sure that what is being said is clearly understood. But basically
we present the facts of the sex response cycle as described by Kinsey and Masters and Johnson and our own data as well. The female therapist talks about female response and the male therapist
presents the facts of the male response cycle.

The diagrammatic materials we use to help explain the female
sex response cycle are based on the charts of sexual response in
Masters and Johnson's *Human Sexual Response*. Some of the important points made are:

(1) Although sexual response follows a natural sequence of events there is a great deal of variation, person to person, and in the same person on different occasions. Individuals do not usually experience all the different body changes.

(2) Sexual response may begin when awake or asleep. A person can be aroused by a wide range of stimuli or only by a limited few.

(3) The very first change in the female is vaginal lubrication. In the young woman this occurs in 10 to 30 seconds, but the lubrication is inside the vagina. She will not feel it until some has worked its way to the outside of the vagina. She or her partner can easily be misled by looking for lubrication as a sign of arousal if they do not understand where the lubrication takes place. Under some circumstances, the lubrication will not work its way to the opening (due to position or some degree of vaginismus). A finger can be inserted to bring out some of the lubricating fluid. It is easy to assume that the woman is less aroused than the male because lubrication is not as obvious as erection. This may lead the couple into efforts to slow him down or speed her up which will turn the sexual exchange into a performance and probably increase spectatoring in both.

There are many changes in the female body during sexual response. Those described include: nipple erection, breast enlargement, increased heart rate and more rapid breathing, changes in the genitals (which are detailed, using diagrams of the external and internal genitalia), involuntary muscle tension, etc. Knowing that certain aspects of normal sexual function are likely to be sources of confusion or anxiety, we mention, for example, the muscle tension which develops in a person's face during the plateau stage and that such tension can be misinterpreted to mean pain when it is in reality a sign of increasing sexual pleasure.

In describing male sexual response we again use the Masters and Johnson diagrams, and start by describing the four stages of sex response, mentioning that the primary changes are due to vascular congestion while the secondary changes are due to increasing muscle tension. We don't hesitate to repeat this message, having just said the same about female response, if only to stress the similarity and analogous changes in the male as compared to the female. The nongenital changes are described: skin flush, sweating, respiratory and pulse change, etc.

The external and internal changes of genital response are described as they occur in excitement, plateau, orgasm and resolution. Erection is an early change. The degree of hardness will normally fluctuate in the excitement phase, reaching a steady state of hardness in the plateau phase. Penile size may change little or a great deal as a man responds, erection being something of a size equalizer. A normal sex response, testicular elevation, can be sudden, especially if there is stroking of the inside of the thigh, and can be a source of discomfort. Orgasm is two-staged—one of the few differences between men and women.

Although hypersensitivity to touch can occur in the refractory period and there is an automatic loss of some of the blood from the penile vessels, there is not an automatic period of flaccidity, and positive sensitivity to penile stimulation can return in a relatively short time so that ejaculation is not necessarily an end-point.

The above is not a complete description of what we teach as our presentations consist of a fairly thorough and complete description of the established observations of human sexual response.

To summarize with regard to the role of sex education in therapy: There is a point in time—before going on to genital touching —when this material is presented. Something like a lecture format is used, the male therapist presenting the male material and the female therapist the female material. Although a video cassette could possibly be used for such teaching, we choose not to, finding a need to stress certain points which we have learned have been particularly significant to a given couple. Approximately one hour of therapy time is taken for such teaching. Other sex education material, about contraception, fertility, pregnancy, etc., may or may not be included in a given case. If it is, that is presented at a later time when the sexual exchange issues are essentially worked out.

We see the presentation of sex response material at this time as part of the process essential to helping the couple work out their sexual difficulties.

Process of Therapy

The process of therapy cannot be spelled out as a precise format. We do follow a behavioral sequence from sensate focus through genital touching and then intercourse; this is the underlying structure on which the therapy process is built but it is not, by itself, the therapy. The behavioral therapy techniques used vary with the presenting dysfunction (see *Human Sexual Inadequacy* for a full discussion [3]). Rather than try to describe in abstract terms what the course of therapy is like, we have provided three case histories, two illustrating the seven-visit format and one illustrating the fifteen-visit format. We have selected varied presenting dysfunctions in order to cover as broad a range of dysfunctions as possible.

Seven-Visit Therapy

Our seven-visit therapy format is a condensation of Masters and Johnson therapy extended over approximately one month's time. As described in the preceding pages, the first half of the process is not very altered. In both seven- and fifteen-visit therapy we have consultation, autobiographies, histories, the Draw-A-Person Test, medical history, physical exam, and roundtable. The main difference is in the time allotted following the roundtable.

Seven-visit therapy is very useful in the university setting where the academic calendar causes special time constraints. We have found that most young couples can be helped and the sexual dysfunction(s) reversed in this length of time. We are likely to use the seven-visit format unless there is a reason or reasons to use the fifteen-visit (see page 200 for an example of this decision-making). Seven-visit therapy has worked well for most cases of an unconsummated marriage, in female orgasmic problems, in cases of vaginismus or premature ejaculation which are too complex to use a symptom-focused approach, and in some cases of ejaculatory inhibition. Seven-visit therapy is not usually enough time in which to treat primary impotence, sexual aversion, or cases in which the couple's relationship tends to work against therapeutic goals.

Seven-Visit Sex Therapy for a Case of Premature Ejaculation (Sandra and Bobby):

VISIT 1. A graduate student and his wife came to see us with a presenting complaint of premature ejaculation. They had been married for three years and the pattern of ejaculating quickly had been present since the beginning of their sexual relationship. He (Bobby) was a fairhaired man of very slight build. His wife (Sandra) was about his height but appeared sturdier and larger.

She tended to do most of the talking at the first appointment and her tone was one of an aggrieved, angry woman. Although she was obviously trying to tone down her complaining, she made several remarks during the hour that were put-downs of her husband. He seemed not to notice. For example, she told us how much more sexual experience she had, compared to Bobby, both before and during their marriage. He was a virgin when they met while "I knew what I was doing." She complained that his penis was too small and, "He just doesn't turn me on. I feel like we're good friends."

We asked what had precipitated their making an appointment with us. Bobby said that they had made an important decision—to try to work on their marriage. Sandra had agreed to call a temporary halt to any sexual or romantic relationships with others while they tried to see if they could resolve their problems.

A few other points of importance emerged in the first interview. One was that Sandra had a job she hated. She had kept it because the pay was good, and they had agreed she would work while Bobby got his graduate degree. Her intense anger about this was so apparent in her body language that we devoted considerable time to the subject. Sandra was now considering applying to a graduate program herself, and they were struggling with the practical realities of their both being full-time students.

The other important fact that emerged was that Bobby's premature ejaculation was extremely variable. He ejaculated within about a minute if they used the male above position, but he could "last indefinitely" if she was above. Yet, for all these years, he had been "officially" labeled as having a sexual dysfunction. When we asked how often they used the female above position, they looked surprised and a little flustered. "Almost never" was their answer, but neither of them could give any good reason for this apparent contradiction.

Both of us felt that sexual dysfunction per se was a somewhat secondary issue in this couple's problem, but we respected their need to focus on it. We told them that we were not completely sure what form of therapy would be best for them and asked if they would each write an autobiographical statement, about five pages in length, which would tell us more about their individual sexual development—their attitudes, feelings, experiences; the influence of school, family, religion, on their sexuality; and their feelings about their problem and current situation.

Sandra's history suggested that she had been very frightened of males and sex as a child and adolescent. Her brother, several years older than she, had terrorized her, once throwing her out of a tree house they were playing in. When she was 10, he showed her what a "bad guy" might do to her—feeling her breasts and genital area. As a teenager, her father showed her his erect penis and made her touch it so she wouldn't do anything just out of curiosity. She had multiple adolescent and adult sexual experiences that were usually impulsive and somewhat self-destructive, including a brief marriage that was annulled, a pregnancy and abortion, and sexual relationships with several older men in positions of power over her —a doctor, a therapist, and a professor. All of these experiences in-cluded—like those with her brother and father—a mixture of ter-ror and arousal for her.

Bobby's family history was one of chaotic, abusive relationships in the context of devout religiosity. His father sometimes beat his mother and sister. Bobby was an unusually small, thin little boy who couldn't use physical force. He developed skill in "managing" (his word) other people to get his way. In early adolescence he became extremely religious and adopted a very mild, gentle demeanor. It was important to him to help others. He found it impossible to be aggressive and even mild self-assertion was always difficult for him. His only experiences with sex prior to meeting Sandra were with an older girl who "showed him a few things."

At the end of her autobiographical statement, Sandra wrote that she had definitely decided she would go on for her degree if she was accepted and that this decision had made her feel much closer to Bobby. She also wrote, "I'm really more the problem than Bobby. I don't understand why I can't turn on to him. I do love him."

VISIT 2. We proceeded to have individual interviews, Bobby with P.S. and Sandra with L.S. Sandra said that she was physically attracted to men who looked "stereotypically macho." She liked their "energetic" approach to sex as contrasted with Bobby's overly gentle ways. She said that he seemed so tentative and didn't *do* much at all, in spite of her trying to show him from time to time what she would like. We also talked about their relationship in general. She felt that she used his nonassertiveness to her own advantage, getting him to make phone calls, for example, that she should make. She realized that she "dominated" him and this made her feel unfeminine and lessened her respect for him.

Bobby's interview revealed that he was very sexually insecure. He was so concerned about coming too quickly that he could think of little else from the moment they began to touch. He was afraid to do much to Sandra for fear this would make him ejaculate on the spot, and he felt he didn't know how to touch her effectively. He was aware that he was, in all ways, "too passive," particularly with Sandra. In the "Draw-A-Person" exercise Bobby drew a Christ-like small male figure and a much larger, angry looking female figure.

A four-way physical was done primarily for educational purposes and to reassure Bobby about his normal penis size. We have found that where there is concern over a physical abnormality no amount of general reassurance is as effective as an examination. Until they are examined, some men can say to themselves, "They may say penis size doesn't matter, but they haven't seen how small mine is!"

VISIT 3. A fairly standard roundtable discussion was the next step. For Sandra, L.S. emphasized the continuing effect of her early, frightening sexual experiences, her almost counter-phobic seeking out of macho males and her ambivalence about Bobby's gentle, nonassertive personality. With Bobby, P.S. emphasized the extreme anxiety about sexual inadequacy which was causing sexual inhibition and lack of sexual assertion and spontaneity.

We suggested that they concentrate a good deal of their energies on new patterns of communication. We encouraged Bobby particularly to say "I think . . . and feel . . ." and to say "ouch" when he felt put down by Sandra. This scared her, but she said she really welcomed it. We encouraged Sandra to tell Bobby when she was aware that she was "dominating" him and ask him to say what he really thought or wanted at that moment.

In sensate-focus we stressed touching for one's own pleasure and letting go without any goal whatsoever.

VISIT 4. We saw them one week later. The communication guidelines were, they said, "revolutionizing" their lives. She had heard that she was accepted in graduate school, and she was feeling "a thousand times less bitchy." She had enjoyed the way Bobby touched in the sensate-focus exercises more than she had ever enjoyed being touched by him. "He didn't lose his gentleness, but he didn't hold back either."

In discussing the facts of normal sexual response (about 15 minutes for female response and 15 for male), they were surprised to learn that ejaculation needn't be an end point for a male. They had always assumed sex was over once he came.

We described the start-stop technique for treating premature ejaculation, emphasizing that he was not really a premature ejaculator but that this technique would help to dispel all concern about ejaculating rapidly.

VISIT 5. A week later they came in and reported continuing progress. There was no problem in using the start-stop technique, and they were both comfortable with his ejaculating from her manual stimulation. They had been spending a lot of time together, doing things and talking. He was working very hard at self-assertion, even carrying it into his contact with others, such as his thesis advisor. Sandra was able to show him some of the ways she wanted to be touched, and she did have orgasms when he was touching her genitals. She said, "That whole big deal I made about not being turned on by him seems silly now. I'm not panting for his bod as if he were Paul Newman, but I *love* it when we do our touching and can't wait for the next time."

Bobby thought that the most important change he sensed within himself was his sense of confidence in his own body and the freedom from worry about failure. He thought that Sandra was being much gentler with him (!) now that he was asserting himself. He didn't have to fear her humiliating him about coming too quickly.

VISIT 6. Bobby and Sandra moved on to the next stage of touching which includes insertion of the penis (in the female above position) and use of the start-stop technique during coitus. Sandra "remembered" how nice the start-stop technique was for her and found she could be easily orgasmic.

VISIT 7. Two weeks later we saw them for a final visit which reemphasized the ways in which they accomplished the changes that had taken place. We discussed how they could keep what they had gained and cope with difficult times in the future.

We asked for a follow-up letter about six weeks later. They were doing fine.

Working with Sandra and Bobby, as with virtually all couples and with individuals, too, we stress not only in-bed communication but out-of-bed communication as well. We believe that improved communication is one of the most important tools a couple can take away from an experience in therapy.

The Xs—An Example of Seven-Visit Therapy
for Nonorgasmic Response

A second-year graduate student and his wife were referred to the SCS because of her nonorgasmic response. Since their marriage two years ago sex had been less pleasurable for her. Since the birth of their daughter, 10 months before, there had been infrequent sex and Mrs. X had not had an orgasm. Mrs. X had been working as a salesperson but stopped when the baby arrived. She had breast-fed for six months.

The Xs were not native Americans. In their first year at Yale, she had considerable language difficulty, had trouble making friends, and missed her home very much. He was preoccupied with and excited about his work and did not give her much emotional support. They had quarrelled a lot and were still angry, although both were happy with the baby, who was planned.

The consultation also revealed that Mrs. X had pain with intercourse. There had been pain occasionally until the pregnancy, but starting quite early in the pregnancy, there had been a new kind of pain which was there every time they had intercourse. They had not asked any doctor about this pain until after the delivery. They had imagined it would "go away," but when they resumed intercourse three weeks after the baby's birth, the same pain was present. At the post-partum check-up the gynecologist diagnosed a monilial vaginitis. Mrs. X used medication and some of the itching which had also been bothering her subsided, but intercourse continued to hurt.

The Xs said they used to have a good sex life, before marriage and their move to New Haven. They were somewhat bewildered by Mrs. X's lack of response because she used to be very "passionate." She missed her own sexual feelings very much.

This couple was scheduled for seven-visit therapy for the following reasons:

1. The gynecologist's medical treatment and sex counseling had not been sufficient to resolve the problem. There was a back-log of some resentment between the couple. Mrs. X was slightly depressed. For all of these reasons, we rejected simple counseling.

2. The indications in favor of seven- rather than fifteen-visit therapy were:

(a) This was a short-duration, secondary problem.

(b) Although there was anger, there was also considerable warmth and total commitment to the marriage continuing.

(c) There had obviously been an important pain factor during the pregnancy and probably there was an on-going vaginismus which we felt confident of reversing (because clinical experience indicated the ease with which vaginismus can be overcome).

(d) Some of the reality factors which had apparently precipitated Mrs. X's depression were now alleviated. She spoke excellent English and had made some close friends.

(e) They were both highly motivated and were not blaming one or the other for the problem.

VISIT 1. Because we had to fit the Xs into a particular time slot that began almost immediately after the consultation, we did not ask for autobiographies as we would ordinarily do. We did the history-taking on one day; same-sex history, 40 minutes, opposite sex history, 20 minutes. Her history was one of a very rigid and sexually repressive family. Her father called her a whore from age 14 onward although she did not have intercourse until age 19. She did, as one might predict from her father's constant "admonitions," go through a promiscuous phase for about one year. During that time she became pregnant and had an illegal abortion. She feared she had VD but the doctor told her she did not. Her feelings about this phase were mingled guilt and anger at her father "for making me so depressed I had to seek comfort outside of my family." She had never really enjoyed sex until she met her husband-to-be. He was nice to her, more gentle than the other men she had slept with. She began to look forward to sex and to have orgasms. She had never masturbated and felt she would not want to. Her sexual fantasies were highly varied, included former and imaginary partners but lately, she noted, stopped short of intercourse.

Although he grew up in the same country as his wife, Mr. X's family had been more "modern" and less sexually repressive. The double standard in their country promoted male sexuality, albeit in the form of machismo. Mr. X felt that he had conformed, throughout his adolescence, to the macho ideal. He began masturbating at age 12 with minimal guilt although he avoided masturbating before sports competitions for fear it would sap his strength. He had intercourse first at age 16 and had many partners over the next several years. He had no worries about his sexual function except that he sometimes came a little too quickly.

When he first met his wife-to-be, he knew that she had been to bed with a number of men but somehow that didn't bother him because he saw her as a fundamentally good and loyal woman. He always took the socially appropriate role (in their culture) of initiator in sex and felt that her pleasure was his responsibility. She never said what she did or did not like sexually except that she would not participate in fellatio. She generally didn't like to have seminal fluid get on her body. His sense of responsibility for her sexuality continued right up to the therapy. He had gone to several book stores and bought books about female response and had read them so that he would know how to help her. She had rejected his offers of help and the books. She had begun to resent his controlling her, what she called his "leftover machismo." She had picked up some ideas about Women's Liberation which had made her see their sex-linked roles in a new light. He agreed with her new ideas at an intellectual level but had trouble with them in daily living. For example, he tended to put down her ideas rather automatically and assumed he would do most of the talking in any social situation. This was also, in part, a carry-over from the previous year when her English had been so poor.

Forty minutes were set aside for taking medical histories and doing physical examinations during the first visit. One significant factor to emerge was that Mrs. X had reacted strongly against the bodily changes of pregnancy and breast feeding. She had an image of her body as very small, tight, and compact. She was upset by her expansion and the "looseness" of her skin and breasts. She felt ugly and "not myself." When she stopped breast feeding (which she had enjoyed) she gradually felt her old form returning.

The medical history also elicited some urinary tract symptoms and a description of some "strong but intensely pleasurable" genital sensations which occurred at odd moments. Mrs. X's menstrual periods had not yet resumed since she had stopped breast feeding. The physical examination confirmed the suspicion that Mrs. X had been in a state of chronic estrogen deprivation, probably as a result of the post-partum breast feeding period (perhaps exacerbated by extra weight loss). She was put on 1.25 mg of Premarin every day and given Premarin Cream to use vaginally. Her urinary symptoms disappeared gradually over the next three weeks and she was gradually taken off medication. She was also instructed in the use of vaginal dilators and told to begin using the smallest.

VISIT 2. In the first part of the roundtable hour—the feedback—we said that we believed a combination of circumstances had led to Mr. and Mrs. X being "thrown off the track" sexually—cultural shock, Mrs. X's feelings about her body during pregnancy, estrogen deprivation in the post-partum period, Mr. X's counterproductive efforts to be helpful by taking over, and a lag time in his recognizing her new strengths. We emphasized the positive aspects of their situation particularly the openness to change which they displayed. We were able to be realistically very optimistic.

Mrs. X had used her first dilator several times with no difficulties.

The remainder of the hour included a discussion of principles and instructions for sensate-focus.

VISIT 3. The Xs were very pleased with their verbal communication. They felt that the issue of sex role stereotypes was finally being aired between them as it needed to be and Mr. X was allowing Mrs. X the time to express her ideas more fully. She was being more assertive with him and in social situations. They had two times of touching which went well. On the second occasion, Mrs. X had gotten "more turned on than I have in so long" and she suggested they go on and have intercourse, which they did. It hurt her and spoiled her pleasure. He ejaculated. They were chagrined about breaking the rules but Mrs. X spoke about this with a grin. L.S. commented on her grin and this led to a discussion of her feelings in her adolescence when her father tried to control her and she rebelled. L.S. said she could understand the feelings, but Mrs. X would certainly undermine herself if she could not get beyond that stage, as she had done when she first met Mr. X and began to have sex for reasons other than rebellion. The negative-conditioning effect of pain during sex was also stressed.

VISIT 4. After hearing about two positive experiences with sensate focus in which the rules were followed, we used 35 minutes to talk about normal sex response. Instructions for genital touching were given. At this stage, as we usually do, we added in the component of communicating more about how one wants to be touched, using hand-on-hand touch as a way of showing what feels nice at some given moment. We spent extra time discussing their feelings about this because we knew it was different from the Xs' established pattern and cultural conditioning. Mrs. X needed to hear her husband say that he would not feel emasculated if she guided his hand.

VISIT 5. Mrs. X had progressed steadily with the dilators. She could now insert the largest comfortably. Her urinary symptoms were gone. The genital touching had gone well except for the fact that Mr. X had ejaculated quite rapidly both times. Mrs. X had experienced an orgasm while she was guiding her husband's hand in genital touching. She had some slight guilt over this being "masturbation" and we spent time discussing this, focusing on the difference between the attitudes learned during her childhood and the very positive attitude she was hearing for the first time in the last year or so. In the instructions we included the start-stop technique, to be used on two occasions with manual stimulation. Since we were not seeing the Xs for 10 days, we suggested that they could move on to vaginal containment during a third time of touching. We recommended a female above position, Mrs. X taking charge of insertion (stopping if there was any pain) and moving for her pleasure. We also explained how they could integrate the stop-start technique into this. We stressed the need not to become goal-oriented because Mr. X seemed so overjoyed at his wife's having had an orgasm we feared she could feel pressured.

VISIT 6. The Xs were pleased with their touching. They had used the start-stop technique twice. In a third session there was no pain (Mrs. X was very relieved and almost disbelieving) and no premature ejaculation; Mrs. X had an orgasm after the vaginal containment from oral stimulation. We spent some time discussing their feelings about oral sex. Mrs. X said she was becoming less hung up about cleanliness and neatness during sex. They had used a condom plus foam for contraception and now talked about using a diaphragm. Mrs. X said she had never before felt confident that she would be able to use a diaphragm but now thought she understood her body well enough to cope with insertion and removal of a diaphragm.

VISIT 7—TWO WEEKS LATER. The Xs said everything was going well sexually. Mrs. X thought her former "sexy" self had returned. This was the most important change for her. They continued to argue about a variety of topics such as housekeeping and time spent with the baby but thought these arguments were different since they were using "I" communication. Their feelings weren't hurt in the same way and they often felt closer rather than farther apart at the end of an argument. We planned on a telephone contact in one month (because they would be out of the area for some time). That call confirmed that things continued to go well for them.

Fifteen-Visit Therapy

This therapy format is essentially the same as the format for seven-visit therapy except that the number of visits following the round-table is increased. We suggest fifteen-visit therapy for cases that we think will require greater input from us. In working with young couples the work of therapy is often helping a couple to *begin* relating emotionally and sexually. One or both may never have had a chance to experience sexual unfolding. Even in this era of pre-marital sexual permissiveness, many young couples who seek help for a sexual problem are naive and inexperienced. But there is usually more to it than that. Sexual information is so readily available today that those young people who choose not to read, question, and explore on their own do so out of inhibition or fear and generally need much more than the names of two or three good books.

By age 25 the majority of young people have gone through the complex process of sexual unfolding. When they have not, they have a great deal to unlearn and a great deal to learn. A fair amount of the counseling and therapy we do with graduate students and other young couples is really a way of helping them to condense the process of sexual unfolding into a period of several months.

A male graduate student came to see P.S. about his wife's sexual problems. They had been married for two years, and she had never had an orgasm. In fact, she disliked sex and was, he said, "very uptight." She was from a southern Baptist family with a very strongly negative view of sex. He worried that she would find it distasteful or even impossible to talk about sex. P.S. suggested that his wife talk with L.S. alone. The husband set up her appointment and on the scheduled day he arrived with her and sat in the waiting room while she spoke to L.S.

L.S. was so intimidated by what the husband had said of his wife and the fact of his escorting her to the appointment as if he needed to support her bodily in order for her to even show up, that she was very cautious for about 20 minutes. L.S. learned that although the wife had had very little sexual experience and was a virgin until marriage, she was a writer who had worked and lived alone for a year in a major city. She was quiet and a bit shy. But she was not a shrinking violet about to bolt out the door. L.S. changed tactics and began asking direct questions about sex—her feelings, what she wanted, how much she knew about orgasm, whether she masturbated. She changed noticeably. When she was not treated as frail, she became more direct and assertive. The alteration in her body language was striking.

Making them aware of their collusion in defining her as helpless and uptight was a first step in helping them to relate sexually. He had projected many of his own fears and anxieties onto her, and she had accepted this role.

One of the issues exemplified by this couple is the difficulty young people are facing in defining their roles as husband or wife. They were both from the South where more traditional sex role definitions are still in force, and they spent the first year of their married life in a foreign country where male chauvinism is alive and thriving. He was studying and had a raison d'etre while she stayed home. She had no friends and no job. In this environment it wasn't surprising that she took on a dependent role. She also felt a conflict between her southern idea of how a woman should behave in bed and her dimly felt desire to be more sexually assertive and abandoned. Returning to the United States and making some friends here, she began to find the role of sexually uptight, helpless female uncomfortable, but, by now, she was fearful of shattering the equilibrium with her husband.

The therapy process with this couple emphasized sex education, including a physical exam at which both were present and sexual anatomy and sexual physiology. He was ignorant about and fearful of his wife's genitals and always felt inept and bumbling in touching her.

In the sensate-focus phase of therapy we asked them (as we always do) to touch for their own pleasure, to find ways of touching that are fun or sensuous or interesting. She had a marvellous time and this astonished him. He never thought that a woman could take pleasure in touching. He still had a young adolescent's view of sex as something a male does to a female. Lying quietly while she touched him instead of being constantly *doing* something, he began to notice how anxious he was. It began to dawn on him that a lot of the uptightness in their sexual exchange belonged to him.

At the stage of genital touching she discovered that she didn't like to touch his penis at all. It scared her. She had no experiences with touching a penis prior to marriage, and after marriage it was something she had done out of a sense of obligation. In the office she suddenly recalled the only other experience she had had with an erect penis. The first time she could remember seeing an erection was one year before her marriage in a bad porno film shown at a girlfriend's pre-wedding party! In that context it had been a shock, but not wanting to make a scene, she hid her disgust and outrage about the film. Because she and her husband were geographically separated during much of their engagement and because of their religious values, she had no opportunity to experience his erect penis in a positive context. In therapy, a gradual desensitization, at her own pace, was all she needed.

The sensate-focus and genital touching phases of therapy were not a corrective re-run of old experiences for this couple so much as totally new experiences. They had "necked" before marriage and "had intercourse" after marriage. The necking, which had been fun, stopped altogether on their wedding day. The transition experiences of being naked together, of touching each other's genitals, had been skipped. Becoming relaxed with one thing at a time, learning a sense of comfort and mastery in gradual steps, were absolutely essential before there could be full sexual response.

This couple, while less experienced than the average young couple today, do represent a sizable minority that often has sexual problems because there was no sexual unfolding process. In our experience, a short therapy or a therapy condensed into two weeks is too fast for these couples. Fifteen visits or so, extended over some months, seems a preferable treatment format.

An Example of Fifteen-Visit Therapy for
Secondary Impotence (The As)

Mr. A., a graduate student, and his wife came to see us because he was unable to have erections when they tried to have sex. They had been on the verge of legal separation, but, a few months ago had decided to "try again." They had seen a minister for counseling, and this helped them to negotiate a number of practical problems and communicate better but they had been unable to relate sexually. Mrs. A had moved back to their apartment just a few weeks ago—the time when they called for an appointment with us. "We'd really like to cross this last hurdle," Mrs. A said, adding that they have an almost one-year-old son and want to try to be a family.

The consultation suggested that there were a number of complex issues which made fifteen-visit therapy advisable. These issues were: the ambivalence on Mr. A's part about recommitting; his expressed lack of any sexual interest in or response to Mrs. A; her expressed anger at his sexual rejection. We should note that these feelings emerged during that part of the consultation in which the couple are *not* together, i.e., L.S. talked with Mrs. A for about 20 minutes while P.S. was seeing Mr. A.

A therapy schedule was planned. We stressed the importance of their giving priority to the therapy and to their relationship during the approximately two month period of therapy. They were told not to have friends or relatives stay overnight, not to plan any trips or conferences and Mr. A was asked to take some vacation during the therapy.

The As submitted written autobiographical statements about one week before therapy started.

VISITS 1 AND 2. (This is a composite of material from the written autobiographical statements and from the history taken during Visit 1 (Mr. A with P.S.; Mrs. A with L.S.) and during Visit 2 (Mr. A with L.S.; Mrs. A with P.S.).)

Mrs. A was very verbal and cooperative. She described her family as lower middle class but always "comfortable." Her father had an extra job and was also active in their small community. Her mother never worked. Mrs. A had two younger sisters. The family atmosphere was warm with lots of affectionate touching. Most subjects were openly discussed but sex was noticeably ignored and *never* discussed. Mrs. A was only slightly aware of competition with her sisters. She was the favorite child of both parents because she did well in school and was well-behaved.

She recalled no childhood sex play. She began masturbating about age eight, spontaneously. She later read that "self abuse" could be harmful and tried to stop but couldn't. Her menarche was later than her friends, at age 14. She was "flat-chested" and very self-conscious about it. "I still am." L.S. asked how she thought this might affect her sexual relationship. She said that in college she was so uptight about it she couldn't relax in many sexual situations. Now she feels it less acutely, but she wondered if her tendency to feel sexually rejected so readily might come, in part, from her needing reassurance that she is "sexy" enough.

High school social life was in groups and did not lead to any specifically sexual experiences.

In college she had no very serious relationships, just some genital petting that was "OK." She never had an orgasm but didn't expect to "yet." In her last year she had intercourse because everyone else had and she was curious. She took birth control pills. There was no pain or bleeding. After a month or so she started having orgasms during intercourse when she was in the above position. Her boyfriend went to another part of the country at graduation. The break-up was not traumatic for either of them.

She was in graduate school for two years. During this time she had intercourse with four different men. At first she felt a little guilty but later came to feel all right about her own moral code. She only slept with men where there was some ongoing relationship. She felt like an adult for the first time during these years.

At the very end of graduate school she met Mr. A. He had worked for a while and had returned to school for an advanced degree. He seemed very worldly and so Mrs. A was surprised to find that he was sexually "conservative and inhibited." He didn't like much foreplay or oral sex. He focused on lasting a long time during intercourse. She found their sexual relationship "good but not great."

They married in 1973. She went to work while he continued in school. Sex was satisfying to Mrs. A. She was shocked and hurt to hear Mr. A say (in the consultation) that he thought sex between them was never good. She always had an orgasm during intercourse. If he ejaculated first, she would continue moving until she came. They each initiated sex about half the time.

During that year, Mr. A had a one month period of unexplained impotence. She felt extremely rejected. Mr. A told P.S. that his wife had been "hysterical" over his impotence, had cried, been furiously angry, and took it as a sign that she turned him off sexually. Mrs. A seemed to want to gloss over this period; in fact, she changed the topic. L.S. returned to it, asking how she had felt. Her voice sounded choked up but she insisted this had been "just a thing that passed." L.S. commented on her holding back feeling. She gave no response. L.S. asked how she felt about talking today. Mrs. A began to cry. She said it was hard to talk about sex. It had been easier to talk with the minister because they talked about "easier" things—"Like, in your family—no talking about sex?", L.S. commented. Mrs. A smiled.

She did then talk more about her hurt feelings and about the fact that the first man she had slept with after entering grad school had been impotent and the relationship had ended. She had felt "unattractive and unfeminine" for months.

(The above details are included because these basic techniques for establishing rapport are sometimes neglected in favor of data gathering when this kind of exchange can be the most important part of a sexual history.)

In the second year of marriage, Mrs. A became pregnant as planned. She stopped working. Her husband was now working as well as finishing his dissertation and was extremely busy. During the pregnancy there was infrequent sex, less than once a month. Mrs. A had become fearful of initiating because Mr. A seemed not to like it when she did. At least this is how it appeared to Mrs. A. They had never discussed it.

Nor had they discussed any aspect of sex. She enjoyed cunnilingus and wished he would stimulate her this way but she never asked. She never showed him how to touch her clitoris even though his technique caused her pain! P.S. heard a similar tale of noncommunication from Mr. A. When intercourse continued after he ejaculated, it was sometimes painful for him but he never said so. Both As said they masturbated sometimes but this had never been mentioned to each other. Mrs. A had made some attempts to introduce variations in their sexual routine but Mr. A rebuffed the suggestions. Mrs. A had begun to think her sexuality might be "too much." She bought a few books she thought might help them but he wasn't interested in reading them with her. She found reading them alone got her aroused and she masturbated. This brought back guilt feelings like those in adolescence. Mrs. A needed reassurance that her level of sexual interest and her masturbation were normal.

The pregnancy and delivery were normal and the As were happy to have a son but their sex life did not pick up and they seemed to fight constantly about trivial issues. Mr. A told P.S. that he had begun an affair when his wife was about six months pregnant. When the baby was three months old, Mr. A's girlfriend threatened to kill herself if he didn't leave his wife. In a panic, he left. Mrs. A had been a bit suspicious but was much taken aback by his suddenly leaving. Six months later, Mr. A's girlfriend had a psychotic break and was hospitalized (then transferred to a hospital in her home town). Mrs. A suggested they try to patch up their marriage. Mr. A had been proceeding with a legal separation but promptly dropped that and began trying to work things out with his wife. They had had several months of counseling with a minister before he moved back.

Mr. A was the only child of wealthy parents who married in their late 30s. The maternal grandmother was part of the household until her death when Mr. A was 16. He described his family as aloof, very "correct," and oriented toward achievement. He felt that he *must* do well in school and athletics. He recalled a pervasive feeling of anxiety throughout his childhood, particularly in a new situation. Once he could figure out what was expected and saw he could do it, he felt more relaxed. However, he did carry a lingering feeling of distrust of women based on numerous interactions with his mother and grandmother. For example, he recalled misreading signals from his grandmother. She had commented (about a bullying teacher), "Someone should talk back to that teacher." He did, but then was met with severe criticism by his grandmother for not behaving properly.

In Mr. A's family women were put on a pedestal. The male role was to make them happy and provide for their needs, needs very often difficult for a growing boy to determine.

Mr. A began masturbating at age 11. He had one episode of mutual masturbation at age 12 with a male friend. He recalled a feeling of repulsion in his early teens for seminal fluid because it was so messy. He had no sexual experiences beyond touching a girl's breast until college. In college he had two relationships. There was heavy petting but he never ejaculated with either girl. He had intercourse for the first time at age 24. He described this sexual relationship as good—he had felt sexually free with her.

Mr. A met his wife at a party and thought she was very attractive. They became "serious" very quickly and then began a sexual relationship. In his written autobiography he made a slip-of-the-pen. He wrote, "She [his wife-to-be] was the second *wom* I slept with." His penmanship made it difficult to know whether he had written "wom" or "mom."

He was surprised to find that, although he loved her and thought she was pretty, sex with his future wife was somehow not very exciting, but it was satisfying enough not to worry him.

Mr. A never understood the brief period of impotence during the first year of his marriage. He vividly recalled his wife's anger and his own guilty feelings about hurting her. He thought the impotence went away when he received an advance from a publisher for a book and spent almost all of it on a fur coat for Mrs. A.

He recalled being very pleased that his wife was pregnant and almost surprised to find himself having an affair. He thought he felt sorry for this other woman who was in psychological and legal trouble. She had a reputation for sleeping around in the past but needed some one person to rely on. Mr. A found sex with her very exciting and was more "experimental" with her. P.S. asked him about the difference in his willingness to be experimental with her, but not with his wife. Mr. A said he had a different image of Mrs. A, that she wouldn't like all these things. P.S. reminded him that Mrs. A had suggested variations and had even bought books (this had come up in the consultation). Mr. A said he might have not seen his wife for what she really is because "she doesn't tell me much." He also said that books scared him. He felt they were a kind of pressure to perform and get an A+.

The months of separation were not happy. Mr. A felt very confused and guilty. He found he was hurting two women at once. He was almost relieved when his girlfriend had a breakdown and Mrs. A wanted a reconciliation. At one point during the separation Mrs. A came to his apartment and made sexual advances to him. He felt pressured and was impotent. When they tried to begin to "patch things up" he continued to be impotent.

The A's gave their medical histories and had physical examinations. There was nothing unusual found in either examination or from laboratory studies. Mrs. A said she felt embarrassed about her small breasts.

VISIT 3. A few major points were made to each partner during the roundtable. L.S. spoke first to Mrs. A. Her low self-esteem was discussed in relation to her body (particularly breasts) and in relation to her not being able to work in her chosen field (due to lack of jobs in the area). The role of wife and mother was denigrated by both Mr. and Mrs. A.

Following the pattern in her family of origin, Mrs. A saw her husband as "more important and more interesting" than herself. This made her particularly vulnerable to feelings of rejection. When she felt rejected, she would tend to become angry or sulky, unable to communicate what she needed to Mr. A or tell him that she was hurt. This communication pattern then triggered Mr. A's guilt and his fear of strong women, causing him to withdraw further.

The lack of effective communication about sex was stressed—again, a repeat of her family pattern. Her continuing guilt about masturbation and a lurking fear of being "over-sexed" or abnormal made it difficult for her to assert her own sexuality unless she was given a very clearly positive response, a response Mr. A had so far not given. L.S. pointed out that some of her efforts at sexual communication—such as buying sex books—had backfired because of Mr. A's interpreting this as pressure to perform up to some established standard.

P.S. emphasized Mr. A's ambivalence about re-commitment, feeling that this issue had best be up front during therapy. He underlined Mr. A's lifelong view of women as powerful people who must be pleased lest they become angry or disappointed. His tendency to put some women on a pedestal and see them as nonsexual while relating in an "exciting" way with another sort of woman was mentioned. Mrs. A was very excited by this interpretation because she felt it helped her to understand aspects of her husband which had always confused her. P.S. also pointed out that Mr. A had never found a way of handling his anger at his mother, his grandmother, or his wife, that he tended to be quietly stoic but was furious underneath.

Mr. A also played into their poor sexual communication through his need to play down eroticism between them and his rebellious feelings about being told what to do.

Last, but not least, both had become spectators in bed, trying to will *his* response.

The concepts that the therapy is based upon were described, i.e., sex is a natural function, there is no such thing as an uninvolved partner (therefore, neither is to "blame" for the problem), feelings are facts, sex response will not come about when there is a goal orientation, learning will come from mistakes as well as from what goes well, people hurt each other when they don't know each other's innermost feelings; then communications guidelines were given, and sensate-focus instructions were given.

VISIT 4. It had been Mrs. A's turn to initiate the first time of touching. She found herself feeling very anxious about it, thinking he wouldn't *really* want to. She waited until he wasn't busy with anything and seemed in a good mood. L.S. repeated the instructions about initiating—to do so when *you* want to, not second guessing Mr. A's mood—L.S. asked how Mrs. A would feel to "interrupt" her husband and say "I want to touch," or ask for attention in any way. This led to a discussion of some themes raised in the roundtable: Mrs. A's sense of herself as less important, her tendency to feel (in this case to anticipate) rejection, and her assumption that she isn't sexually desired. The actual touching, in the two times they had, went fairly well and both found it enjoyable. Mr. A said he was relaxed but ticklish. On both occasions he enjoyed being touched more than touching. Mrs. A said she had felt hurt by Mr. A's "cursory treatment of my body." It made her think her body was ugly. L.S. supported Mrs. A's direct expression of hurt feelings and urged her to try to do it when the feelings were actually happening.

Mr. and Mrs. A were told to have two times of sensate-focus, Mr. A to initiate the first, Mrs. A the second.

VISIT 5. The A's had gotten into a "heated discussion" after Mrs. A won several games of gin in a row and Mr. A had become grumpy and withdrawn. He felt enraged at his powerlessness against "Lady Luck." P.S. encouraged him to explore this feeling and he got in touch with his fury at people—especially women who have power over him. "It makes me feel so small"—pause—"Hey, you don't think that could have a sexual meaning, do you? Hmm. Maybe next time I should just say I'm not enjoying the game and stop. Would that be all right with you?" he asked Mrs. A. She said she'd much rather he do that, that she didn't like being a "whip cracker."

Their touching sessions had gone well. Mr. A had felt a little "freer" and more aware of feelings and less ticklish. He mentioned he hadn't had an erection yet.

P.S. discussed normal sexual response. Mrs. A was surprised to hear that erections can normally come and go and that erection occurs at an early point in sexual response. She commented that she was always very focused on Mr. A's erection as a sign that he was responding to her. She hadn't realized that erection didn't always mean a man was very excited and its absence or lessening might not mean that he was just not interested. The A's were asked to have two times of sensate-focus, trying the use of a body lotion. Mrs. A was to initiate the first session, Mr. A the second.

VISIT 6. The A's had a good experience with their first time of sensate-focus, using the body lotion a small part of the time. They were both luke-warm about touching with lotion. (We should comment here that we use lotion as a means of extending sensate-focus and to confront possible aversion to wetness but it is not an essential element in sex therapy process). Mr. A had only touched Mrs. A's legs and lower back in these two sessions. He said he "sensed" that she wanted the rest of her body touched, was impatient with him, but, "you [the therapists] said I was to do what I wanted to do." Mrs. A said she was disappointed, but she didn't feel hurt this time. She had the feeling that he would "come around when he was ready." Mr. A said he was grateful for her not being angry or trying to hurry him up. He then spontaneously recalled how he used to second-guess his mother's demands. For example, if he thought she would ask him to cut the grass he would make elaborate plans to be away all weekend to avoid even being asked. Mrs. A said, "You second-guess me a lot. I'd better start telling you more about what I *do* feel."

L.S. discussed normal female sex response. Mrs. A was surprised to learn that many women regularly had orgasm with their partners from manual or oral stimulation. She had a more stereotyped view of sex in which everything was foreplay, leading up to the "real" thing, intercourse.

VISIT 7. The A's one and only touching in the past week was going well, they said, until Mrs. A saw how aroused Mr. A was when she was touching his penis. She "jokingly" said, "Let's screw." Mr. A was furious and they had a fight. L.S. asked them to review the entire time. Mrs. A had enjoyed being touched. She was eager for a response to genital touching but was "very nervous about telling him (Mr. A) what to do." L.S. asked if she was referring to the hand-on-hand communication. Yes, she was. L.S. asked, "Is that the same as telling him what to do?" Mr. and Mrs. A had a spontaneous discussion of this crucial issue, with Mr. A encouraging his wife to show him what felt good to her. She said, "I guess I was only partly joking. It would have been easier for me just to go back to the old familiar screwing." P.S. reminded the As that it was important for them to have satisfying alternatives to "screwing" so that they would not feel pressured to have intercourse if either or both wanted to have an orgasm.

VISIT 8. The A's felt they had made some important breakthroughs. Before any touching had begun they had a long talk about lots of things, including sex. They each told the other that they sometimes masturbated. The touching had felt more spontaneous than ever before. Mrs. A did guide Mr. A's hand from time to time and did have an orgasm. They were both pleased. Mr. A felt very aroused but did not have an orgasm. The second time the A's touched was similar to the first. Mr. A said he wasn't trying not to come, but he was aware of mixed feelings about it. He recalled an adolescent experience of coming in his pants that was "icky and embarrassing" and he thought maybe he was doing his "old stubborn-resister number" because he sensed Mrs. A wanted to make him come. She said she had been, maybe, trying to prove she could do it. She thought she would "stop playing that game . . ." in the future.

VISIT 9. The As were seen separately for about 15 minutes, L.S. with Mrs. A, P.S. with Mr. A. Mr. A said, "Everything seemed to go back to square one but we recouped." In the first time of touching he had become focused on producing an erection and had gotten very tense when there was no sign of hardness. They stopped in the middle and both were almost in tears. Two days later she had said she wanted to touch. Mr. A asked his wife to use body lotion in touching his genitals and found himself concentrating on the new feelings so much that before he realized it, he was coming. Mrs. A told the same story. The interview continued as a foursome. L.S. and P.S. underlined the strengths the As had demonstrated in dealing with the nearly universal slipping-back phenomenon which takes place in therapy. When a couple experiences what feels like a complete set-back but can share their feelings and work through to a positive touching experience, this is a very good prognostic sign. Mr. A added that his wife didn't have an orgasm in their touching and he thought this was important; he hadn't been afraid she would be angry. He had, instead, asked how she felt and he believed her when she said she felt completely satisfied.

The As were told to try touching simultaneously. Either one could invite for either time. P.S. suggested they see if they could observe Mr. A's erection subsiding and returning if Mrs. A discontinued stimulation for brief periods.

VISIT 10. Mrs. A said, "The main change is how much more fun we have now." Both times of touching went well. Mr. A's erection had come and gone a few times without either of them feeling worried. They had one "near fight" when Mr. A put down Mrs. A for not liking a play they had seen. Mrs. A said that in the past, she would have sulked in silence and felt like a dummy. This time she defended herself and said, "My opinion is as valid as yours."

Instructions for vaginal containment of the penis were given.

VISIT 11. There had been one very long "lovemaking" time, Mrs. A said. She asked him to stay in bed although she thought he might want to get to work. He stayed, happily. There were no problems with vaginal containment. We suggested Mrs. A feel free to move more after she guided the penis into her vagina.

VISIT 12. Everything went very well. We suggested a new position for intercourse, the lateral position (as described by Masters and Johnson in *Human Sexual Inadequacy*).

VISIT 13. The As were not able to use the new position. They did try intercourse with Mr. A above.

VISIT 14. The As tried the lateral position and liked it. No problems. They did notice that they had fallen into an early morning pattern for love-making, but Mr. A felt this was not his old fear that he would only have erections in the morning but was a matter of convenience and preference.

VISIT 15. Two weeks later, the As reported that there had been a few bad days with the return of some old feelings. Mrs. A found herself unable to tell Mr. A what she was feeling—that he was not spending time with her now that the therapy was over. She had forced herself to be honest with him when she felt herself getting into a sulky mood during love-making. "I was afraid I'd undermine everything we gained and that was too high a price to pay." Once she had expressed her feelings of hurt, the sulky mood went away and the lovemaking was very satisfying. We felt reassured to see that the A's were able to use the guidelines of therapy to work themselves out of a potentially destructive situation.

The above summary has focused on the part of the therapy which deals directly with the couple's experiences in sensate-focus, genital touching, and intercourse. In doing this we have given a distorted picture of the real content of therapy hours. In almost every hour, time is spent talking about other issues, particularly out-of-bed communication. There is special emphasis on this for a few sessions after the roundtable because the self-assertive and self-protective communication system we outline for the couple is new to them; they often have trouble using the system and they make mistakes. By about visit 6 or 7, many couples have a feel for the verbal communication and are using it fairly effectively. Even then, we do not omit discussion of communication, usually focusing on problem areas the couple pin-point.

In the case of the A's, Mrs. A had a great deal of difficulty with verbal self-assertion (which paralleled her difficulty with assertion in bed). She wasn't able to express disagreement or state her wants if there was any chance this would stir conflict with her husband. She couldn't say something as simple as "I'd rather not go out tonight." She began to see that her reluctance to speak up and cause conflict stemmed from her own family's style of handling issues. Her father had been very "opinionated" and didn't take kindly to any disagreement. The entire family maintained a kind of rule of silence about things that were uncomfortable, keeping up an image of happy agreement that denied real conflict. We have already alluded to Mr. A's trouble with "strong" women and his tendency to put Mrs. A down. Prohibiting "you" statements helped to clarify this dynamic. Mr. A kept making "you" statements in disguised form, e.g., "I think you haven't really thought about what you're saying." The As actually had more difficulty than the average couple with the communication system. Their difficulties did help them—and us—to get at important issues which might otherwise have been overlooked only to surface later in their sexual interaction and later in the therapy process or when therapy was completed.

Individual Therapy for Sexual Problems in the University Setting

Sexual Dysfunction

A man or woman with a sexual dysfunction may come for therapy without a partner for a number of reasons. Each situation needs to be evaluated carefully in deciding whether to proceed with individual sex therapy, insist on working with the couple, or refer to some other treatment modality such as a pre-orgasmic group, another type of individual therapy, or general couple's counseling.

In the university setting, it is not uncommon for couples to be geographically separated and to see one another only on weekends or at much longer intervals. Rather than telling such couples that nothing can be done to help them, we have attempted to work with the available partner, seeing the out-of-town partner once or twice if possible or working entirely with the partner who is at the university. This is certainly a compromise but we have had some success in this approach where the absent partner was willing and able to cooperate.

We would only attempt this approach if we felt the couple did *not* have major problems in communication or conflict over commitment and if the sexual dysfunction was not too severe. This would probably mean ruling out cases of primary impotence, or very severe premature ejaculation. We would also be less inclined to consider working with one partner in cases of secondary sexual dysfunction which originated in the course of this couple's relationship because of the likelihood that interpersonal dynamics are at the root of the problem. On the other hand, where external factors such as vaginitis or reaction to medication seem to have been the prime precipitating factor, we would consider treating a secondary dysfunction by working with the dysfunctional partner.

Vaginismus is the one problem which yields readily to couple's therapy but which we have not been able to treat "long-distance," i.e., when only the male partner has been available. However, even then, one visit for the woman can be enough for diagnosis and beginning treatment.

When a person has a regular partner who is geographically available but the person chooses to come alone, this issue needs to be evaluated with special care. Is a young woman anxious to become orgasmic so as to please and hold onto a man who is drifting away? Is a man with premature ejaculation, whose partner is sexually uninterested, trying to do the work for both of them and shielding her? In our experience the most common reason for one partner to come alone is that the other partner is reluctant, fearful, or unmotivated. When that is the case, a common feeling of the partner is that sex therapy couldn't begin to deal with their problems because they are so complex. In addition, there is a fear of opening up areas which are too painful to deal with. We usually attempt to have a direct contact with the other partner. We suggest that he or she call to make an appointment to talk with a therapist (of the same sex) alone. Sometimes the reluctance to participate in sex therapy is due to misconceptions about what sex therapy involves. Clarification, seeing the therapist face-to-face and having a chance to talk about feelings may make it possible for the partner to enter sex therapy willingly.

Students who are not married or living together but who have an on-going relationship may come for help with a sexual dysfunction. This presents something of a dilemma. If therapists pressure the couple to work together they run the risk of coercing the nondysfunctional partner into more involvement in this relationship than he or she wants. (The partner may also have a dysfunction but this is not presented to the therapists as part of the problem). It is very important to respect the partner's feelings, needs, and boundaries, either by not seeing them at all or seeing them alone to explore what sex therapy as a couple might mean for this individual and for this twosome.

Our experience in this regard with one diagnostic category, premature ejaculation, has been interesting. Nine men with premature ejaculation have asked to be treated alone although they had girlfriends in the area. In two instances, the girlfriends agreed to enter couple's sex therapy. They were both worried about their own sexual response—not having an orgasm—but neither was motivated at that time to deal with her own problem or to participate in therapy except superficially. Both cases fell apart in the early stages. In four cases, the girlfriends came in for a consultation and were diagnosed as having vaginismus. These four cases worked out well, and the premature ejaculation was reversed. In three cases, the girlfriends did not become involved in the therapy process directly because they felt this meant more investment and commitment to the relationship than they were prepared to make at the time. In these three cases the male was able to work out the problem of premature ejaculation through individual sex therapy.

If there is a lesson to be seen in these cases it would be that a partner who is self-motivated to participate in sex therapy is an asset (or at least not a deterrent) while a reluctant partner is potentially destructive of progress in therapy. Since it is possible to achieve good results without directly involving the partner, it would seem that, in a student population at least, it may be preferable to work in individual sex therapy unless there is a highly motivated partner.

There are sometimes very special circumstances which present the option of working with one partner or doing nothing at all. These special circumstances involve cultural values which make it impossible for the couple to seek help together. We have worked with four such situations—all graduate students from foreign countries with unconsummated marriages. In each instance it has been the female who has sought help. For the husband to admit "publicly" (we stress total confidentiality but, apparently, even one outsider equals "the public") that he has been unable to have intercourse with his wife would be such a humiliation that he cannot consider even a telephone conversation about it with a therapist or doctor.

Three of the four couples have been from the Near-East and one was from India. In three cases, the problem was vaginismus and it was possible to treat the vaginismus successfully by working with the woman alone. One of these women could not be examined by P.S. (the physician half of our co-therapy team), because her husband would not permit her being examined by a male. A nurse mid-wife was brought into the case to examine her. One case involved vaginismus and severe premature ejaculation. The vaginismus was reversed but attempts to treat the husband's dysfunction via the wife were only partially successful—although the marriage was eventually consummated.

A fairly large number of young men (but very few young women) ask for help with a sexual dysfunction although they do not have any one sexual partner at the time. We have observed an important and interesting phenomenon with these young men. The majority manage to form some kind of outside relationship as their individual therapy gets under way. This is true even for individuals who have been terrified of relationships and avoided them for months or even years. We suspect that the same change in motivation which led to making an appointment with a sex therapist led to a willingness to risk a relationship. Also, the anxiety reduction accomplished in the first one or two interviews helps to encourage reaching out to another. Lastly, of course, is the acknowledged fact of *sex* therapy (a fact shared with the individual) that one cannot accomplish very much behavioral change without a partner.

When an individual in therapy has not found a sexual partner in the course of therapy, the goals and outcome are different. In three or four visits the therapist can take a full sex history, rule out medical causes, help the person to understand his or her sexuality and the causes of the dysfunction, look at the question of what a sexual relationship means to the person (hopefully making it more likely that a relationship will occur in the future) and, when appropriate, refer for individual psychotherapy, group-therapy, social skills training, or other forms of help.

How do we do "sex therapy" with one person? We always have a female therapist work with a female, a male therapist with a male. We time-structure the therapy, as we do with couples, and we follow many of the same procedures. There is an initial consultation. If the plan is to go ahead in individual work, the person is asked to write an autobiographical statement. A fixed number of appointments, usually seven, is set up. At the time of the first visit following the consultation the history taking is completed and the person does the Draw-A-Person test. These drawings are used as a diagnostic aid and as a springboard for discussion. The therapist helps to delineate the past and present factors contributing to the dysfunction. There is education about sexual response. Unless there is no sexual partner available at all (which is very seldom) there are specific instructions given about touching.

The following is an example of this mode of sex therapy.

A 24-year-old divorced graduate student with a problem of premature ejaculation had isolated himself socially. He felt that in the singles scene and at his age it was expected that meeting a new woman would probably mean going to bed with her that night. After his divorce he had made several forays into the singles scene. Each time it was the same. He never told any of the women he was anxious about his sexual performance. He always came quickly. Finally, about one year before P.S. saw him, ejaculation occurred without erection. Panicked and humiliated, he couldn't bear to face another woman.

In the first two interviews he presented a fairly full account of his sex history. He was also able to get in touch with his fears of hurting a woman physically and emotionally, his tremendous performance pressure to achieve simultaneous orgasm whenever having intercourse and his basic fear of rejection and failure as a result of losing control of his sex response. At the end of the second interview, P.S. suggested that they meet again in 10 days. If, in the interim, the opportunity arose to relate to a woman, it was suggested that he start by telling her his fears and that he not have intercourse before we could talk again. He said that wouldn't be a problem since he really hadn't felt any desire for intercourse in more than a year. In the 10 days between appointments he did pursue a friendship which had started just before he saw P.S. for the first time. He did tell the woman about his sexual anxiety and that he was getting help from a therapist. She accepted his statement. They petted and did not try to have intercourse. He had an erection and felt "My body's coming back to life."

During the second appointment he had talked about the terrible fear he had felt when he had ejaculated without an erection. By the third visit he felt he was ready to have intercourse. P.S. made four suggestions: that he only have intercourse if he felt comfortable; that he not try to control the premature ejaculation; that both he and his woman friend only do sexually what was pleasurable for themselves; and, if she did anything that was uncomfortable for him or if he did anything she didn't like, then they were to protect themselves through verbal communication. P.S. also presented a mini-lecture on male sexual response to him.

At the fourth visit a week later, he reported that he had had intercourse three times—"the first time with an 80 percent erection, the second time with a 90 percent erection, and the third time with 100 percent erection," "100 percent erection" meaning she had had an orgasm during intercourse. Then we talked about "what if" the premature ejaculation should re-occur. P.S. described both the start-stop technique and the Valsalva maneuver* but stressed that the most important way to deal with anxiety was to be able to relate as openly as he had in the previous weeks. There were two more appointments in the next two months. At no time did the impotence or premature ejaculation recur. At the end of the therapy he decided to enter psychoanalysis to help him better understand his basic fears of hurting, of losing, and of achieving "in order to make the right impression."

The following is an example of individual sex therapy with a woman. L.S. worked alone with her.

Jane, a junior, asked for help because she had never had an orgasm in intercourse or in petting. She was easily orgasmic in masturbation and had been masturbating for many years. She had been having intercourse for two years (in three different relationships) and before that had had several relationships in which there was mutual genital petting. She had been in a relationship with another junior, Bert, for four months. They were both upset by her lack of orgasm but she didn't want him involved in therapy. "It's my problem," she said, "and besides, this relationship is probably not going anywhere." His feelings were similar and he did not want to be involved in therapy though he was willing to help out in any other way.

The autobiography plus the history as she told it revealed a young woman with very low self-esteem except in the area of intellectual achievement. She thought that she was very unattractive and that no male had ever enjoyed sex with her. This belief seemed to be part of a larger conviction that no one liked her. Jane had one semester of individual psychotherapy in her sophomore year which focused on this and "some other issues." She had found it slightly helpful.

---

* In this maneuver, a man holds his breath and bears down, as if to move his bowels, when he feels close to ejaculating.

After the first of our scheduled visits, L.S. asked her to spend time in pleasurable touching of her entire body plus looking at her body and noticing what she liked. She was able to do these tasks and found they were helpful. She also felt it had helped her to review the origins of her negative feelings in early adolescence.

During the second visit we discussed some specifics of her present sex relations with Bert. She never showed him what she liked because she felt she was imposing on him—that he couldn't possibly get pleasure from touching or stimulating her. She knew that there was one way she could probably have an orgasm with him—by touching her own clitoris while they had intercourse with her on top but, she said, "I could never bring myself to do that. I'd be much too uptight about it." I asked her to do two things, to talk with Bert about how he felt about stimulating her and to *imagine* stimulating her clitoris during intercourse.

During the third visit Jane said she had talked to Bert who said he really liked touching her but she found it hard to believe. She had been "sort of" able to fantasize clitoral stimulation and intercourse but got distracted easily. She spontaneously told a dream in which someone was trying to kill her. Some questions brought out the fact that this was a recurrent nightmare which she had experienced for years. These nightmares and her fear of death were some of those "other issues" which she had discussed in psychotherapy the year before. Jane said that she had a way of handling the nightmares: She always woke herself up just as the man was about to kill her. "You don't think," she asked, "that I could think orgasms are like dying?" She then made a connection to the fact that she cries after orgasm when she masturbates. She feels "suddenly completely alone."

During the fourth visit Jane reported that she had let Bert stimulate her much longer than ever before but that "It got too intense and scary, so I stopped him." L.S. commented on the similarity between that and her awakening herself from her nightmares. During this hour the term *make love* was used; Jane said she never called sex "making love" because she had never loved or been loved. She used terms like, *being friendly* or *have sex.* Bert preferred it that way too. The instructions given Jane during this part of the therapy focused on the communication guidelines we use in couple's therapy. L.S. particularly emphasized not second guessing Bert (because of her tendency to project her negative feelings about herself onto him and others) and the need for self-protection and saying "ouch" if she didn't like something.

The fifth visit was focused on the subjects of trust and commitment in relationships. Jane had always felt she dragged Bert into this relationship and he would be just as happy to breakup. He had said to her in the previous week, "Maybe I do sort of love you." She wanted to hear this but found it frightening. She didn't want to let herself fall in love with him because it might not last and she could get hurt. She didn't want to find herself thinking in terms of marriage because years ago she had "decided" she was "too ugly and too intellectual to ever get married" and always thought she would be a self-sufficient career woman. L.S. asked if she thought having an orgasm with a man might make her fall in love. She thought it might.

The sixth visit began with Jane saying she had decided on a plan of her own and had gone ahead and done it! She was very proud of herself because she had masturbated to an orgasm with Bert at her side. He had been very supportive and encouraging.

During the last visit Jane said that she and Bert had had a more open discussion about sex than they'd ever had. He had confessed that he hadn't wanted to have intercourse with her as early in their relationship as they had. He had felt social pressure because he was a virgin and didn't know how to say he felt overwhelmed and scared himself. Jane was more impressed by his willingness to tell her this than she had been by his saying he might love her.

She had been able to have an orgasm by stimulating her clitoris during intercourse. Although she was very pleased by her progress she still wanted to be able to have Bert stimulate her to an orgasm or to have an orgasm during intercourse without clitoral stimulation. We discussed the question of adding on one or two interviews past the seven we had agreed upon. Jane said that although she could possibly use it, she felt she had gotten over the real hurdle in letting down her guard with Bert.

Therapy With Individuals for a Variety of Sex-Related Concerns (Other Than Sexual Dysfunction)

Students have come to the Sex Counseling Service for help with issues that are related to sexuality but not particularly to sexual dysfunction. Several students, men and women, had essentially no sexual experience with another person and sought help in making first steps. Some of these students have worried about their total lack of sexual interest. Others, who were moving toward having sexual intercourse, wanted to further understand the meaning of their virginity and the potential significance of "losing" it. At the other end of the spectrum there have been several men and women caught up in sexual behavior that they themselves labelled "promiscuous" and that they wished to better understand and change. Some students have been concerned about a "hang-up" having to do with a particular sexual behavior, for example, a male student who couldn't "get into" oral sex with his girlfriend. Several men and women have sought help in overcoming their inability to masturbate.

There have been about 25 students who sought help with issues relating to sexual orientation. For some, the focus has been on understanding what their orientation is—or could be—homosexual, heterosexual, or bisexual. Others, who have accepted their homosexuality, have needed help with adjusting to early homosexual experiences or with the process of "coming out of the closet," i.e., with dealing with roommates, friends, and parents, with career issues and with learning about and entering the gay community.

We have seen about a dozen students who had been raped—including three men who were sexually assaulted by women. The issues have ranged from such straightforward concerns as the possibility of pregnancy, venereal disease, or bodily injury to more psychological dimensions such as fear of relating to another person, confusion over having sexually responded when attacked, and repressed anger at having been violated. In all of the above situations, we offer an open-ended therapy which is really short-term focused psychotherapy. The seven- or fifteen-visit format is not applicable although, after a first or second exploratory interview, we and the student usually arrive at an understanding of how many visits will be scheduled—sometimes just 2 or 3—at other times, a full semester of once-a-week hours.

In order to illustrate the kinds of situations we are referring to, the following cases are presented. As each has involved a very individualized approach—in keeping with a psychodynamically-oriented approach to psychotherapy—we have not included the details of therapy process.

Penny, a first year student, came to see L.S. with what sounded like a very grave problem. She was experiencing something she called "flashes" or "images" throughout her waking hours. These near-hallucinatory images consisted of "seeing" a sharp object, like a razor knife, slashing at her bare breasts or genitals. The flashes had begun two months before, about the time that she became emotionally and sexually involved with Mike, a young man who was a senior at a university in another city. She had little previous sexual experience beyond some necking with clothes on in a car, but with Mike she was having intercourse and mutual oral-genital stimulation. She described Mike in glowing terms, and, in describing their sexual relationship, said she always let him take the lead because he was so sophisticated and experienced. She did whatever he wanted and was only worried about disappointing him.

The nature of Penny's symptoms were worrisome, so L.S. consulted with one of the more experienced psychologists on our staff. He felt that Penny's problem seemed to be directly related to her current sexual experiences and thought L.S. should continue to see her. In the series of weekly interviews the goals were:

1. to help Penny to see the extent to which she was self-effacing in relation to Mike;
2. to help her to begin to define what she wanted and did not want;
3. to facilitate communication between Penny and Mike, or, in other words, once she had some ideas of her own, how might she tell Mike about them without driving him away;
4. not really in contradiction with goal (3), it was crucial that Penny be able to face the thought that Mike might, in fact, be driven away by her newly assertive behavior.

It was not difficult to accomplish these goals, and over a period of about three months, Penny was able to discover and then assert what she wanted and did not want in her relationship with Mike. Not surprisingly, this involved many spheres besides the sexual. With the exception of one visit to his school, all the communication between Penny and Mike was by letter and an occasional phone call. When he did visit Penny, they came in for an hour together. They were, at this point, petting to mutual orgasm instead of having intercourse or oral-genital contact. Mike was "perfectly willing," he said to go at Penny's pace now that he understood her better. Her symptoms had gradually subsided and then disappeared altogether.

For the sake of brevity, we have not included the full history in this and other cases but we want to make it clear that in on-going therapy we do ask about individual history and family relationships in addition to a sex history. This may be limited to a few facts about family composition, religion, and family attitudes toward sex. In Penny's case, which is more typical, more detail was elicited. Sometimes, in our experience, this sort of in-depth understanding is directly relevant, sometimes not. Even when some facet of history seems important, the therapist must decide if and how to make use of it. In Penny's history, there was a suggestion that some unconscious response to family dynamics may have played a role in precipitating the course of events and symptomatology. In the summer before Penny left for college her mother had a long talk with her in which she confided that she and Penny's father were having a sexual problem and that sex between them had almost ceased. Penny was very upset and "felt sorry" for her mother. The counselor can opt to follow up or drop such a line of inquiry. In this instance, as in much sex therapy, the dominant focus is on the present situation and the method of choice is to stay with that focus. With Penny, the material about her parents' relationship was not followed up.

Tim presented the problem that he was afraid to relate sexually to women and had, as a result, become isolated and lonely. He had what he felt to be a normal childhood and adolescence. He had a girlfriend for two years with whom he had had intercourse. There had been no sexual difficulties. The relationship ended when, in his second year in college, she went away to school in another part of the country. He continued to date during his last two years in college. There were a few sexual intercourse experiences, most of which were without difficulty although, on a couple of occasions, he did ejaculate rapidly.

The current problem developed in his senior year. He was dating a woman who was a bit older than he and who was much more sexually experienced. One night they decided to try a "game" of bondage. She tied him to the bed and then approached him "menacingly" (with a knife in her hand) as part of the game. He became very frightened, and then panicky. It is not clear whether she did or did not understand the depth of his fright. She carried out the "rape." To his dismay and despite his panic, his erection was firm, she easily inserted him in her vagina, and he ejaculated almost immediately. Afterwards, he felt angry but also shocked at his own response. He did not date her again nor anyone else for the next two years. The scene was often relived in his masturbatory fantasies. He concluded that he had a "weird" sexuality which he was reluctant to impose on another person especially since he was reaching a time in his life when he was feeling the need for a permanent relationship.

In tracing back his sexual history, it became clear that he had learned to masturbate lying on his back in very much the same position in which he had been bound. The kind of muscle tension which had triggered his earliest ejaculations was also present when he was "raped" as was the anxiety which had accompanied masturbation during his early adolescence.

He did not know that a wide range of emotions can be attached to ejaculation. At the end of the first hour, P.S. asked him to draw a set of pictures of a man and a woman. Looking at his pictures, he described seeing an angry but resolute man. The woman was larger than the man and drawn in a side view. He felt she was evasive, strong and yet vulnerable. P.S. asked him to write a sex-oriented autobiography before his next visit and to read Kinsey's chapter about childhood sexual experiences in the volume on the male sexual response [4].

He was seen two weeks later. He no longer felt that his sexuality was so weird—partly as a result of reading Kinsey, and, as he said, partly as a result of the way in which he felt P.S. had accepted his story and made some sense of it. Obviously, he needed boundaries when relating sexually and needed to protect himself from getting into situations in which he was made helpless but this did not seem to be such a difficult task. Within a short time he was dating again. There were two more meetings to discuss what was happening in his present relationships. The sado-masochism disappeared from his masturbatory fantasies.

Robert was a graduate student who came to see us. He had not had any sexual experience with anyone except an occasional date in high school and college when he kissed a girl good-night. Since puberty he had found he was most turned on by men. His masturbatory fantasies were entirely homosexual. He told his family that he felt he was gay although he had not eliminated the possibility of being bisexual. Several of his closest friends were women. He had frequently engaged in mutual massage experiences with these women but he did not regard such times as being sexual and had not been sexually responsive to their touch or his touching their bodies. His family was accepting of his gay identity, as were his friends and faculty advisors. Robert had not had any homosexual experiences. He wanted help in initiating a relationship with a man so that his homosexuality could lead to something more substantial than a series of one-night stands.

We first dealt with his feelings about gay bars. He found he was attracted to large men with muscular bodies but was afraid he could get hurt if in bed with such a man. In a gay bar, he felt that he was sexually objectified and not regarded as a person. He also felt that "sex" meant going all the way and he was frightened at the thought of body penetration. During the time P.S. was seeing him, Robert was attending our course on human sexuality. In the course he saw the film, "Vir Amat" (which shows a male-male couple relating sexually). In one way it was helpful. There was no anal sex and yet the couple seemed to make love in a way that was fulfilling to both of them. It showed the kind of relationship which was his "ideal." In the therapy hour after he saw the film he talked mostly about trust. He felt that he was so defensive about himself, so careful in everything he said and did to avoid people's thinking ill of him, that his defensiveness was a formidable barrier for anyone who might want to develop an intimate relationship with him. In that hour we also talked about the importance of developing a sense of trust on a body level and that if he could do that with someone, perhaps that would help him be less defensive in other ways.

He stopped going to gay bars. Instead he started attending gay alliance meetings. A friendship developed with a man a little older than Robert who turned out to also be at the beginning of his homosexual relating. It was not possible for P.S. to see them together. However, it was possible, by giving instructions through Robert, for them to initiate touch following the basic guidelines of sensate-focus, i.e., to touch without a goal, to avoid genital touching, to touch for one's own pleasure, and to stop when touching became physically or psychologically uncomfortable. During the time when P.S. saw Robert, he and his friend became lovers. It was a gradual process, taking about two months before they were both comfortable being naked together and extending their touch to include genital touching. When he ejaculated with his lover, Robert felt his "letting go" in that way represented a major breakthrough for him with regard to his defensiveness in the presence of others. He subsequently did have intercourse with a woman and enjoyed the experience. However, he stated when last seen that his preference was for men. He and his lover had an "open" relationship. Neither, however, had any extra-relationship sex except for Robert's heterosexual intercourse, which they both regarded as a kind of experiment and not a threat to their primary relationship.

Ejaculatory Inhibition

The material on ejaculatory problems is being presented as a separate entity because it presents some unique features. The sexological literature has not had as much to say about male ejaculatory difficulty as about other dysfunctions. Kinsey barely mentions the syndrome [5]. Masters and Johnson reported only 17 cases of "ejaculatory incompetence" [6].

Although Helen Kaplan states, "it appears that mild forms of this disorder may actually be highly prevalent," she does not state how many cases she saw, mentioning only that the number had been small [7]. More recent reviews of the literature list but a few small scattered series of patients treated by different approaches [8].

In contrast, this problem, in one form or another, had not been unusual in our clinical practice and is consistent with the survey findings among University of Rochester male students taking a course in human sexuality in which 11 percent report inability to have orgasm [9]. We believe the main reason we have seen so many men with ejaculatory inhibitions is that we see younger men for whom having an ejaculatory experience is one of the hurdles of psychosexual development. Some have solved their problem as a result of one visit. Others have responded to the seven-visit format—some by themselves, others in couples. At other times, more extensive couple's sex therapy or individual therapy has been necessary.

A 24-year-old man who was able to ejaculate in masturbation, but who had never been able to ejaculate during intercourse wrote these questions:

When I'm having sex with my partner, should I just relax and let it come naturally, or are there specific things that I should do to help me achieve orgasm? I've read the steps that Masters and Johnson suggest in their book, *Human Sexual Inadequacy*—man masturbates, woman stimulates man to orgasm by hand and inserts penis into vagina before ejaculation, intercourse.

Just what is orgasm like during intercourse?

Could part of my problem be that I'm reluctant to lose control?

Can frequent masturbation "condition" one to a certain style of orgasm, thus making it more difficult to achieve orgasm through intercourse?

They are reasonable and pertinent questions. For him sex was not a natural function but, instead, something he had to work at and figure out just what to do. He believed his problem had something to do with the fact that by the time he was 17 he had lived in 10 different places and had never had a peer group relationship from which he could learn about sex. He had an image of intercourse needing to be fast with deep thrusting—a little bit violent—to achieve orgasm. Many men have that image and they are ambivalent about it and their holding back keeps them from having the experience. He was on to something important when he brought up the issue of losing control. Having an orgasm can mean losing control and trusting and being vulnerable to another person. His last question also touches on a widespread aspect of sex response—that behavioral conditioning is involved.

This young man's questions were not unusual and neither were his circumstances. We have talked to more than 100 men—most in their 20s or younger—whose presenting problems had to do with either never having ejaculated or not being able to ejaculate in a particular way. We prefer to use the term "ejaculatory inhibition" to cover the spectrum of this problem.

Men Who Have Never Experienced Ejaculation in the Fully-Awake State

We have not seen any men who have *never* ejaculated but it has not been unusual to talk to men whose only ejaculatory experience has been nocturnal emission. Some have not masturbated nor desired to and have not had an opportunity for sexual stimulation with someone else. Others have tried to masturbate or have been sexually stimulated by a sexual partner but have not experienced ejaculation for one reason or another. Most have been young men who fit Kinsey's findings about adolescent orgasmic outlet: that about 12 percent of males do not masturbate prior to age 20; that nocturnal emission is the source of first ejaculation for about one-eighth of adolescent boys and can be the primary if not the only sexual outlet. Another related finding is that among boys who do not mature before age 15, about 20 percent take more than a year before they have their first ejaculation and an even longer time before establishing regular sexual outlet. This is in contrast to "early-maturing" boys (age 11 or younger) who usually ejaculate in the first year of maturation and who establish a regular sexual outlet by the time of age 15 [10]. The picture of the normal range of development then is one of some boys establishing their sexual behavior before other boys have taken their first steps. Most of the men we have seen who have ejaculated only in nocturnal emissions are taking those first steps. Our role has usually been to reassure the men that their experience is not atypical and will evolve into a satisfying sexual pattern especially if they can avoid putting too much pressure on themselves to catch up to others sexually.

We have also seen four older men who had had repeated sexual experiences (masturbation, petting, intercourse) in which they had never been able to bring about ejaculation. The four also had impotence problems. In each it was possible to trace the sexual history back to adolescence, the feeling of being less sexually experienced than other boys, and the pressure to perform sexually to "catch up" to their peer group. Although other factors were important in these cases, the sexual feelings generated at puberty had set the stage for the complications and conflicts which followed.

Men Unable to Ejaculate in Some Particular Way

The most common ejaculatory problem we have seen is *difficulty* reaching orgasm during intercourse. Forty-five minutes to an hour or more of continued coital thrusting are necessary for these men to "achieve" a climax. By the time they do, they frequently feel it hasn't been worth the effort, nor do their partners. The women can become exhausted and physically irritated. Not infrequently they feel angry as they regard their partner's pattern an indication of personal rejection or of their own lack of sexiness. Sometime a woman partner's problem of recurrent urinary infection has been our first clue to ejaculatory inhibitions as the prolonged time of intercourse results in urethral and bladder irritation.

A married couple in their early 20s were first seen because of the woman's recurrent urinary infections. Multiple courses of antibiotic treatment had been prescribed and several urethral dilatations had been done. Nothing had helped. Because more than a year had gone by during which intercourse had always been associated with pain, the couple had been referred to us. The woman had been orgasmic throughout the first two years of the marriage but had not had an orgasm in the past six months.

Intercourse had been prolonged from the onset of their sexual relating. The first time, while still undergraduates, the husband-to-be had been extremely fearful of discovery. Although it was the first intercourse for both, he could clearly recall being only partially involved as he listened and watched for intruders. After about an hour, he "let his guard down" for a minute or so and ejaculated. This happened repeatedly over the course of the next years of their courtship.

At first, she thought sex was great. She became orgasmic and then multiorgasmic, and then irritated and fatigued. After a while she started to wonder if her husband (by that time) wasn't so much a super lover as someone who wasn't very turned on by her.

He, in turn, no longer worried about being intruded upon, and wanted to come faster but found that no matter how hard he tried it seemed to make matters worse.

By the time we saw them, their relationship was in trouble. Both were angry and depressed. They were considering divorce. Fortunately, careful attention to the biological factors and the interpersonal issues in sex therapy enabled the couple to get back together again and establish a satisfying married and sex life.

Although lasting a long time in intercourse can be considered a form of "super-studdism," it has not been unusual for men with this pattern to feel the problem is an indicator of homosexuality and to express this belief to a counselor or therapist. The issue is one of not performing up to some expectation of normal male response and when that is the case—especially in adolescents and young men—homosexual anxieties are stirred. Interestingly, in the Masters and Johnson series, only one of the 17 men had a homosexual history and in that case Masters and Johnson concluded that the man's dislike for his wife was the predominating factor in his holding back ejaculation. They felt that conflict over sexual orientation is a minor factor in this syndrome.

Men who take a long time to ejaculate are frequently unaware that there is anything different about their pattern of response. Several students were seen after reading Kinsey's statistics that indicate that "normal" males have a median response time of less than five minutes. Only then did their 45-minute pattern strike them as different. Most commonly, the prolonged pattern has been brought to the man's attention as a result of his female partner's feelings or medical complications. In this regard, our experience is different from Helen Kaplan's in that she dated patients' awareness of their ejaculatory difficulty to their first intercourse [11].

The same issues are present when a man cannot ejaculate at all during intercourse. In addition, however, there is the issue of fertility. This is an issue which not infrequently leads to consulting us either when couples are contemplating marriage and are concerned about future family or are already trying to conceive a child. Both Masters and Johnson and Kaplan found that couples with ejaculatory inhibition were often first seen in infertility programs. Frequently, the sex history was not taken or the problem was denied when first inquired about.

Some men find that they cannot ejaculate from a particular form of sexual stimulation. The most common has been inability to ejaculate in fellatio. It has also been common to see men who have been unable to masturbate. Some develop pain during masturbation. Some find no pleasure in self-stimulation. Many have been 18- and 19-year-olds who ejaculated in petting or intercourse experiences but who never learned to masturbate. They have come to us feeling "abnormal" because they don't do what they think everyone else does. Extrapolating the Kinsey statistics to today's adolescent population would indicate that at least 2,000,000 American males have not masturbated by age 20. Still, the men feel they are 1-in-a-million, not 1-in-10!

Some men can only ejaculate during intercourse. This can be a problem when the partner has pain with intercourse or, for many, when there is a menstrual flow. The men get turned on, the women feel guilty if they don't have intercourse because they know the man can't ejaculate any other way. They have intercourse. The sex is not very good for the woman—or for the man for that matter. They have a problem.

Some men have to have intercourse in a particular style or position in order to ejaculate. For example, it is not unusual for men to be slower or unable to come in a woman-above position but have no problem in a male-above position. Two men could only ejaculate if they used a rear-entry position with their girlfriends lying on their abdomens.

Several men have had difficulty ejaculating in homosexual relating. That too can be very specific. Three men had no difficulty coming with fellatio but could not with anal penetration. Two other men presented the problem reversed.

We have also seen men who had been able to ejaculate in the past but who later developed ejaculatory problems. In this regard, our experience is similar to that of Masters and Johnson in that determining factors have included specific traumatic episodes, problems of an interpersonal nature between sexual partners, drug effects, depression, and so on. We have been particularly impressed by the experiences of four men who stopped ejaculating after single episodes of ejaculation without an erection. This experience, which is a response many males have at some time or other, without being upset, is very frightening for other men.

It is obvious that what one man might consider an ejaculatory problem to bring to a sex counselor, another man might not even notice. Thus, many men will simply shrug off the fact they can't ejaculate in masturbation or in fellatio or in some particular coital position and live their sex life without that particular option. In fact, most of the men unable to ejaculate during intercourse hadn't been particularly bothered by their response until the difficulty ejaculating gained some particular significance.

Themes in the Histories of Men With Ejaculatory Difficulties

Whatever the setting for sex therapy, working with a man alone, short-term therapy with a young couple or longer-term, more intensive therapy when there has been an established pattern of ejaculatory inhibition, we begin with individual history-taking to develop an understanding of that particular individual's sex value system. Sometimes the men can readily relate their problem to its origins in a particular experience or in the way their sex response pattern initially developed or as a result of cultural/religious values. Often they are able to connect their sexual response pattern to the ways in which they do other things such as eating or athletics or public speaking, thus recognizing that their sexuality is clearly a dimension of their personality. More often, however, the men have not made these connections. They feel their sex response to be separate from the rest of their experience and thereby feel all the more confused about, and resigned to, their condition. The therapist's first role, therefore, is to carefully develop the sexual history, finding the various threads which can be brought together in order to make the development of the presenting complaint comprehensible. Certain sexual experiences and particular messages about the meaning of ejaculation have been prominent in the histories we have elicited. Because we think a therapist needs to know what to look for and because not very much has been said in the professional literature about these factors, we have included illustrative material drawn from the cases of men we have seen.

THE BELIEF THAT EJACULATION IS THE GOAL OF SEX. Before their first ejaculatory experience, boys can learn, in an emotionally laden way, that achieving ejaculation is *the* goal of any sexual experience. If their neuroendocrine system has not yet matured to the point of biological capacity to form and release an ejaculate, attempts at sexual stimulation are "unsuccessful" and the boys can become anxious about achieving what they have been taught is the "normal" response. They become anxious spectators from the very beginnings of sexual unfolding.

A 17-year-old who had never ejaculated except in wet dreams recalled: At age 11 he hung out with his 13-year-old brother and the brother's older friends. On several occasions the boys played "circle jerk," forming a circle and masturbating to see who could "shoot" the farthest. Our patient always lost simply because no matter how hard he tried, even though he would have something happen that he thinks must have been an orgasm, no ejaculate came out. Biologically he was capable of orgasm, but his glands could not form and release an ejaculate. He described many attempts of stimulating himself to a point of skin irritation but no ejaculate. By the time he was 13 and starting to have wet dreams, he was already spectatoring his masturbation so much he was still unable to ejaculate in the awake state. Interestingly, in therapy he was soon able to ejaculate with his girlfriend. Only after success in heterosexual relating was he then, with further insight, able to stop spectatoring during masturbation and be able to ejaculate through self-stimulation.

A 26-year-old married graduate student was unable to ejaculate at all. He and his wife had intercourse regularly. They had become concerned because they wished to become pregnant. He recalled: At age 12 he had intercourse for the first time—with a 16-year-old babysitter. She apparently had tried very hard, in pelvic thrusting, to make him come. He, having never ejaculated before, really didn't know what was going on. The whole experience was frightening to him. He remembered clearly that the girl became very angry at him and verbally abusive because he hadn't come. After that he read about masturbation and tried to make himself ejaculate, but couldn't.

An 18-year-old freshman had learned about masturbation from his father. At age 13 his father sat him down and explained the "facts of life." Ejaculation was described as pleasurable and a little bit messy but nothing to be ashamed of and something which every boy does. This discussion sounded innocuous enough and, in fact, was the sort of father-to-son talk we ordinarily think of as helpful. But it wasn't for him. He subsequently tried hard to make himself come, not so much as an erotic experience but because he felt it was something a normal boy *should* be able to do. He was unable to ejaculate in masturbation. In high school he held back from relating to girls because he felt he was sexually abnormal. When he came to see me, he was really more interested in initiating dating than in learning to masturbate. While in sex therapy he began to date, found that he was comfortable with kissing and light petting and then with genital stimulation. He was quite amazed the first time he ejaculated. He was with a girlfriend, and came from rubbing against her genitals. It happened rather easily and spontaneously and felt good. Caught up in erotic feelings, he hadn't been a spectator.

THE BELIEF THAT EJACULATION = SEX = SOMETHING DIRTY OR SINFUL. A 21-year-old senior was brought up in a religiously strict family. He was taught in parochial school that masturbation was a sin for which he would certainly go to purgatory. The teacher was very specific, using the expression, "spilling seed on the ground" and clearly indicating that masturbation meant ejaculation. The boy, aged 14 at the time, concluded that as long as he stimulated without ejaculating he was not committing a sin. He developed a self-stimulation pattern which purposely stopped short of ejaculation. He later found, in petting, that his girlfriend felt his non-ejaculatory response was a rejection of her. He also began to worry that not ejaculating with his girlfriend was a sign of homosexuality although there were no other experiences or feelings to support such a belief.

Several other men we have seen presented variations of the basic theme that for them ejaculation was the single event that *meant* sex and that anything which was sexual was something to be avoided. As one man said, "For me, sex wasn't just dirty—it was filthy—scum bags [condoms] floating in the gutter—that kind of thing."

THE BELIEF THAT EJACULATION MEANS PREGNANCY. One student first ejaculated (at age 13 while masturbating in the bath). When he saw the ejaculate floating on the water, his immediate thought was, "My God, now I can become a father." He came to us with the question, "Can a girl get pregnant if you don't have intercourse?" He had not been able to ejaculate in petting.

A black student complaining of ejaculatory inhibition had never been able to ejaculate when with a girl. He had no problem masturbating. Among the questions he asked was, "Can you get a girl pregnant if you come outside of her?" He thought it was impossible but admitted that for many years he didn't know how a girl got pregnant. The only sex education he had been given as a young boy was, "Don't go getting in trouble." That meant, "Don't go getting a girl pregnant." He remembered going to a library and reading about sperm and eggs and fertilization. His determination to keep out of trouble was reinforced when his best friend's girlfriend became pregnant. The other boy got married, they had the baby, and he dropped out of high school. "I'm sure he would've gone to college if that hadn't happened. He was a lot smarter than me except in one way—sex." And so he never allowed himself to let go. He could have intercourse and pull out before coming. But once he pulled out, he was unable to come. On several occasions he developed testicular pain. He finally was able to ejaculate with a girlfriend if he masturbated himself. Still it was a poor substitute. Their therapy started with her initiating birth control pills. A month later we counseled them in the standard approach to treatment of ejaculatory incompetence [12] and he was readily able to ejaculate from her manual stimulation and then with intercourse.

THE BELIEF THE EJACULATION MEANS LOSS OF CONTROL. Increasing sexual tension can trigger fears of loss of self-control in some men. As they approach orgasm they become frightened that with orgasm they might thrash about and hurt their partner or that they themselves might be hurt. One man who had never ejaculated in the awake state was brought up in a family in which "no one ever lost control." Anger was never expressed. Joyous outbursts were also forbidden. This man feared that ejaculation could mean a loss of control leading to aggressive behavior. He had known all his life what it felt like to start to feel angry, to get "hot under the collar" and then to suppress the feeling, "to stop it before I killed someone."

Another man, brought up in a very wealthy family, remembered being "completely under control" by age 3. He behaved exactly as his parents felt a little boy should behave. By the time he reached college he was afraid to even go near a woman, fearing he might lose control and ejaculate. Still another student had been told by his father that his (the father's) first ejaculation had been a "terrifying experience." The student wasn't sure what there was to be terrified of, but he wasn't going to try to find out. Indeed, in therapy when he did ejaculate, he too felt terrified, but after a few times it started to feel pleasant and then his anxiety decreased sharply.

The fear of loss of control then is a fear of the unknown. It is *not knowing* what it is they have to control that leads to being so controlled—and so panicky when there is a hint that control might be lost.

THE ASSOCIATION OF SEX RESPONSE WITH UPSETTING OR UNCOMFORTABLE FEELINGS. Some men have described a feeling of "overstimulation" when sexually aroused. One man said, "When she licked the end of my erect penis it was incredibly exciting. The sensation was sort of pleasure-pain. My body twitched all over. I asked her to stop because I couldn't take anymore. I didn't ejaculate." Another man describing his feelings said, "I tried to achieve orgasm rubbing against her pubic hair but I couldn't. I thought at the time that it was just because the stimulation was so intense that I couldn't relax."

Sometimes the discomfort is more strictly physical although it can be difficult to differentiate the physical from the psychosocial: One man felt pain in the rim of the foreskin when he was very aroused. He was found to have a tight foreskin. It retracted or at least tried to when he was preorgasmic and this sudden stretching caused the pain. The pain had been there from the time of his first masturbation as a young boy. He responded to circumcision. Another student complaining of pain in the penile shaft found that our talking about his feelings of sex as dirty and sinful—feelings he thought he had "outgrown" years before—helped him. He was able to ejaculate once the pain, probably an hysterical symptom, disappeared. Several men with pain in the tip of the penis have been found to have an engorged prostate gland. Their problem is a circular one. The pain in the penis is referred pain from the prostate; the prostate is a source of pain because it is engorged as a result of sexual arousal without ejaculation. Ejaculation, however, is inhibited by the pain. After ruling out the possibility of an organic problem and establishing prostatic engorgement as the underlying factor, we have recommended (if the man is accepting of the idea) masturbation as an approach to treatment. Three men have been successfully treated in this way, finding that with more frequent orgasmic release their penile-tip pain disappeared.

Angry and Aggressive Feelings

Angry and aggressive feelings seem to be more prevalent, and constitute a psychodynamic to be dealt with more often, in cases of ejaculatory inhibition than in other dysfunctions. This is not to say that overt or suppressed anger is not present in other dysfunctions. Nor are we saying that anger and aggression are the central dynamics in *all* cases of ejaculatory inhibition as, for example, men who have been behaviorly conditioned to coming close to but not ejaculating or men whose partner-interactions lead to spectatoring and performance demand. In these instances, the men may be frustrated but do not harbor the kind of angry and aggressive feelings we are talking about. We have been impressed by cases in which the men have a depth of anger of which they are usually unaware that keeps them from fully relating to another person. This is an anger usually born of years of being put down and controlled. The history may be traced through childhood, adolescence, and early adulthood; the man who was so controlled by age 3 that he knows he never made a mistake, in his parents' eyes, after that; the man in whose home there had never been expression of anger, or joy for that matter. His parents chose his school, chose his clothing, chose his friends. "They cut it off," he said, as he himself could readily correlate his ejaculatory inhibition and subsequent impotence with his upbringing.

These are furious men. In the confidence of the history-taking, they describe murderous feelings which they fear they could unleash if they ever let go. For some, their anger has reached the end-stage of "anger-limpness" [13]. They do not defend themselves when they feel hurt. They offer a smile or a weak joke. Their anger builds and they don't ejaculate. We think the two correlate.

Sometimes the anger is generated by the occurrence of a tragic happening—one man paralyzed by a spinal cord infection, another terribly injured in Viet Nam. Their bodies have recovered, but psychologically they are handicapped. Why me? What did I do to deserve the pain and then the humiliations of illness and treatment? In these last two cases, the men have been calm, even gentle. They have been pleasant people to work with—unless you cross them. A word out of place, a challenge to what a good guy they are, a hint that they are holding back and not giving their all to making the therapy succeed, then the fury is unleashed, the shoulders tense, the smiles disappear, the fists form—right there in the office.

When there is a problem of ejaculatory inhibition in the context of an established relationship, there is often a hostile relationship, sometimes very overtly hostile. One couple had communicated only by written note for months prior to therapy and, each evening, she greeted him at the door of the house and handed him the day's garbage! The woman's anger may be understandable, but its unyielding persistence keeps alive the sexual difficulty.

It is interesting to us that in most of the cases of ejaculatory inhibition, all men in their late 20s or older (many of whom are not students), the aggressive feelings have been depicted in the Draw-a-Person testing. As mentioned elsewhere, we use this test at the beginning of therapy and then during the course of therapy as a way of monitoring body image change in the context of the behavioral changes being reported to us. Angry men frequently draw people whose hands are clenched in a fist. When they do, the pictures offer a clear indicator of a psychodynamic which we have already suspected. In the course of therapy, the pictures almost invariably show the fists until after the ejaculation has occurred and then the hands open up. We should mention that there are many other features of the drawings which indicate anger and defensiveness. The hand-clenching, however, is an easy feature to follow and is one which is also often present in the therapy hours.

A 24-year-old with ejaculatory inhibition had a long history of feeling misunderstood, controlled, and determined by his parents. It was also a history of feeling engulfed but, at the same time, rejected by them. Apparently his brother had similar feelings—and also had confided in him that he had a problem of impotence. We felt that although he was "cooperative" in the therapy, he really was so defended that we were not getting through to him. He was content to view the therapy as for his girlfriend. She was nonorgasmic. We were convinced that her not letting go was affected by his not letting go, and that unless his feelings were dealt with the therapy wouldn't get very far.

His original drawings and the drawings after sensate-focus all showed men and women with clenched fists. We were also aware that, in the office, when we sought his greater participation, he would usually smile, say something cordial, and make a fist. We also knew, from his girlfriend, that there had been rare occasions, at home, when he would lose control and have angry, destructive outbursts. He walked a fine line.

We decided to use the drawings as a way of helping him gain insight into the underlying dynamic. At first, he resisted the interpretation—"That's just the way I draw hands." About a minute later his girlfriend suddenly pointed out to him that his hands were clenched in fists. Only then could he start to recognize that he was feeling threatened, and he was getting angry but that he had no way to deal with these feelings, especially with people he cared about. He feared rejection, by us and by his girlfriend, if he let us know how he really felt about being there and being in therapy.

That session proved to be the turning point. He finally realized he could share all sides of himself and still be accepted. Subsequently, he was able to use the communication tools to express hurt and angry feelings, was able to respond in a more sexually spontaneous way and to ejaculate, and the fists in the pictures disappeared.

The importance of anger and aggressive feelings in ejaculatory incompetence is discussed directly by Kaplan and indirectly by Masters and Johnson. Kaplan states: "We have noted in our admittedly limited experience with this syndrome that some of these men seem to have problems with hostility and aggression. More specifically, conflict about expressing anger, along with defenses of 'holding back' expressions of such impulses, seems to play a role in the pathogenesis of some retarded ejaculators" [14].

The same theme pervades the Masters and Johnson case material in the details given for almost all of the men they worked with in this category. In some, the anger is specific and directed at the partner. In others, it is more diffuse, an anger generated by the ways in which they were brought up and taught to behave. For example, in one of their cases of religious orthodoxy-determined ejaculatory incompetence, Masters and Johnson give this description: "At age 13, the first occasion of nocturnal emission was soon identified by his mother. His father whipped him for this 'sin of flesh' and thereafter his sheets were checked daily to be sure he did not repeat this offense" [15].

In another case reported by Masters and Johnson of a religiously orthodox man, the first intercourse attempt did represent a break with his religious beliefs. But there was also another factor in his loss of control of aggressive feelings: "He not only forced physical attention upon, but tried to penetrate, a young woman somewhat resistant to his approach. She stopped him with a plea that she was menstruating" [16]. He was one of the three men (out of 17 treated by Masters and Johnson) who did not respond successfully to sex therapy. The other failures were a man who had walked in on his wife and her lover and another man who had "no personal regard for, no interest in, and no feeling for his wife." His refusal to ejaculate intravaginally was a direct decision to deprive her of the pleasure of consummating the marriage. Once the depth of the husband's personal rejection of his wife was recognized, the therapeutic attempt was helped [17]. In another Masters and Johnson case, in which fear of pregnancy was a determining factor, the history includes the following:

The mother had been in full control of the son's every major decision until his marriage . . . his mother insisted upon total control of his social commitments. She chose his school, his college, and his clothes. She also chose his female companions . . . time and again she embarrassed her son by her obvious demand for dominance. He grew to hate his mother but lacked the courage to let her know his level of rejection. Particularly, he was careful not to offend her too deeply, for she controlled a considerable amount of money. . . . His constant fantasy (after marriage) was of revenge upon his mother [18].

Treatment in Ejaculatory Inhibition

Any one or several of the themes we have described may be important to understanding why a particular man has ejaculatory inhibition. The history-taking therefore is a careful eliciting of behavior details as well as an exploring of personality development. Special attention is also paid to interpersonal relationships in the present and the past. What does he feel when sexually aroused? Is there ejaculation at any time? If so, how does he bring it about and how does he feel when it happens? What is erotic to him? If he has fantasies, what are they made up of? Does he have wet dreams? If so, what happens in the dream? They may *not* be obviously erotic, but they are for him and they may give an important clue to helping him resolve his problem.

The developmental history should include his relationship with his parents, paying particular attention to the issues of self-control, anger, and expression of angry feelings. What values and attitudes about sex and about ejaculation have been internalized? What was his first ejaculatory experience like? If he can't remember, that question must be returned to later on. In taking more than 600 male sex histories there have only been a few occasions when men could not recall the circumstances and feelings of their first ejaculation. When they could not, it usually turned out, as disclosed later on, to have been important in the development of their sexual difficulty. It is usually possible to obtain information which can be used in determining subsequent behavioral tasks.

During the client's recounting of experiences, attitudes, and values which relate to his sexuality development, the therapist can identify major themes and make connections to the presenting problem which the man had not made by himself. A bond is formed between patient and therapist when the knowledge of such private feelings and experiences is shared, understood and accepted. The therapist is a role model for a different way of understanding and appreciating sex. Especially for a young man, the therapist is a transitional person between a problematic past and a more hopeful present. Even in the first history-taking hour(s), attitude change can become evident. It's the beginning of a therapeutic relationship.

Particularly in treating young men whose ejaculatory problems appear to be a developmental hurdle, education plays an important role. A man who has never ejaculated needs to understand, first of all, just what happens when a man does ejaculate. This can be described verbally or he can see a film of male masturbation or of ejaculatory response during intercourse. One man couldn't believe the man in the movie had ejaculated because it didn't look "violent enough." Another man, seeing the same film, was surprised it wasn't as "messy" as he had imagined. When such feelings surface, the man can talk about his feelings and what they mean to him. Sometimes the issue seems resolved in minutes while at other times the men need several hours to talk about their associations and feelings.

Teaching about sex response and sex behavior is included in the second or third visit. The sequence of physiologic changes which make up the sex response cycle is described: "An orgasm is part of the sequence you've already been experiencing; the two parts of the orgasm are the moment of inevitability and then the ejaculatory release. An average ejaculate contains less than a teaspoon of fluid." Straight facts are given which often serve to reassure, desensitize, and establish new sex values. Information is provided about the range of male experience—how many do and don't masturbate, how many males are still virgins at such and such an age, how frequently males have had homosexual experiences, etc. The importance of unfolding sexually and not trying to rush the process is stressed.

A physical examination is almost always done and utilized for medical assessment as well as education. The genital anatomy is carefully explained in terms of embryologic development. Many of these men have held misconceptions about what was what and often worried about the normality of their genitals. Another value of the examination has been to desensitize the men to genital exposure and to being touched. For several, this was their first genital examination since childhood.

Sensate focus has been particularly valuable in breaking men out of spectatoring and goal-orientation behavior. The simple guideline in touch—"touch for your own pleasure"—works two ways for men with ejaculatory inhibition. First, without a goal, they are able to focus erotically and many for the first time find what is sensuous to them in touching, smelling, or looking. Perhaps more important, when the man knows that his partner is touching him for her own pleasure and *not* to make him have an ejaculation, he can stop worrying about her and also not push himself toward an end-point.

When there is an ongoing relationship and a couple is in treatment, all of the usual sex therapy principles about working with both partners apply. If the patient is a young man in the early stages of a relationship then, whether treating the couple face-to-face or indirectly through the young man, it is important to help them establish ways of sharing feelings rather than defending against them and playing games. In this context he will be more likely to relax and truly experience his sensations.

Several different issues have been raised when touching has been extended to include genitals. The Masters and Johnson positions (woman in front of man when he touches her genitals, man lying on his back with the woman approaching him directly from a sitting position between his legs when she touches him) are used. For young men (and most of our older patients, as well) the positions mean increased vulnerability and greater initial anxiety. But, the protective clause "you must stop your partner from touching you if you feel physically or psychologically uncomfortable," seems to be all the safeguard needed to allow initial touching and then more erotic direct stimulation. The men are told to show their partners what feels good to them. At the same time the partners are advised to adhere to the guideline of touching the men in a way they like, *not* with the goal of inducing ejaculation.

The young man we mentioned at the very beginning of this section on ejaculatory problems wrote down four questions. He had read Masters and Johnson and wanted to know if there were specific behavioral tasks that would help him overcome his problem of not ejaculating during intercourse. In our experience, young men like him do not need to employ any special or vigorous stimulatory techniques to overcome their problem. The process of relating to a therapist, the decrease in anxiety and in spectatoring, the greater comfort with their female partner seem to be sufficient. Biology seems to be on their side and the hurdle is not yet so high.

The exception to this treatment approach for young men would be those cases in which inability to ejaculate has been conditioned through hundreds of experiences of *almost* ejaculating. This history puts the hurdle several notches higher, and then the behavioral treatment regime described by Masters and Johnson as one part of the overall treatment of the problem is indicated.

When ejaculation occurs in the partner's presence this is the important breakthrough for many of the young men. Fears of loss of control, of humiliation, of anger and hurting are dispelled. Self-assertiveness, acceptance of erotic pleasure, and intimate sharing are accomplished. Extending to intercourse and ejaculation within the vagina may be a simple addition. But, it may not. There can be specific fears about penetration or extra performance demand when intercourse enters the scene. In therapy, it should be possible to discuss these feelings.

The next step is usually to have the couple figure out the easiest way to quickly insert the penis once the orgasm has started (i.e. the moment of inevitability). When that happens, new feelings about penetration, the ejaculate, pregnancy fears or hurting the female may surface.

Follow-up has tended to be short-term with the possibility of returning for help should there be problems in the future. A number of men have returned for different reasons. One man, mentioned earlier, came back to learn how to ejaculate in masturbation now that he had no trouble in intercourse. Another man found that, on occasion, he was still unable to ejaculate during intercourse. He was seen for three further visits in which it was found that his anxieties about a set of particular circumstances were inhibiting his response. It does appear, however, that once an ejaculatory pattern is established, it is readily maintained.

References

1. Kaplan, Helen Singer, *The New Sex Therapy*, New York, Brunner/Mazel, 1974, pp. 305-307.
2. Paper in progress by the authors and Dr. Sidney Berman.
3. Masters, William H. and Johnson, Virginia E., *Human Sexual Inadequacy*, Boston, Little, Brown and Co., 1970.
4. Kinsey, Alfred C., Pomeroy, Wardell B. and Martin, Clyde E. *Sexual Behavior in the Human Male*, Philadelphia, W. B. Saunders Co., 1948.

5. Kinsey, [4], pp. 580-581.
6. Masters and Johnson, [3], p. 116.
7. Kaplan, [1], p. 316.
8. Wright, J., Perreault, R., Mathieu, M., "The Treatment of Sexual Dysfunction" in *Archives of General Psychology*, Vol. 34, August 1977, pp. 881-890.
9. Babineau, R. and Schwartz, A., "The Treatment of Sexual Dysfunction in a University Health Setting" in *Journal of the American College Health Association*, Vol. 25, 1977, pp. 176-181.
10. Kinsey, [4], pp. 300-302.
11. Kaplan, [1], p. 316.
12. Masters and Johnson, [3], pp. 129-133.
13. Verbal Communication, Ernst Prelinger, Ph.D.
14. Kaplan, [1], p. 316.
15. Masters and Johnson, [3], p. 116.
16. Masters and Johnson, [3], p. 117.
17. Masters and Johnson, [3], p. 134.
18. Masters and Johnson, [3], p. 123.

8

A Sexological Approach to the Medical History and Physical Examination

We are not alone among sexologists in finding that the physical examination is a potential diagnostic and therapeutic goldmine. Almost every man, woman, or couple who consults us is examined as part of the assessment process. In addition to its usual role in medical evaluation and treatment, the physical serves other purposes. Invariably, the medical history and physical shed light upon the issues and problems presented and contribute to our formulation of the dynamics to be dealt with in counseling and therapy. We have also found that the examination provides the opportunity to elicit further history, to observe emotional reactions, to educate visually as well as verbally, to reassure, and to further the "patient-professional" relationship.

Doing physical examinations for people who come for sex counseling and therapy has been an education for us. A number of new biophysical findings have emerged that are relevant to gynecology and sexology and we have gained further insight into the processes of sexual unfolding in late adolescents.

Medical Findings in the Physical Exam

Careful and complete medical evaluation was the original rationale for including the medical history and physical examination at the

Sex Counseling Service (SCS). At first, students' appointments were made primarily for contraceptive services. In addition, we were often the first professional contact for such crisis situations as pregnancy, sexual assault, exposure to venereal disease, and unprotected intercourse. Most of the remainder of our patients came for annual check-ups or for evaluation and treatment of problems such as irregular menses, vaginal pain and discharge and other typical gynecological complaints.

About 10 percent presented a "sex problem" as their reason for seeing us. All of the conditions mentioned, except perhaps the sexual, required a pelvic examination for optimal care. We soon came to appreciate the degree of underlying sexual conflict and confusion among patients presenting with nonsexual complaints. We also started to realize the incidence and significance of physical factors among the "sex problem" cases.

In recent years, as we have become more identified as sexologists, the primary reason for an appointment usually has something to do with sexual function or interpersonal relationships, although annual checkups, contraception and the gynecological problems are also presented by many of those seeing us. Thus, there is still this indication for the medical evaluation. Another reason for including medical evaluation almost routinely in a sex counseling service is the fact that medical conditions are frequently found in situations when there have not been the usual signs and symptoms of pathology. Vaginitis is the most outstanding culprit in this category, often presenting with such minimal signs and symptoms as vaginal dryness or numbness or simply lack of sexual response. There has not necessarily been an odor, pain, burning, or itching. We feel that the prevalence of vaginitis warrants the examining of most female patients, with or without sexual problems.

Involuntary muscle contraction leading to narrowing or occlusion of the vaginal opening—vaginismus—is another condition which can be present and significant enough to require treatment. At times the diagnosis is obvious when the couple complains of inability to penetrate. However, complaints may be minimal. The only indication may be a feeling of pressure at the opening of the vagina or a slight burning sensation. It is also not unusual in a sex clinic for vaginismus to be present when the presenting complaint is in the male partner, most often either premature ejaculation or impotence. The following case example is illustrative.

Mrs. and Mr. S., both aged 22, presented a chief complaint of premature ejaculation. Mr. S stated that he ejaculated almost the moment his penis touched the vulva. Married 16 months, the couple had been unable to have intercourse at any time. Mrs. S. had been referred by her gynecologist who had not been able to examine her because she was too tense during the office visit. The gynecologist did not know about the premature ejaculation problem or the unconsummated marriage. He referred her to us as he knew of our approach to examination of women who were not easily examined. The first visit was simply an interview and an eliciting of the sexual history. Both husband and wife were seen together. The basic format for an examination was described, including delineation of the all important role for the woman during the examination. She was told by P.S. that "I will examine you to the extent that you are comfortable. It's more important that you are able to protect yourself than that the examination be completed."

At the time of the first examination with her husband and the female therapist present, she was able to sit in the pelvic position and let her thighs spread apart. It was possible to touch her thighs and vulva with a cotton applicator before she complained of pain. She, watching in a mirror, was amazed at her reaction as she did not feel the muscle contraction. Needless to say, her husband was also impressed, having placed the entire blame for their sexual inadequacy upon his problem of premature ejaculation. She was instructed to use the mirror and to insert the cotton applicator twice a day, being certain not to hurt herself or put up with pain.

She gradually was able to insert larger objects, vaginal dilators. About two weeks after the initial examination—a time during which there had been steady progress and three office visits—she recalled the early painful pelvic experience. At the age of nine, while riding a bicycle she had fallen forward and bruised the area around the opening of her vagina. There was some bleeding and considerable pain. She told her mother about it and was reassured that she would be all right but neither her mother nor anyone else looked at her genitals. After the initial conversation nothing was said. She was left with the feeling that she had permanently damaged herself. Once she became aware of the early event her progress with the dilators was rapid. The usual treatment for premature ejaculation was also employed. The couple had no difficulty having intercourse. At the time of the follow-up visit they appeared to have no further sexual problem.

A particularly interesting finding in some cases of vaginismus has been the presence of a hymeneal strand subdividing the hymeneal opening. In 200 women examined specifically for either the presence of a tissue band or for evidence that there had been one (i.e., the presence of tissue stumps), nine cases were found. The band was significant clinically because vaginal penetration was usually accompanied by severe pain. A number of the women had been examined by a physician before seeing us but the band had not been detected. In one case, a woman examined by P.S. had a hymeneal band which went unnoticed. Months later, when P.S. was aware of the care necessary to detect the bands, much to his surprise, it was found upon re-examination. Indeed, hers was a fairly significant piece of tissue thinned out and flattened against the side wall of the vagina, but easily separated manually. At first, there were times when she could have intercourse without pain, times when the tissue stayed flat against the side wall of the vagina. However, during sex response there were times when, as a result of increasing sexual arousal, muscles on either side of the vagina and vulva contracted causing the opening to the vagina to become wider. Apparently, at those times the tissue would fall loose from the vaginal wall creating a second smaller opening along side the main vaginal entry. Inadvertent attempts to penetrate this smaller opening resulted in a sharp knife-like pain. The fear of this pain then led to a vaginismus reaction with all attempts at penetration, so that there was some pain at all times.

The effects of drugs on vaginal physiology is another major area in which pelvic examination, coupled with an understanding of sexological concepts and guidelines is especially helpful. The association of oral contraceptives and vaginitis is well-known. We have also been impressed by the drying effects that a number of psychiatric drugs cause. Antihypertensives can also inhibit vaginal lubrication. Indeed, it is reasonable to suspect that any drug that can inhibit erection can also block vaginal lubrication. A recent case is illustrative.

Mr. and Mrs. B., a couple in their 40s, after 20 years of a sexually satisfying marriage developed the problem of impotence. For about a year both were aware of his increasing difficulty in maintaining an erection and finally, during the past eight months, of his inability to develop an erection at all. There were no precipitating crises. If anything, having been through a number of serious illnesses and other life events, the couple felt closer to each other and under less pressure than in the past.

In therapy a number of intra- and interpersonal dynamics had to be dealt with. Most important, however, was the finding during the medical history that Mrs. B had started antimigraine medication—clonidine hydrochloride—two months prior to the onset of the problem. Within a short time she developed difficulty in experiencing an orgasm—a response she was accustomed to and with which she had never had difficulty. On examination the vagina was dry. Mrs. B., aged 43 and with no signs of menopause, nevertheless equated the dryness with menopause and lack of femininity.

Mr. B is a husband exquisitely attuned to his partner, her words, her movements, her odors, and her secretions. Her lack of response led to his spectatoring. The increasing anxiety on his part led to his loss of erection.

Her drug was discontinued and within 72 hours Mrs. B was aware of lubrication. Within another week both had regained their capacity to respond sexually.

The above case presentation is meant only to illustrate the importance of the medical history and examination especially in cases where a drug of any kind is being ingested.

It is not unusual to find couples who have a sexual dysfunction who present a fairly healthy interpersonal relationship and whose individual psychological assessments appear quite normal. In such cases the medical history and physical examination often reveal one or more of the female conditions already described or a physical finding in the male partner. Certainly, when one adds together the incidence of drug-induced effects, vaginitis, hymeneal septa, and vaginismus, a significant percentage of the patient population is involved.

We conclude that except in the rare instance when a person is unable to psychologically or physically cope with being examined, an examination on medical grounds should be done.

The Physical Exam as an Educational Experience

Prior to our work with university students several years had been spent conducting a comprehensive care program for pregnant teenagers. As reported previously [1], one of the most impressive observations in that experience was the degree of ignorance about their bodies that the young women had. Most had never looked at their genitals in a mirror. Those who had did not understand what they were looking at. The great majority did not accurately understand how they became pregnant or even what the definition of intercourse was.

We imagined that university students would be more knowledgeable about themselves, but we soon learned that, although they knew a little bit more, theirs was far from an adequate understanding. When we asked a group of 300 first-year college students to define intercourse, we received no less than 16 different definitions ranging from "when a man touches a woman" to "true intercourse is simultaneous orgasm which leads to pregnancy."

The majority of female students are misinformed about some aspects of their genital anatomy [2]. The most common misunderstandings have to do with the hymen. In two different series one year apart, each of 100 consecutive women patients was asked to describe the hymen and its location. Over 50 percent of the women in both groups placed the hymen high up in the vagina—

"sort of in front of the cervix" and imagined it to be a closed membrane. When actually showed their hymen or the remnants of the hymeneal ring in a mirror they were very surprised. Even those who intellectually knew where it was were nevertheless surprised to *see* its actual location.

Although there has been some change recently, misunderstanding and lack of appreciation of their genital organs—the labia, the clitoris, the vagina, the uterus—continues to be widespread among women, including the highly intelligent.

The labia minora, the erectile skin on either side of the vaginal opening are often felt to be abnormal—too big, too small, too lopsided. Women have had no easy way to compare their anatomy with others to learn what is normal. The assymmetry of the body, so much a source of concern in feelings about breasts, extends to the labia. Some of the women had been told their labia were "peculiar" or big from masturbating too much. (We have not been able to correlate labial size with masturbating activity although we have specifically inquired about this.) Others have been concerned about the clitoris: "It seems so small" or "It's so big it's almost like a little penis." These remarks have been stated often enough that we routinely comment (while examining) on the normality of these structures and usually indicate that the part of the clitoris seen is but the tip. It is a much more substantial structure than most women, or most physicians for that matter, appreciate.

To most women the vagina is a hole and a hole is nothing. Women may think the vagina is black or raw. They don't have a clear perception of it as it is, i.e., a warm, wet, pink, soft, pouch-like potential space. Seeing it, watching the space expand, and contract as a speculum is opened and closed, realizing that it is not a nothing, this is the kind of basic self-understanding which is so important to impart during the pelvic examination experience.

During previous examinations women have often been told confusing things about their uterus, e.g. "You have an infantile uterus," "Your womb is tipped," "You're underdeveloped," etc. Also, the uterus is often thought of simply as a source of bleeding and pain. In other words, nothing positive had been associated with it. All the more reason to allow a woman who accepts the opportunity to see her cervix and feel her uterus. It is often possible to lift the uterus during an examination in such a way that the woman can feel it with her own hand as it presses against the wall of the abdomen. The message is: Everything is there that should be there. These are important, vital organs to be understood and appreciated.

Men often verge on total ignorance of female anatomy. As we are seeing so many couples, we often have the opportunity to teach the male about female anatomy. We frequently use the examination to teach both partners. Because many men misunderstand and are concerned about their own anatomy, we incorporate an explanation of male genital anatomy in our description of the female (see below).

We originally talked about normal female anatomy only during the interview. It soon became obvious, however, that the only way we could really communicate information such as where the hymen was or what the cervix and vagina looked like was to show women their genital anatomy and enable them to feel their uterus and ovaries whenever possible. The response of the first women with whom we tried this was so positive that we ourselves gradually became convinced of its value. As the number of women grew into the hundreds we became enthusiastic about doing this. In recent years we have come to feel so strongly about the value of teaching a woman about her body and using her physical examination to do it, that we practice the use of the mirror and the anatomy lesson routinely. Only rarely, when we feel it not a good idea psychologically, do we omit it.

We have offered the opportunity to use the mirror to over 1500 women. *Two* have declined the invitation. The response has ranged from "intellectual interest" to enthusiasm. There have been some fairly emotional scenes when women for the first time have had a positive message about their genitals, often finding something in their anatomy "completely normal" which they had always felt was terribly abnormal.

Using the Physical Exam
to Promote Sexual Unfolding

The pelvic examination can be an opportunity for promotion of self-understanding, self expression and identity formation [2, 3].

The use of the mirror combined with a basic lesson in female genital anatomy has proved a useful way to deal with body-image. The woman sits in a position so that she can hold a mirror and watch the procedure. Reassurance is given that everything is normal (unless it is not). The attitude towards the body is a positive one. For example, when gloves are being put on the examiner explains that their purpose is to protect the woman from any organisms the doctor might be carrying, not to protect the doctor from her body, which is basically healthy. Except in the very rare instance when venereal infection is present (five cases in nine years, among literally thousands of pelvic examinations), the statement is a true one.

Careful attention is paid to teaching a woman how to examine and thereby protect her breasts. When there is assymmetry, which is more often the case than not, comment is made to reassure that differences in the size and shape of the two breasts are normal.

It is possible to do an examination without hurting physically. However, certain precautions must be taken. Most important is the preliminary description of what is to happen and the careful delineation of the role the woman herself is expected to play in protecting herself: "I need to know if you are uncomfortable at any time. There should not be any pain during this examination." Direct eye contact is maintained during the examination by eliminating the leg draping and elevating the woman's head and shoulders. If there is any kind of pain, the examiner pauses, and the woman is given the opportunity to say exactly what she is feeling.

We do not believe the examination has to be completed in one visit. The avoidance of pain and the promoting of the self-assertive role for the woman will, in the long run, yield a more reliable and worthwhile examination. One group of women we have worked with, 25 women altogether, were referred to us because they could not be examined by others. Although several visits were necessary in some of the cases, all have been examined following the approach described.

Aside from the actual physical contact aspect of the examination, there is the significance of the experience from the point of view of an interpersonal interaction.

Going for a pelvic examination is an adult act—one of the earliest for a young woman. It is important that she be treated in an adult fashion, not as a little girl. Therefore, the tone of the interview and the examination is one which should say, on the doctor's part "I can't guess what is best for you. I can tell you the options. You are of an age when you must make decisions for yourself." Each patient is given choices relative to the examination. She may be examined if she feels ready. She doesn't have to be examined if she wants time to think about it. She may or may not have a nurse present—whichever is more comfortable for her. She can bring a friend along (male or female) if she wishes. The use of the mirror, similarly, is optional although we carefully explain the rationale for its use. By presenting options we are also maintaining that doctors are not omniscient and patients must play an active role in the delivery of their own health care. Thus, we respect the intelligence of the patient, recognizing her as an independent person in this exercise in self-expression and self-understanding.

To digress for a moment, something should be said about the optional use of a nurse. Consultation with several lawyers has confirmed that there is no legal reason why a nurse must be present. Other doctors have told us they fear the disturbed woman who will sue them for assault. Our experience has been that most young women are more comfortable if another woman is not present. They feel she inhibits them from asking questions that are the private concern of her doctor and herself. She may feel embarrassed about her body being displayed to a woman. Women may also resent the use of a "chaperone." If a doctor is someone to trust, then why should you need a chaperone?

Inclusion of a boyfriend or husband during the examination is a practice we have found worthwhile. It provides an opportunity to dispel myths and to enhance male/female understanding of their own as well as the complementary sex anatomy. However, it should not be done automatically. Many women are concerned about how the male will react—will he be upset to see another person touch his partner's body? Will he be turned off by seeing her vulva and vagina? We raise the possibility of the partner being present when the partner has accompanied the woman to the interview. We ask her how she would feel if he were to be present. We ask him how he feels about joining her when the examination is done. The response is variable. Some reply that the reason their partner is present is because they heard, usually from roommates or friends who have seen us, that he would be allowed in the examining room. For some that possibility played a role in their finally making an appointment to see a physician. Others state they would prefer not to have their partner present. We leave the discussion at that and do not feel it appropriate at that time and place to explore the meaning of the reply.

Procedure

To maximize the value of the office visit, body issues are dealt with during the preliminary discussion, the physical examination itself, and the after-discussion.

There is almost always an opportunity to talk before the actual physical examination. In the past there have been "emergency" situations—pregnancy, post-coital contraception, fear of venereal disease, sexual assault—when patients have been fitted into a busy schedule and an examination done without a preliminary office discussion. More recently, there have been fewer such emergencies. We have also become convinced that a talk beforehand is potentially so helpful to being able to do a proper physical examination that it is rare for us to examine a woman without such contact.

We schedule appointments to allow 20 to 30 minutes, before the examination, for discussion. The sort of material covered includes contraception, sexual response, personal development, family and peer relationships, etc. The questions that deal with the physical examination are woven into this discussion, sometimes determining the directions that seem most relevant to explore.

We ask about previous experiences: Have you had a pelvic examination before? What were the reasons for seeing the physician? Was there a pre-existing relationship between you and the physician—your pediatrician or family physician? your mother's gynecologist? a friend of the family or relative? Did anyone go with you? Was the visit in any way different from what you expected? Did you have any particular worries or fears before the visit?

We have found that many girls have had their first pelvic exam when they were quite young and without any forewarning or preparation. The doctor may have decided she was old enough to be examined. Parents sometimes get "paranoid" when a daughter first starts dating and immediately drag her off for a pelvic examination. Because there is a menstrual problem or a vaginal discharge, a young girl does not automatically assume she will have to expose herself for treatment to be given. She is surprised to be led into a little room and told to undress completely and lie down on the table. There is often no acknowledgement of the potential embarrassment of being examined with the mother present or a family friend or relative. Before we make it all sound too bleak, we should say that there are often good past experiences. Examinations have been conducted sensitively with an awareness of the extreme privacy need and self-consciousness of the young adolescent. When this is the case, we usually only have to ask if the patient has any questions about the examination and then describe our approach.

We also start to lay the groundwork for the woman's being self-assertive during this visit: "Did the doctor ask you to let him know if you were uncomfortable? Did he give a choice about whether or not a nurse was present? When you were examined were you in a semi-sitting up position or were you flat on your back?" In other words, was she treated as an adult, as a person? Or was it a dehumanizing, humiliating experience?

We then turn to questions exploring her understanding and appreciation of her body: "Did the doctor use a mirror to show you your anatomy? Have you ever looked at your genitals in a mirror?

Do you use tampons? Have you ever had any difficulty inserting one or taking one out? Have you ever been concerned about or had any questions about the secretions that come from your vagina in between periods?" We also use a life-size model of a uterus to indicate uterus size and consistency. It clearly demonstrates the cervix and the endometrial cavity. Most women are surprised to see how small the normal is. They are also impressed by the firmness of the muscles.

Finally, we turn to the examination process as it is done in the SCS. "Do you know anything about the way we do an examination here? We have found that most women appreciate the opportunity to hold a mirror during the examination and watch what is happening. At the same time the different parts of your anatomy can be pointed out. How do you feel about doing that?"

In the last year many women have come to us because they have heard from friends and roommates about our approach. They have been expecting us to offer the opportunity for using the mirror. Many of the first- and second-year students who see us have not had intercourse and many of them have not had a prior examination. We feel this is an ideal opportunity for an approach such as ours.

At the end of the interview and as an introduction to the physical examination each woman is told that she has an important role to play to make the examination worthwhile. We ask that she clearly let the examiner know if she feels pain or any kind of discomfort at any time. The doctor will stop and wait and only continue if she is comfortable. She is also urged to ask questions, especially if something that is said is not clearly understood.

This discussion phase of a visit to the SCS is usually conducted by a team (L.S. and P.S. or another team which may be part of the Service). The physical examination is usually done by the physician alone. In the case of Yale's Sex Counseling Service, the physician has always been a male gynecologist.

Technique

The examination is done in an examining room. Each woman is given an opportunity to undress and put on a gown in private. The room has a buzzer which the patient (or nurse) pushes when she is prepared and is sitting upon the examining table. Before taking pulse and blood pressure both hands are held and examined. The "hand-on-hand" thus is the first act of touching by the physician. A statement is usually made about the diagnostic significance of hand appearance, thus engaging the patient as a student. When the blood pressure is taken an explanation is given: "The upper level indicates the height of the column of mercury that the pressure sustains when the heart is contracting; the lower level, the pressure when it is at rest." The words "systolic" and "diastolic" are used.

Examination of the head, eyes, ears, nose, and throat follows and then the breasts, heart, and lungs. Self-examination of the breasts is taught. Each woman is shown how to systematically palpate the glandular tissue to gain an appreciation of "normal" irregularities. The position is changed for the breast examination, still basically a sitting position but lying back somewhat with her legs straightened out. Abdominal examination, leg evaluation, and reflexes are checked in routine fashion.

For the pelvic examination itself the woman is in a semi-sitting up position, shoulders elevated to above the level of the knees. Foot supports extend from the end of the table, the buttocks positioned at the edge. A drape is not used except to cover the lower abdomen. In this way, with her legs spread apart, each woman can have direct eye contact with the physician and vice versa. When she holds a hand mirror angled at her knees she can also view the vulvar area. First touch is to the inside of the knees and then the inside of the thigh. A repeat is given of the directive, "I need you to protect yourself. If I touch any area that hurts I need you to let me know about it." Even women who have not been able to relax for previous examinations have responded to this sequence designed to give her control of the situation. Vulvar inspection is accompanied by a lesson. Using a cotton applicator as a pointer, each of the vulvar structures is identified and its embryologic counterpart in the male mentioned (labia major/ scrotal sac, labia minor/corpora cavernosa of penis, hood over clitoris/foreskin, clitoral body/corpora spongiosa). The labia are then spread to reveal the hymen. Placing a finger through the opening and touching the wall of the vagina, the point is made that many women misunderstand the anatomy and position of the hymen. "It is the boundary between the vagina on one side and the vulva on the other. It normally has an opening in the middle through which a finger can pass." The essentials of a pelvic examination are then done, including bimanual and speculum examination and rectovaginal evaluation.

When the speculum is inserted the woman is shown how to angle the mirror so that she can see her cervix and the walls of the vagina. She is also able to watch the Pap smear being taken. When the speculum (a plastic one) is removed she can see how the walls of the vagina naturally fall together. When the bimanual examination is done, the body of the uterus is elevated by the fingers within the vagina. The woman's hand is applied to the abdomen so that she too can feel her uterus and not infrequently the ovaries on either side. After completing the pelvic part of the physical, the patient sits forward lowering her legs. At that point she is asked if there is anything further she wants to know about her body and if the lesson was clear. She is also asked how she feels about seeing herself in this way. She is then left alone to dress and rejoin us in the consultation office.

The discussion which follows the physical examination is a brief one. "Are there any further questions about what has been discussed today or about the examination?" Usually there are none but occasionally there is a further question about contraception or about something seen or said during the physical. We also explain that the people we see have found it worthwhile to schedule a follow-up visit in six to eight weeks either to discuss contraception or some issue that first surfaced during the preliminary interview. In this regard, of course, we are talking about the individual who has presented no particular problem either medically or sexologically. When there is an issue which requires return sooner, issues which could range from a diaphragm check to the more complete taking of a sexual history, the "after-discussion" is the time when we make these arrangements.

Examination of Males

The majority of students coming to the SCS are seen for contraception or counseling and this involves examining only the female. But in sex therapy cases both the male and female are examined, usually at the same time, and the co-therapist is present for the physical examination. In our case, L.S. is not a doctor and cannot do any medical procedures (which would be the ideal) but she can do the educational parts of the woman's examination.

Essentially everything we have said about the meaning and significance of the medical history and physical examination for the female holds true for the male. Men seem to be as confused, anxious, and ignorant about their genitalia as women despite the fact that their genitals are external and thus more available for self-scrutiny. More men have refused to hold a mirror during their examination than women, and the two patients who have ever fainted from the emotional stress of the physical have been men! We have also found that there is some history of genital trauma or abnormality in a high percentage of men who are involved in sex therapy and this holds true for cases in which only the female has a specific sexual dysfunction. Often the history of trauma or the genital abnormality has been "forgotten" by the man and only became known in the course of the examination. For example, a graduate student on examination suddenly recalled having had mumps as a young teenager that had resulted in loss of function of one testicle. Until that moment, despite extensive history-taking, that fact had not emerged.

Males have many vague anxieties about their genitals which can be dispelled during a physical examination. Several men have expressed the idea that the line which runs up the underside of their penis was a scar from some surgical procedure they imagined was performed in infancy. More common sources of anxiety are about penis size, the epididymis which may feel like an abnormal growth on the testicle, the way the testicles hang, or the tortuous veins on the shaft of the penis.

We have been amazed to see how many men who have gone through the educational genital examination have expressed the same enthusiasm and sense of relief that so many women have expressed. Perhaps this kind of examination should be more routinely available to young men.

Summary

Careful attention to the medical history and physical examination format has proved a valuable asset in our sexual health program. We relate to the person as an adult. We offer the opportunity for personal understanding as well as medical assessment. Feedback from the people who have been through the program indicates its appropriateness. It is almost unheard of for someone to fail to return for follow-up. Often, a friend is told about the experience and he or she, in turn, makes an appointment.

We realize that a number of potentially controversial practices are being advocated. One should bear in mind that it is only in the last 50 to 75 years that the use of the speculum has been widely accepted. Prior to that time it was felt that it was unprofessional for doctors to see a woman's genitals. Interestingly, it is probable that the main reason for barring the use of the speculum was not so much the modesty of the Victorian and Edwardian eras, but the basic observation that doctors didn't know what to look for or what to do with the information obtainable by such an examination. The development of the Pap smear with its proven value in detecting disease did more to promote the use of this instrument than any change in moral attitude.

The approach we are using has naturally evolved from an orientation that is medical as well as being psychological. Techniques such as the pre-examination "give and take," the use of the mirror, patient-doctor eye contact, the presence or absence of others, each of these fits into the understanding of young people's need for establishing independence and sexual identity. We feel it is a model of how a sense of trust is promoted when people are given the opportunity to exercise their right to self-assertion and self-protection. In this regard, the medical dimension has been consistent with the basic principles which guide us as therapists.

References

1. Sarrel, Philip M., Teenage Pregnancy—Prevention and Treatment. *SIECUS Study Guide*, No. 14, September, 1971.
2. Sarrel, Philip M. and Sarrel, Lorna J., *A New Approach to the Pelvic Examination*, Network for Continuing Medical Education, Television Tape, New York, 1974.
3. Sarrel, Lorna J. and Sarrel, Philip M., "Your Most Intimate You," *Redbook*, Vol. 150(5), March, 1978, p. 82.

9

Contraception and Pregnancy

Contraceptive services have been an integral part of the Sex Counseling Service (SCS) since the beginning of the program. Between 1969 and 1975 almost 1,200 women have been seen for whom contraceptive information has been provided, a physical examination done, and a contraceptive method prescribed.

Our aim has been to do more than give contraceptive information and prescriptions—important as those services may be. From the beginning, the contraceptive appointment has been regarded as an opportunity to initiate a patient–professional relationship for the promotion of sexual health.

We are now convinced that providing contraceptive services in the broader context of a sexuality-oriented program is worthwhile. Almost without exception, students who see us for contraception need and want to discuss sex related issues either during their initial visit or subsequent follow-up appointments.

We are convinced—but what about the students? Although our contraceptive services at first filled a vacuum, there are now alternatives for students. Contraception is available from the gynecology clinic or from their assigned internist. Many students do choose these alternatives. However, we still see approximately 20 percent of all the undergraduate women students at some time for contraception (approximately one third of the sexually active female students). We think there are a number of reasons why students choose to see us for contraception—who we are, what we do, what they have heard from other students about the SCS. Many come to see us after taking the course in sexuality; some, as a result of reading *Sex at Yale*. A number are referred by their "primary" physician or the gynecology clinic because they have expressed a need to talk about a personal concern. But, most come to the SCS referred by a friend.

Our ideas about patient treatment have evolved from an understanding of student psychosocial and developmental needs. These ideas have led to the development of an approach which is consistent with student needs but differs from the standard approach to delivering contraceptive services. We believe that our approach is an important factor in the finding that over 98 percent of patients have returned for follow-up care and that in nine years only six women who have seen us for contraception have subsequently become pregnant as a result of unprotected intercourse.

Our years of working with young people in a contraceptive and sex counseling service have been an education for us. We have learned lessons about the prescription of contraceptive methods. We have also learned that a student's use of contraception is a very meaningful act in both practical and symbolic ways, with important psychological, developmental, sexual, and social implications.

The average young woman, including those who are at college, does not use birth control as effectively or maturely as she could. In their early studies (1971), Kantner and Zelnik, demographers Johns Hopkins University, found that a staggering 81.6 percent of unmarried girls age 15-19 who were having intercourse, frequently had intercourse without any contraceptive protection [1]. In their second study (1976), the authors found an increase in the use of contraception (although 70 percent of girls 15-19 were still not using contraception at all or were using it "sometimes"). Kantner and Zelnik's 1976 study also showed an increase in the use of more effective methods as well as more regular use of all methods. Another pertinent finding was that few teenagers begin use of contraception at the time of initiating intercourse and many won't until after they have had a pregnancy [2].

Let us look at the student who is coming to a doctor to ask about contraception for the first time in her life. We know that in most birth control clinics and private offices she is a nonvirgin who has been having unprotected intercourse, perhaps using a form of rhythm or withdrawal. Her seeking contraceptive advice often seems almost fortuitous: her friend was coming and brought her along; her period was late last month and she became nervous; her boyfriend insisted she do something; her mother asked some pointed questions; a friend became pregnant. There is a passive quality to the event. A third party or outside force was the precipitant.

The "typical" Yale student who comes to the SCS presents an interesting contrast, a contrast which we have seen at other colleges where there are sex counselling programs offering contraception. Over the years, between 10 and 15 percent of the female students requesting contraception have been virgins who want to have effective contraception before they even start to have intercourse. Of the 85-90 percent who have had prior coital experience, the extent of this experience is usually small and they have tended to use a means of contraception (such as condom and/or foam) consistently. When they have had intercourse without contraception, this has usually happened on only one or two occasions. Only about 10 percent of the female students with prior coital experience have had repeated unprotected intercourse and repeated pregnancy scares before they come to the SCS.

About one third of the students who want contraception come in with their boyfriends. By and large, they seem to be taking an active, carefully thought-out and self-initiated step.

Why is there this difference and what can be learned from it? Yale students are a fairly special group—intelligent, goal-directed, planful, able to delay immediate gratification for future ends, verbal, and accustomed to using medical care. They are predominantly middle-class and white. But they are not radically different from other college students in the U.S. today. Their contraceptive behavior is the product of several factors: (1) Widespread changes in attitudes and knowledge about sex and birth control which influence all students, perhaps to a greater degree at the more "liberal" colleges and universities; (2) the campus milieu with respect to sex, which can be (and is at Yale), influenced by official policies, courses in sex education, and so on; and (3) the availability and quality of birth control services, including the attitudes of personnel offering the service and the campus reputation of such services.

The first of these is largely beyond control but the last two are not. Students, like most (young) people are very strongly influenced by their peers. During adolescence they must continuously find a balance between peer acceptance, which tends to mean a good deal of conformity, and the expression of their individuality. Sex is certainly not immune to peer pressure—a point we stressed in Chapter 2. As anyone who is familiar with the field of contraception knows, each community has shared attitudes, beliefs and myths about sex and birth control that are important influences determining contraceptive use or nonuse—often more influential than rational appeal or even the desperate consequences of nonuse.

On campus today there are trends and fashions which strongly influence sexual attitudes and behavior, including contraception. There are important fads and swings of opinion which may be nation-wide, campus-wide or dorm-wide. One such influence, which is more or less nation-wide, is the Women's Liberation Movement. Women's Liberation seems to have had a role in liberalizing attitudes toward many aspects of female sexual experience—lesbianism, bi-sexuality, masturbation, female sexual pleasure, an active female role in initiating sex and in touching, and nonmonogamous sex. Insofar as acceptance of and comfort with sexuality influence contraception—and there is no doubt that it is a vital factor—this liberalizing effect would tend to promote good use of birth control.

The "liberated" female not only accepts her sexuality, she understands and respects her body and takes responsibility for it. She is savvy about male chauvinism and paternalism in medical care and will assert her rights and needs vis-a-vis the "establishment" in medicine. At Yale, the local Women's Lib organization has exerted some direct pressure on the student health services and a list of "male chauvinist pig (MCP)" doctors to avoid was placed on file in their headquarters.

The Women's Movement has also played a part in promoting

nancy risk and the ability to protect herself and her partner from this unwanted consequence.

When a student takes such a step, especially when she does it apart from parental help, she shows a certain level of mature functioning. In making the decision and in carrying it out she will usually grow in her feeling of independence, assertiveness and her sense of herself as a sexual being.

When she makes the decision or comes to the doctor with a boyfriend, this shared responsibility both reflects and extends psychological intimacy. They must talk about the need for contraception, discuss and negotiate about a method, and plan an appointment or a purchase. If they see a doctor together, they are making a kind of public statement about their sexual relationship. Certainly, the treatment they receive, medically and as people, should take these factors into consideration. If the doctor leaves the young man in the waiting room or ignores him in the consultation room, a great opportunity is missed, an opportunity to enhance contraceptive utilization and psychological growth in one 20-minute appointment!

When a student requesting contraception comes in with her boyfriend, he is included in the discussion of methods and any other issues that arise. The couple is offered the option of having the boyfriend present during the examination (which is used for educational purposes as well as medical). A growing number of student couples tell us that they have chosen to come to the SCS, rather than the regular gynecology clinic, because they liked the idea of being able to share the experience of the physical exam.

Just as the initiation of contraception is a significant step, so too is changing birth control methods. Although students, like any other group of women, often change their method of birth control for medical reasons, it is not at all unusual for them to change methods for nonmedical reasons. This means that a student's revisit to a contraceptive service may be as important, in terms of psychological, sexual or interpersonal issues, as the first visit.

Switching from the pill to the diaphragm has been extremely

common among Yale students, mostly because of concern about taking any medication for long periods of time. But this switch can also occur for a number of other reasons. Many women, young and old, believe, correctly, that the pill can affect mood, libido, or sexual response. But the pill is easily scapegoated for a wide variety of concerns. If a young woman blames her nonorgasmic response on the pill, it is certainly more helpful to be able to talk about the issue of sex response directly and not simply agree with her in blaming the pill if there is no rational basis for this blame.

Switching from the pill or an IUD to a diaphragm sometimes carries another implication that it is useful for doctors or counsellors to understand. This contraceptive method change sometimes reflects a young woman's feeling that she is having intercourse with too many men partly because her being on the pill makes things too easy. She feels that a diaphragm will help her to say "no" on some occasions because its use requires more forethought and is an active step. She can also use lack of contraceptive protection as an excuse with a very persistent man.

Contraception and Sexual Experience

The woman who becomes nonorgasmic after starting birth control pills is just one example of the many ways in which different methods of contraception may affect sexual interest and response. In prescribing contraception or in evaluating complaints about a method, we are alert to the possibility that important determining factors may be real or fantasized sexual meanings of the method in question.

A senior recently came to the SCS for contraception. She began the appointment talking about her fears of pills and IUDs. We were surprised when she then said she thought she "had better" use the pill anyway. She and her 23-year-old boyfriend had had intercourse just twice, using a condom plus foam. He had been unable to ejaculate either time and told her that in his one previous experience, also using a condom, he had not ejaculated. He told her that "situational" methods were not so good because of decreased sensitivity and the interruption. Both of them had believed that a diaphragm would need to be inserted at the last moment, like a condom, and would be interruptive.

When she was told that a diaphragm could be inserted two hours before intercourse she began to think that might be the best method for her. If she hadn't been concerned about his response, she said, she would have wanted a diaphragm. Her older sister used one and liked it, and the pills really worried her.

She wasn't completely reassured that a diaphragm would be okay with her boyfriend and so she was given two prescriptions—one for a diaphragm and one for birth control pills. She returned a few days later to have her new diaphragm checked.

It is certainly possible that she could have used pills successfully, but we suspect that a busy doctor who never got past her early statement of "I guess I'd better use pills," would have seen her a month or two later, complaining of nausea or some other problem—a reflection of her strong ambivalence about the pills.

Each method has its own particular drawbacks with respect to its impact upon sexual behavior and response. The following observations are drawn from the experiences of our patients:

Birth Control Pills
Birth control pills can cause mood changes and decreased sexual interest and/or response in some women.

The newer low-estrogen pills can create a variety of side effects because they cause a relative deficiency in the hormone. These side effects mimic the problems seen in post-oophorectomy and post-menopausal women with insufficient estrogen. There may be little or no vaginal lubrication in spite of sexual arousal. The low estrogen level can promote symptomatic monilial vaginitis or make the vaginitis more resistant to treatment. Low estrogen levels are also implicated in recurrent cystitis and urethritis. All of these side effects can seriously impair sexual function.

We are impressed by the frequency of sexual problems in young women using the very low-dose birth control pills. Because of the many social and psychological issues involved, it is not possible to pinpoint the cause of dysfunction as being due to the low estrogen dose. However, the addition of a small amount of estrogen to the already existing dose has at times resulted in a reversal of sexual dysfunction—most notably of dyspareunia and nonorgasmic response due to persistent vaginitis or cervicitis.

IUDs

The IUD may cause post-coital bleeding which can be frightening. It may create some uterine cramping at orgasm although the newer IUDs seem not to create this side effect. The IUD can be a source of unpleasant vaginal odor which can be a deterrent to sexual relations, especially oral sex but also petting and intercourse.

Diaphragm

An occasional woman is allergic to jelly or cream and develops itching or swelling of the vagina or vulva. The need to insert the diaphragm can be a deterrent to sex if the woman is anxious about inserting it for any reason—squeamishness or fear of hurting herself or concern about her ability to do it properly or being in a situation in which it would be socially awkward to suddenly produce and insert her diaphragm. The odor and taste of jelly or cream may interfere with oral sex. An occasional couple complains that the jelly or cream makes the vagina too slippery and decreases pleasure during intercourse.

Condom

The condom is a problem for many men because of the need to interrupt sexual stimulation prior to inserting the penis. The interruption can cause loss of erection, premature ejaculation or difficulty in ejaculating. Some men, and even some women feel that condoms decrease pleasurable sensations in intercourse. If the man or woman is tense about using the method—about the condom tearing or about leaking or spilling of seminal fluid—then they may find their sexual response is decreased.

Withdrawal

Many young people today are aware of the dangers of this method. They know that sperm will usually come from the penis in the lubricating fluid emitted during the plateau phase. Even if they don't know this, they tend not to trust the method and may be too tense to enjoy intercourse completely. The need to focus carefully on his stage of response can create anxiety for the man, leading to some form of sexual dysfunction. The woman's expectation of an abrupt end-point can interfere with her responsiveness.

Unprotected Intercourse

What of the approximately 10 percent of students for whom exists a considerable lag time between initiating intercourse and seeking birth control? Their pattern of intercourse is generally infrequent and irregular, which probably explains why there are so few pregnancies in this group. In addition, they do tend to take some precautions against conception—a rather haphazard combination of rhythm, withdrawal and occasional use of condoms or foam. When they do finally come to the SCS for birth control, we try to find out the reasons for their previous behavior and for their deciding now to change that pattern.

Some, of course, are freshmen or transfer students who cite the nonavailability of service as the crucial variable. Freshmen say they feel differently about things now that they are away from their families. But many go beyond these external reasons to a realization that they were not emotionally ready to have a regular method of contraception. One student related this to the relationship she was in. Although she and her "boyfriend" were having intercourse, they weren't all that close, didn't see one another very frequently, weren't committed to the relationship and, in fact, didn't have intercourse very often, sometimes just necking or petting. When the relationship progressed, and sex became more regularized, they started to talk about birth control, and some planning for future intercourse, which was now a more predictable event, seemed called for.

The psychological determinants in having unprotected inter-course are complex and highly individual. They have been the focus of research, debate, and clinical interest for a long time. We have been particularly interested in one very practical facet of this complex question; is there anything that can be done (on a col-lege campus) to reach out to this group? At Yale there is already a complex web of services and education—but what more could we do?

One idea has recently occurred to us, stimulated by the observa-tion that female students who delayed getting birth control often described themselves as socially isolated, having few, if any, close girlfriends. This social isolation is particularly acute for freshmen women, and we know that approximately one quarter of them will have their first intercourse experience sometime during this year. Obviously, this is a high-risk group.

The correlation between social isolation and an individual's non-use of birth control is not simple and direct. A case example may help to make the point. In her junior year, a student came to the SCS to get pills or a diaphragm. When we asked about her pre-vious use of contraception, she said she'd been very erratic about it. She thought her "messed-up" sex life had something to do with her being unable to deal with things like contraception. In her fresh-man year she had had intercourse for the first time. She thought it would be perfectly simple because she had had some experience in petting and being naked with her boyfriend. She knew that her parents expected her to be a virgin for a long time, probably till marriage, but she hadn't ever felt much guilt about sex and didn't expect to in the future. She was very surprised by her own reac-tion to intercourse. It wasn't painful, but it wasn't very pleasurable either. She became "hysterical" afterward, though she didn't know just why. The young man was very upset, told her she was "crazy," and offered little support or understanding. Her parents "just happened" to be visiting that weekend, but she didn't feel any guilt or discomfort when she was with them.

That Saturday night, at a party, a girl from her home town who was very "straight-laced" came up to her and said, "You look different, like you're becoming a woman of the world." This remark shocked and startled her. It accentuated her feeling that she was different from others around her. In all-female student groups she found herself preoccupied with the thought that they were all virgins. The only sexually experienced students she knew were *very* experienced, not at all like herself.

She had dealt with her inner conflict and her fear of parental disapproval by projecting the two sides of her ambivalence onto the outer world. The females around her then represented her innocence and virginity on the one hand, and her guilt, sinfulness and sexual experience on the other. The fact that she was socially isolated (probably, in part, a result of her defenses) heightened the potential for projection because she received little or no feedback from other females about their actual attitudes and life experience. It is interesting that she snapped out of her confusion about sex, about a year later, after having her first frank discussion about sex with a female friend.

She and her boyfriend saw one another on and off in a very stormy relationship, breaking up frequently and then reconciling. She had been completely unable to think about sex or birth control because she felt so overwhelmed and confused. She was unable to integrate the concept of herself with the concept of a "female who has intercourse." The friend in whom she finally confided instinctively said the right things. She wasn't shocked or upset by what she heard and she remarked, "Well, it's not such a big deal; you're still the same person after all."

As a result of talking with students like this young woman who have gone through periods of confusion and isolation in part because of their conflicts over sexual behavior, we have concluded that our next effort should be to reach out on a dormitory-by-dormitory basis, to small groups of freshman students (about 30 at a time) in small informal sessions. This would both make the SCS more real and visible and would help to break down the barriers between freshmen, providing an opportunity for reality to replace fantasy and stereotyped ideas about what everyone else is or isn't doing sexually.

Sex Counseling in a Contraceptive Visit

We have always used the contraceptive appointment as an opportunity to educate about sex, to find out if there are any worries, conflicts or questions, and to begin an on-going counseling process when that seems warranted. We believe that this practice should be more widespread. In clinics and offices throughout the country doctors and nurses could, without spending very much more time, expand the scope of discussion with patients who are seeking contraception, particularly with adolescents and young adults.

One stumbling block to making discussion of sex a natural part of the contraceptive interview has been doctors' lack of expertise about, and comfort with, the subject. As this changes, due in part to the inclusion of human sexuality in most medical school curricula, doctors are more willing to consider raising the subject with patients. Many, however, feel unsure of how to do this. How quickly can one launch into talking about something as personal, private, and sensitive as sex? Will young women or couples be shocked and put-off? What words can be used?

The reactions of patients seem to have a lot to do with the doctor's sense of comfort. If the doctor really wants to open up a discussion and feels able to answer questions that may arise or will at least know where to refer patients with complex problems, the doctor is likely to find that patients welcome discussion of sex and can talk comfortably about intimate details quite quickly when it is relevant and appropriate.

The interview below is offered as an example of how to shift discussion from contraception to sex. This student couple came together to the SCS. Contraception was their uppermost concern but, as it turned out, they had some concerns about sex as well. They could easily have backed away from the matter of sex if the way hadn't been opened by the professional team. The total time for this single appointment, including gynecologic exam, was one half hour.

An undergraduate couple, they said that they wanted contraception but were uncertain about which method. Her doctor at home was generally "anti-pill," but she wasn't sure what to think.

As we routinely do, we said we couldn't make the decision for them and asked if *he* had any thoughts, thus making him an active part of the decision making process and the interview. He felt a bit anti-pill himself because it could "change your body." She then discussed her own reluctance to take any medication and the fact that her mother had become depressed while taking birth control pills. She guessed she really wanted a diaphragm.

Another routine question was asked. Had they already had intercourse? Yes. What method, if any, was used? A condom once and then nothing. How many times had they had intercourse? Just twice—very recently. The first questions about sex were thus tied to the subject of contraception.

After this there was a discussion of the diaphragm, its use, care, etc. A model of the female pelvis was used to demonstrate insertion and this again brought up some aspects of sex very naturally. For example, we mentioned that it is better to insert the diaphragm before a high degree of sexual arousal is attained. It's less interruptive and it is mechanically simpler because the inner two-thirds of the vagina balloons and the cervix elevates during the sexual plateau. This couple was already familiar with many aspects of diaphragm use and with the terminology of sexual physiology from reading the booklet *Sex at Yale*.

We often ask about parental attitudes with a question like, "Would you tell your parents you were having intercourse?" This couple said that his parents were very liberal and they would probably not hide anything from them, but her mother and father were divorced. Her mother was very far away and wouldn't understand. She didn't discuss private things with family members very much.

L.S.: Do either of you have any questions or concerns about the times you had intercourse or about any aspects of sex?

L.S. (to her): Any concern about bleeding or pain?

SHE: There wasn't any bleeding but it did hurt—less the second time.

L.S. (to her): Did it worry you?

SHE: Not really. I guess I wasn't stretched out.

There followed some discussion of the hymen, its location, how it stretches with intercourse and the fact that the first time or so is often, though not always, painful. We stressed that after this, intercourse is *not* usually painful or uncomfortable—that pain is often caused by involuntary spasm of the muscles at the vaginal opening. If discomfort persisted it could disrupt sexual pleasure, and they should come back to see us. In all probability, we said, there will not be a problem.

P.S.: You know, most men don't know that much about a woman's body. Can you talk in bed—about what to do, your feelings?

HE: Well, we're not very open with each other—but we're not terribly unopen either.

P.S.: For example, you might like her to guide your penis into her vagina so you won't have to guess how—or whether it's comfortable.

HE: That would be good.

SHE: But I'm so naive myself!

L.S.: Do you use tampons comfortably?

SHE: Yes.

L.S.: So you can insert something in your vagina—and you will be using a diaphragm?

SHE: I guess I could do it.

L.S.: In what ways do you feel naive? Do you understand about female sex response?

SHE: Well, no. Like, what's an orgasm anyway? I know the technical stuff—but how would I know if I had one?

L.S.: No one can really describe it very well. It's some seconds of intense feeling at the end of a cycle of arousal. Very few females have an orgasm when they're just starting to have intercourse. It takes time for you to learn about what feels good—to learn together. Lots of women find that they respond as much or even more to stimulation around the clitoris (pointing to model) than to intercourse. You'll have to learn what turns you on. Don't get too focused on having an orgasm. Most likely it will just happen.

[Pause, in which the male patient seems about to speak, hesitates, then does speak.]

HE: Is there anything I can do about coming too soon?

At this point P.S. made several points: Abstinence tends to increase speed of ejaculation; anxious focusing on "Will I come quickly?" is not helpful. You should concentrate on your own bodily feelings, your penis—the female above position often helps in delaying ejaculation. L.S. interjected that it's also a good position for a woman; she can do most of the moving and explore her own sensations. The start-stop technique was described in a few sentences. We suggested that they could come back to talk again if they felt it was a persistent problem. The physical examination followed. A diaphragm was prescribed.

We have purposely included this detailed description of counseling in the chapter on contraception because we want to promote the idea that this is, or can be, business-as-usual in a contraceptive appointment. The professional should show the way, by referring only to sex, talking about sex response, using words like *penis*, *vagina*, *orgasm*, *come*, or *ejaculation* and mentioning some aspect of sexual exchange (such as the suggestion that the female might take responsibility for inserting the penis). These interviews can be a model of primary prevention in the area of sexual health. A bit of information, reassurance and frank communication at a time like this can make an enormous difference to the course of an unfolding relationship.

Program Procedures

Program services include those usually offered in the care of the contraceptive patient—a medical history, physical examination, and appropriate laboratory testing (Pap smear, cervical, and vaginal culture). Routine procedure also includes several practices which have developed out of our understanding of psychosocial and developmental needs of students and our commitment to a sexuality-oriented approach to contraception.

The principal reason for the team approach is that one of us brings medical skills to the program and the other the counseling experience. The interview part of the contraceptive appointment is divided between us as the physician focuses on medical issues and the social worker discusses sexuality. We both have had considerable experience with the medical and sexual dimensions of contraceptive care of students. Either of us is capable of discussing the issues that arise. But it has been our experience as co-therapists in sex therapy that has been the most educative for us. In that situation, we have come to appreciate the value of a male professional dealing with the issues of the male patient's sexuality, and a female professional relating to a female patient. The question of how to staff a sex counseling and contraceptive service should be considered in terms of how best to meet patient needs as well as the relative efficiency and cost of different staffing options.

When a female patient is alone

A female doctor trained in counseling, interested in and sensitive to psychosexual factors would be ideal for the female alone, requesting contraception. Such women doctors have been hard to find, but as more female doctors are trained, the task of finding such a professional will become easier.

What about a sensitive, psychologically trained, male doctor? Certainly he can do a great deal toward meeting the medical and counseling needs of a female patient, but a great many of the young women we see have not felt comfortable raising questions such as "Why don't I have orgasms?" "How does a female masturbate?", or "Why are my labia so large?" with a male doctor. The on-going sex counseling process, which almost always includes detailed discussion of sexual experiences and feelings, should be female-female. Of course, the traditional model of medical care delivery can be used, the male doctor "referring" all female patients who need counseling to a female counselor, but there are so many issues and questions that can be dealt with at the time of the initial visit—and perhaps *only* then—while the young woman is already *there*. If she does raise serious questions, it is so much better to have the female who will be her on-going counselor there at the time rather than to bring in a new person a week or two later. So, although it is a relatively expensive form of health care, we continue to use the team approach because we feel it is the optimal way to meet patient needs. There are, of course, intangible benefits that are more difficult to assess, in having a young woman talk to a male-female (perhaps married) team of professionals. Some students have spontaneously commented on their feelings about this, e.g., "It's been a little like talking to my parents—only different—because you can be objective and, anyway, I just couldn't talk this way with them." The presence of a team may also defuse some of the potentially threatening aspects of a gynecologic visit for a young woman such as fears of being hurt or the sexually charged nature of the discussion and examination.

When a couple comes for contraception

When a couple comes to the SCS to discuss contraception, the young man often presents questions and concerns of his own. Although we hold a four-way conversation, the male member of the team responds to the male's questions and concerns and the female responds to the female's questions. This male-male, female-female alignment can then continue into any sex counselling or therapy which may follow.

As in the case of the female patient alone, a single doctor-counsellor of either sex could be fairly effective, especially in a contact limited to one or two visits. However, when the contraceptive appointment leads into on-going counselling, we believe in the advantages of co-therapy. It would certainly be useful to have some investigation of cost-effectiveness of different modes of professional staffing but, so far as we know, this has not been done.

Confidentiality

In the late 1960s very few colleges and universities were providing contraceptive care for students. Those that were, tended to be very quiet about it. Students were loathe to use their college health services for any situation in which their nonvirginity might become known. Students generally did not believe that college doctors and administrators would maintain confidentiality. The doctors, in turn, were nervous about the legal implications of dispensing contraception without parental consent.

In the past decade this climate of fear and mistrust has altered considerably. Doctors feel secure in their legal position in prescribing contraception for college students and students are certainly less paranoid about their college health services than were students in earlier years. When we started the SCS in the fall of 1969, it was apparent that we needed to stress confidentiality. The Mental Hygiene Division had an established reputation for confidentiality. Becoming part of that division, we benefited from that reputation. We let it be known that the SCS would maintain completely separate records. No records of a visit to us or of the fact that a student was using contraception would appear on her medical record. If a doctor or a parent wanted to know about this, they would have to ask the girl herself. We wouldn't even acknowledge to a parent that their daughter had been to see us. Interestingly, this policy was never put to the test. No parent, doctor, dean, draft board, or CIA agent ever tried to get information from us!

The doctors in the health service at Yale were rather concerned about the fact that medication was being prescribed without notation on the medical record. We were not totally happy about this either but felt it was a trade-off worth maintaining. Beginning in 1975 we have altered our policy. We now tell students that we will make a notation of their visit, the physical examination, and prescription, if any, in their medical record unless they object. The fact that almost no students raise an eyebrow to this is a measure of the altered climate about sex.

We still maintain our own files in which we record material about sexual response, relationships, or problems. This material is never entered in a student's medical record.

Continuity of Care

In the SCS, continuity of care stems from the multiservice nature of the program. When the same staff is available to students for a variety of concerns which relate to sex, e.g., for the treatment of vaginitis, for couples or individual sex counselling, for dealing with an unwanted pregnancy, there are many opportunities to reinforce trust in the professional relationship and to have an ongoing dialogue. For example, a student seen for contraception might return two months later for treatment of vaginitis. The treatment of vaginitis usually involves three or four short visits during which the student might talk about having pain with intercourse or being nonorgasmic. Her boyfriend might accompany her when the vaginitis is treated, thereby presenting the opportunity to talk about interpersonal issues.

In order to achieve continuity of care we have had to be accessible to students in several different ways. Early morning appointment times are kept open each day for quick visits. Students seen at these visits have semi-urgent problems such as a diaphragm check, vaginitis diagnosis or treatment, post-coital assessment when contraception has not been used, irregular bleeding, or some side-effect of the pill. Not infrequently, in this 15-minute visit, a student will mention some issue that requires more time and counselling, and arrangements are then made for another appointment.

The telephone has also been very useful in maintaining continuity of care. All patients are given our office and home telephone numbers. Often, when there are fairly straightforward questions or concerns, they call our office and our secretary is able to handle the matter. We have trained our secretaries over the years to be able to answer some common questions; for example, what to do if a birth control pill is missed. In fact, it was our secretary who thought to give students an extra package of pills for "fill-ins" when pills were dropped or lost. We seldom receive more than one or two calls each week at home. This has not been an inconvenience, and we do feel the calls are warranted.

Working in a team has also allowed a flexibility which means greater availability to students. For example, a student seen for an early morning visit might need further counselling as soon as possible. A crisis in a relationship or the possibility of pregnancy have been reasons for needing immediate help. We have always been able to fit such a patient into our morning's schedule, by the two of us splitting, i.e., one taking one appointment scheduled and the other seeing the student in crisis. In that way, the continuity of care is maintained through crisis situations. These are particularly important times to have a professional available who knows the student and who can appreciate the crisis situation in a broader perspective. For students who first see us in crisis situations, it is particularly important that continuity of care stem from the crisis treatment. Until recent years, students who were pregnant were diagnosed, counselled about pregnancy and abortion, aborted, returned to the counselling situation afterwards and then seen for years of follow-up—all these services stemming from the same office and the same people. For many students, our participation in the human sexuality course is a kind of continuity of care. We sometimes suggest to students who see us that they take the course. Afterwards, an office visit may pick up with ideas generated during the lectures or small group discussions.

Some Basic Observations

Having seen over 2,000 young women asking for contraception in the last nine years, having discussed in depth many aspects of contraceptive choice, relationships and sexuality, having seen many of the same women repeatedly over a span of years, we have made some observations about the prescription of contraception in this age group that we think are particularly useful for clinicians involved in contraceptive prescription but should also interest others whose concern is more with psychology than medicine.

There is no one contraceptive method that is clearly best for this age group. Many doctors have tended to promote either birth control pills or perhaps IUDs for all unmarried females because these methods provide more certain protection against pregnancy. In so doing, the professional may be allowing his or her own feelings about the meanings of a possible out-of-wedlock pregnancy to color his or her medical advice. We have found that students often sense when one or another method is being "pushed," and, more and more, they are rejecting this somewhat paternalistic approach in favor of one in which their felt needs and desires are seriously considered in choosing a birth control method.

The level of sophistication varies greatly. Some students have gone to the *Index Medicus* and reviewed the recent literature on several methods before their appointment. A few know little beyond hearsay. But everyone we see has some ideas of her own and, if there is a "steady" boyfriend, as there usually is, he has some ideas too. We believe that the patient's ideas, prejudices and feelings are important. If they are explored, if myths and misinformation are dispelled, if idiocyncrasies are respected and the patient feels that she has been able to choose the method best for her—all of her—then contraceptive utilization is enhanced.

She may be influenced, in her choice of method, by extraneous influences that are unscientific but are none the less real. If her mother became pregnant while using a diaphragm she may not be able to trust it. If her sister likes being on the pill, she may favor pills. The method of contraception needs to fit with the totality of her self-image as well as her reality situation.

The medical history which is part of the evaluation for choice of a method often yields information which should be considered not only for its medical relevance but also for its psychological relevance. For example, in the college-age group, between one-fourth and one-third of all females still have some menstrual irregularity. Not uncommonly, a student is worried about the implications of this irregularity. She may have doubts about her future fertility, her femininity, or her maturity. If she is put on the pill with little or no comment about the meanings, to her, of her menstrual pattern, these anxieties may persist and contribute to contraceptive discontinuance.

In the course of several years, students often need or want to use a variety of contraceptive methods. The first follow-up appointment (about six weeks after starting pills or having an IUD inserted) is a time when initial side effects can be evaluated or a change considered. More often it is a question of changing need due to a change in frequency of intercourse or a change in attitude. As mentioned earlier, changing birth control methods can represent a significant developmental step or may signal a problem, and its meaning should be adequately explored with the patient or couple.

There is a wide variation in reaction to side-effects so that an objective measure of a particular side-effect may be misleading; the subjective response must also be considered. Obviously, pain threshold and tolerance vary. Some students cannot cope with minor cramping from an IUD while others go too far in the other direction. They are so determined to have an IUD that they tolerate levels of pain that may indicate a problem without complaining to the doctor. Knowing a bit about the individual personality in this regard can help the doctor to tailor instructions about side effects to the person. We have also been impressed with the intense response some young women have to a slight alteration in body configuration or weight gain due to the pill. In this age group there may be particular hypersensitivity to such issues. Some students have been unable to cope, emotionally, with a weight increase of even three pounds. These are generally young women who appear to border on being anorectic. Their body-image is precarious and their sense of ego integrity is tied to maintaining a particular body image. A minor alteration for such a young woman is a major psychological stress and should be recognized as such. This might be a fruitful moment for discussion of feelings about the body, anxieties and preoccupations, and possibly an opportunity for suggesting counseling or therapy.

Follow-up is an important ingredient in good contraceptive care. A day or two after getting a diaphragm, the female returns with her diaphragm in place to have it checked. Does it fit properly? Has she inserted it correctly? Approximately 10 percent of students have *not* inserted the diaphragm correctly and need to be taught again how to do it. The value of this extra reassurance about the method may also be important in promoting its regular use. The six-week return visit for students starting on the pill serves a reassuring role and provides an opportunity to talk about the initiation of intercourse, as is often the case when the student has come for pills just before having intercourse for the first time.

Unwanted Pregnancy

Between 1969 and 1975* 85 pregnant undergraduate and graduate students were seen in the SCS. We believe that this number represents almost all students who became pregnant during those years. In 1971, the Yale Health Plan went into effect. It provides abortion for all members (which included almost every student), and it is unlikely that many students chose to seek and pay for their own abortion. In 1969-1971, some students may have arranged for abortions on their own although this was not easy to do, in those days, and the SCS was known to be a resource for legal abortions.

Between 1969 and 1975 the SCS provided comprehensive care for pregnant students. They generally saw us from the time of suspected pregnancy through diagnosis, abortion, and follow-up. Only two students chose to continue the pregnancy. One arranged for adoption, the other kept her child. Since 1975 P.S. has not done abortion procedures and the majority of pregnant students are now seen in the gynecology service of the health plan. The availability of on-going counseling which was built into the system

---

* We were on sabbatical leave in the 1975-1976 academic year.

has thus been lost, although students who are obviously distressed or develop emotional or sexual problems are referred for appropriate help.

We believe that the comprehensive approach that was used by the SCS was a good model of care for all pregnant students, not only those who show obvious signs of emotional upset, and is worth describing. The care involved can be broken down into seven steps.*

Pregnancy Test

Pregnancy tests are provided through university health services. In the early years of the SCS when unwanted pregnancy had a heavier stigma than it does today, students would sometimes submit a urine sample under a false name to assure absolute confidentiality. Recently, though, almost no students have done this.

Preliminary Discussion

If the result of the pregnancy test is negative, we still suggest an appointment to see us (95 percent of the pregnancy tests done for undergraduate students have been negative). Almost invariably, those who have had a negative test warrant counseling time to discuss their anxieties and, perhaps, their contraceptive needs. Some had intercourse one time and feared being pregnant. Others had not had intercourse at all but were relating sexually in new ways. Still others had been having unprotected intercourse for a while. For them seeking professional help, albeit just a pregnancy test, represented a first step in dealing with a conflict. If the test is positive, an immediate appointment is made to discuss the situation. In this circumstance, as in most others, the SCS encourages participation of the partner if the woman wishes it. Of the 85 pregnant women, 78 were seen with their partner. Usually both P.S. and L.S. are present.

This is obviously an important discussion. Since the vast majority of students seen by us have already decided they want an abor-

---

* See also Philip Sarrel, *Teenage Pregnancy, SIECUS Guide #14.* September 1971.

tion, most of this hour-long appointment does not need to focus on alternatives, although we do always review alternatives and discuss the reasons for choosing one or another.

Although the decision about what to do has usually been made, there is almost always some underlying ambivalence about abortion. These lurking doubts, feelings of repugnance about the act, guilty feelings, and wishful fantasies that the situation were different and the pregnancy could be carried through should be heard. Helping the young woman and young man to talk about their ambivalence is not the same as insisting that they *must* have mixed feelings or forcing them to view the situation as the doctor or counselor views it. We disagree with the attitude expressed by Whittington: "The counselor must help the applicant face a painful existential dilemma: whether to kill one nascent human being in order to enhance the quality of life of another person" [3].

The couple (and we use this term loosely, as some are in the earliest stages of a relationship—more potential than actual) is focused on the immediate situation. Before going on to discuss procedures, a physical exam is done to reconfirm pregnancy and establish the duration of gestation. This examination can serve as a kind of prelude to the abortion procedure and should be done with sensitivity. The male partner may be present during this examination if the couple so chooses.

After the examination, details of the procedure are described. We also try to cover questions of family involvement. Should a parent or parents be told? This is not legally required but it may be desirable. Or it may not. At times students have not thought through the pros and cons of telling their parents about their pregnancy. Most often, as we have talked about their parents' situation and their basic relationship with their parents, the decision has been for the students to talk to someone at home about the pregnancy. However, there have been times when it has become clear that the students should keep the information to themselves. For example, one student's father had recently had a heart attack. She planned to tell her mother. When we talked about the home situation, it became clear to her that her mother, as well as her father, was already under great stress. Her boyfriend agreed that her parents shouldn't be told but did suggest that his parents would be accepting of the problem and helpful. The couple did talk with his parents who also agreed that it was no time for either her mother or father to be put under extra stress. By the time of the one year follow up, the pregnancy and abortion had become a thing of the past. The couple eventually married. Although it had been difficult for the girl to keep a secret from her mother—it was the first time that she had done something about which she didn't confide in her mother—not sharing seemed to have worked out best for all concerned. In another situation, a student felt she had to tell her father that she was going to have an abortion. When she did, he told her he no longer considered her his daughter. Fortunately, her mother supported her decision and stayed with her through what was truly an ordeal. Finally, after six years, her father accepted her back into the household.

What about friends? Should they be told? Is there at least one friend to stand by? This is particularly important when the male partner cannot be continuously available.

During this hour we are learning about the couple's relationship and the circumstances surrounding the conception. In 20 to 25 cases out of the 85, the conception was certainly or probably due to contraceptive failure. When no birth control or very ineffective means were employed, we want to understand something of the meaning of unprotected intercourse for this twosome. We do *not*, however, focus on this during the preliminary visit unless the woman or couple wants to. This is a time for gathering impressions, not for giving interpretation.

There has usually been a difference with regard to psychological and interpersonal issues when the pregnancy represents contraceptive failure and not the result of failure to use any contraceptive technique. However, it is important to recognize that even in those situations where the pregnancy is indeed a failure of a contraceptive method, the fact of being pregnant and having to terminate the pregnancy engenders feelings and conflicts which should be given an opportunity for expression.

During this preliminary interview the male half of the couple is often rather quiet and a bit removed although anxious to be supportive and helpful. One can easily be fooled into thinking that the experience is basically hers while he is a sympathetic bystander who can cope with this situation on his own. Our experience suggests that this is not true. In follow up visits in the early months of the SCS we were impressed by the extent of upset the young men expressed and so we began to focus on *his* needs as well. Before the actual procedure he may not be very aware of his own feelings. He feels called upon to play a strong, supportive role, allowing the female to cry and be openly unstrung.

If he is given an opportunity talk on his own (in our case, to P.S.), he can focus more clearly on his own feelings and let go a little. One of the feelings frequently expressed by these young men has been extreme guilt and an envy of the female for being able to "have it out" through the physical experience of the abortion—a kind of catharsis. Young men may also be frightened by the potential escalation in commitment to the young women. This has been particularly true when the pregnancy has occurred within the first five times the couple has had intercourse. Three of the couples we have seen became pregnant the first time they had intercourse; two other couples had had intercourse twice! Although these are the more dramatic situations, there is often a male feeling of having been "trapped." We will not deal directly with relationship issues at this early visit but do start to develop an understanding of what is at stake with regard to the relationship, knowing that we can pick up on these issues at subsequent visits.

The Abortion

Abortion procedures can be traumatic. In follow-up discussions women have most often described as traumatic any sudden pain *for which they were unprepared.* It was the surprise and fear engendered by the pain that upset them. It would seem important then for anyone doing an abortion to be honest about possible pain and to prepare the woman for it.

In recent years abortion centers have taken over the majority of abortion procedures. There are certainly many advantages to these centers, but one disadvantage, we feel, is a tendency toward an anti-male atmosphere. Although the majority of students go to the abortion center with their male friend, he is often excluded from the proceedings. All-female groups, while supportive of the woman in crisis, may be openly furious at all men and indulge in stereotypes about male selfishness or how men just use women for one purpose and then cop out. While this does represent some women's reality, it is not universal. Such a discussion at a moment of extreme emotional vulnerability may be harmful for young women who are learning about male-female relationships and sex. We are in favor of consciousness-raising but not in this super-charged context. There is also the young man to consider. His exclusion is not likely to make him less of a male chauvinist nor help him in coping with the crisis of an unwanted pregnancy.

At the time of the abortion, along with the routine medical advice, the woman should be told that she may experience a depressed, shaky period starting about 48 hours after the procedure. It may last from 12 to 24 hours. This reaction is not uncommon and is probably related to the sharp drop in hormone levels. It is more likely to occur when the pregnancy has lasted longer.

Telephone call after the procedure
If P.S. did not do the abortion himself, but was the physician providing continuity, this call was scheduled for the night of the procedure. When he was the doctor who did the procedure, this call was scheduled for two days later. There is a variety of medical concerns at this time. Two women have needed to be seen on an emergency basis because their post-abortion emotional reaction was very intense. Almost all of the women have welcomed the reassurance that depressed or anxious feelings are a transitory phenomenon. This phone call is the time to check on whether or not there has been a temperature elevation which might indicate a low-grade infection. If a vacuum curettage has been done, the most common procedure, there may have been little or almost

no bleeding. It has been important to reassure that this is normal. Not infrequently basic questions about tampons, bathing, sexual intercourse, and so on, have been asked and answered two days earlier, but the advice had not been appreciated in the midst of everything else that was going on. It is also important at the 48 hour contact to let patients know about sudden heavy bleeding which often occurs about a week after the abortion procedure. Thought to be a part of the healing process, the bleeding can be frightening especially if by that time the woman has had no bleeding and feels the crisis is over. This bleeding is usually of short duration and is usually treated simply by bed rest for a few hours.

TWO-WEEK FOLLOW-UP VISIT. A physical examination is done. At this visit feelings about the experience are aired. The majority of women (and partners) say they feel "fine" and have no very strong emotional reaction. Although studies have shown that abortion does not usually have serious emotional sequelae, it is, none-the less, an important emotional event, particularly for young people. Even when there are few conscious conflicts after the procedure, we have learned that almost all the women and some of the men can recall one or more dreams that clearly reflect the themes of loss and sorrow. Asking specifically about recent dreams has helped to bring these feelings into awareness.

By this visit attention has shifted to the meaning of the conception and abortion for the relationship. Sometimes the pregnancy has occurred very early in a relationship and causes a premature cementing in of guilt. On the other hand, sharing this experience may genuinely deepen an early relationship. These couples need the opportunity to sort out and air their feelings.

There may be a need to discuss future contraception. Sometimes it was a conflict about contraceptive method which led to the unwanted pregnancy. The conflict can reflect deeper problems, for example, his insistence on using condoms to maintain control or her anger at being "the female, who bears all burdens in this male chauvinist society." Previous carelessness about birth control is important to talk about at this stage. It probably reflects some un-recognized ambivalence about the birth control itself or about pregnancy.

There are many possible unconscious reasons for wanting a pregnancy and it is not always appropriate for a professional in a doctor's or even a counselor's role to try to ascertain these dynamics. On the other hand, certain themes are recurrent and fairly close to consciousness. It can be important to clarify these dynamics if a repeat pregnancy is to be avoided. In a university environment one recurrent theme is a more or less conscious conflict between career and marriage-family. At crucial junctures (such as graduation from college or after passing orals but before doing a doctoral dissertation) a young woman may act out one side of her mixed feelings by getting pregnant [4].

Another theme which is frequently encountered is a persistent anxiety about femininity and fertility. This is an example of a situation in which it is helpful to have had continuity of medical care. If the doctor doing the abortion has seen the young woman before and knows the history of her concerns about irregular periods, lack of orgasms, or small breasts, the possible meaning of the pregnancy as proof of feminine adequacy will be more obvious. We have found that this area can be opened to discussion by stating the positive side. "Now you know you are fertile. How do you feel about that?"

The assertion of femininity may also be an assertion of adulthood and independence. Here too, one would like to separate the underlying wish, which is healthy, from the form of its expression, unwanted pregnancy, which is not. One can help a young woman or couple to use the pregnancy-abortion experience to enhance feelings of independence, maturity, and mastery. In the college-age group, an abortion may be the very first major decision and act taken apart from parents. The intercourse itself may not have been a thought-through decision at all and not a genuine act of independence. The experience of painful but thoughtful deliberation, discussing the situation with professionals and going through the medical procedures can be positively maturing.

Pregnancy in the context of promiscuity has already been discussed (see section on promiscuity in Chapter 4.)

An unexpected pregnancy can also be a cry for help or at least a situation in which emotional disturbance comes to the attention of a professional. Of the 85 women seen by us, almost one-fourth entered psychotherapy. Many more were seen by us in some kind of on-going counseling, alone or with their partner.

Any of the themes mentioned above may be applicable to the male. He was, after all, one half of the unwanted pregracy. He may be ambivalent about marriage or be worried about his masculinity, fertility, or independence, or be promiscous or have a problem for which he should see a psychotherapist. The lack of emphasis in professional thinking on the male's role in unwanted pregnancy is quite remarkable. Even someone as experienced and thoughtful as Sadja Goldsmith, the Medical Director of Planned Parenthood in San Francisco, seems to fall into this trap, laying blame for unwanted pregnancy entirely on the female's doorstep and then reminding us that young men do foolish and harmful things, too, to prove their masculinity. "Racing around in cars or motorcycles is a typical example—the young man may precipitate an accident that causes as many problems as the girl's unwanted pregnancy" (5).

The expression *bad boy* can have many meanings, but we all know what a "bad girl" does!

THE SIX-WEEK FOLLOW-UP VISIT. By this visit the impact of the pregnancy experience upon the relationship and upon sexuality is becoming apparent. There are reality factors following an abortion which may contribute to a sexual problem. Changing hormone levels may affect mood and libido. While hormonal levels usually return to normal within four to six weeks, it can take longer. Some women do not resume their menstrual pattern for as long as three months. Cervicitis and vaginitis seem prevalent in the weeks following abortion (possibly due to the temporarily low hormone levels). Finally, making an adjustment to a new form of contraception which may or may not be trusted and may cause side-effects can be very disruptive of sex life.

Some individuals or couples stop having intercourse or stop relating sexually in any way. A strategic retreat to regroup psychic forces can be helpful but it may also signal the beginnings of a chronic withdrawal from sex. In two instances we have seen young women move in the direction of celibacy and a puritannical public image in the year following an abortion.

When intercourse is resumed, there may be some sexual dysfunction. The most common problem we have seen is vaginismus. Considering the meaning of the abortion, the shock of the experience, and the physical procedures involving the vagina, the occurrence of vaginismus is not surprising. Treatment should involve discussion of feelings about the experience, the current sexual relationship, fears of a repeat pregnancy and anger as well as a behavioral approach to the muscle spasm.

Occasionally, we have seen male dysfunction following an abortion. As with the female, there is a need to understand the meaning of the abortion experience and current anxieties.

A couple's relationship may be at a crisis in the weeks following an abortion. Again, as at the two week visit, there should be an opportunity to talk about this with a doctor/counselor.

LONG-TERM FOLLOW-UP. Approximately one-third of the young women or couples seen by us need some kind of on-going counseling or treatment. Even when this is not necessary, we try to have at least some long term follow-up. A visit three months after the abortion is often scheduled. We have also learned that an emotional crisis very frequently occurs about the time of the "due date"— when the baby would have been born had the pregnancy continued. Without consciously recognizing any relationship to the abortion, young women often become depressed or emotionally labile on this "anniversary." This is an opportunity for emotional closure. We try to schedule revisits at about the due date, without specifying why this time is selected. Then, if the young woman or couple are having an anniversary reaction, it can be clarified.

Results

Probably the most impressive result is the occurrence of only three subsequent unplanned pregnancies among the 85 women. Two-year follow-up was possible for almost everyone and up to four-year follow-up for many. Two of the three women who became pregnant again had seen us first after they had had a previous pregnancy and abortion. This experience is in contrast to other studies which have shown very high rates of repeat pregnancy in an adolescent population. For example, in one study 95 of 100 teenagers had a repeat pregnancy within two years [6]. That was a study of a noncollege population. Even among more highly educated women there is a repeat rate which has been estimated to be as high as 25 percent in the two years following an abortion!

Contraceptive continuance has been almost 100 percent. Interpersonal issues have been able to be dealt with by the same counseling team that first dealt with the pregnancy crisis. We think sex problems have been avoided through such an on-going approach.

References

1. Kantner, John F. and Zelnik, Melvin, "Sexual and Contraceptive Experience of Young Unmarried Women in the U.S. 1976 and 1971" in *Family Planning Perspectives*, Vol. 9(2), 1977, p. 62.
2. Kantner and Zelnik [1], p. 67.
3. Whittington, H. D., "Role of the Counselor in Abortion" in *Abortion Techniques and Services, Excerpta Medica*—Amsterdam, 1972, pp. 117-119.
4. Sarrel, Philip M. and Lidz, Ruth, "Contraceptive Failure—Psychosocial Factors: The Unwed" in Calderone, Mary (Ed.), *Manual of Family Planning and Contraceptive Practice*, 2nd Edition, Baltimore, William and Wilkins, Co., June 1970.
5. Goldsmith, Sadja, "Teenagers and Abortion: Some Special Considerations" in *Abortion Techniques and Services*, pp. 147-150.
6. Sarrel, Philip M. and Davis, Clarence, "The Young Unwed Primipara" in *American Journal of Obstetrics and Gynecology*, Vol. 95(5), July 1966, p. 722.

10

Sex Education

Ten years ago sex courses were uncommon, if not rare, on the college campus. They had been there. In the 1930s and 1940s, many schools had lectures in hygiene or physical education which dealt with sexual issues. Some schools had "marriage courses," many of which were well presented and well received but, for one reason or another, were dropped. Most notable was Kinsey's experience at Indiana University. The university authorities gave him the choice of either continuing his sex research or his "marriage" course but not both. The sex research had been a direct outgrowth of his need to find accurate information for presentation in his course. He chose to continue the research. The course was dropped [1].

At first our commitment to teach sex on campus was questioned by experienced sex educators. In 1966 the emphasis was on developing sex education programs in elementary schools. It was felt that college students "knew it all" and that, by that age, it was really too late to teach anything that could be helpful.

Still, the time was ripe. New information was becoming available. 1966 saw the publication of Masters and Johnson's *Human Sexual Response*. The laws were changing: in 1967 contraception became legal in Connecticut and Massachusetts. It then became legal to teach contraception. And there was the pill. The sex revolution had not yet hit with full force, but the evolution certainly had speeded up. Our first experience as sex educators was at Yale Medical School in the fall of 1966. One of us, Philip Sarrel, organized a multi-disciplinary series of lectures on various topics related to sex: contraception, abortion, sex response, etc. The lectures were followed by small group discussions in which faculty and students were able to react to the material presented. Although the course caused much discussion within the medical school and did serve to bring members of the faculty together who ordinarily would not have the opportunity to know one another, it really wasn't a very good course. The basic areas were covered, sometimes adequately, sometimes not. The small discussion groups were top heavy with three experts in each: from psychiatry, gynecology, urology and other fields. In one of the small groups five medical students met with two full professors and a dean! Needless to say, it was all very intellectualized and never got beneath the surface. But it was a beginning, and we learned from the experience. We learned basically that students *want facts* and *need* to talk about their *feelings*. A course should be able to provide the opportunity for both.

In the next two years we focused on developing a program for college students. It was really a matter of fortuitous circumstances, as a military obligation required moving to an Air Force base in Massachusetts. We met with a group of students and faculty at Mount Holyoke College and presented our proposal to initiate a sexuality course. They were enthusiastic and the course was held in the Spring of 1968.

Since 1968, more and more colleges have recognized that there is a need and a place for sex education on the campus. Some schools offer a full credit, full semester course complete with lectures, reading assignments and exams. Among the best known were the course by the late Dr. Leslie McCary at Houston and the Lunde-Khatchadourian course at Stanford. At Amherst, Dr. Haskell Coplin offers a course which includes a full series of lectures and the option to participate in small group discussions, an option which most students take. The Sex Attitude Restructuring (SAR) course originating in San Francisco through the Glide Foundation and further developed at the University of Minnesota is another approach. Thousands of students have participated in the intensive two-day exposure to lectures, films, body movement, and small group discussions. The feedback from students is very positive and more and more schools are adopting the SAR approach. Many schools have had "sex-ins"—a day or a week-end of lectures about various topics given by national authorities. Some schools have been very innovative, including in their presentations an exhibit of erotic art, an original play by students on a sexual theme, contraceptive exhibits, etc.

While we have had the privilege of participating in many types of sex education programs, what we have done on our own has been to continue to develop and refine an approach stemming from the first efforts. The process is one of continual change, but let us describe what we are doing at present and why.

At Yale, the course in human sexuality is just one part of an ongoing program. Before describing the course in detail, we want to place it in the context of this broader program. The other facets of the program are: (1) the Sex Counseling Service; (2) the booklet for students, "Sex at Yale"; and (3) a student-run counseling service.

The Sex Counseling Service has already been described. It is through our work in counseling that we learn about students and sex—their experiences and development, their dilemmas and dysfunctions. Without this familiarity, we couldn't begin to give as relevant and interesting a course. The course also encourages students to use the counseling services. There is always a marked increase in calls for appointments during and after the course. This is a point to be noted because some schools offer a course but have no counseling back-up. We feel strongly that sex education and individual counseling should go hand in hand whenever possible.

Soon after establishing the Sex Counseling Service, we decided to offer a course in human sexuality at Yale similar to the type of course developed at Mt. Holyoke and Smith. In those courses we had learned the value of establishing a Committee on Human Sexuality. Made up of students, other interested faculty, and us, the Committee is responsible for organizing and conducting the course. Two students from each class serve on the Committee. They register students for the course, distribute and collect course materials, readings, questionnaires, etc., organize the training day for the group leaders, arrange for classrooms, audiotaping, film projection, etc. After each course meeting they collect the student evaluation forms. At the weekly meetings of the Committee they contribute their own criticisms and ideas about course content and make suggestions for course improvements. The Committee is also responsible for the *Sex at Yale* booklet and has played an instrumental role in the establishment of the Student-to-Student Counseling Program.

Sex at Yale is a 64-page booklet for Yale students. The idea originated in the late 1960s with the appearance of a Canadian booklet about sex written by students for distribution to students in Canada and the United States. For a number of reasons, the Canadian pamphlet was not usable on our campus. We got together with a group of students and decided to write our own booklet, based on the needs and experiences of Yale students. The first edition, called *Sex and the Yale Student,* came out in 1970. In it we wrote a section on most commonly asked questions about sex and our responses to those questions. The remaining sections of the book, on genital anatomy, contraception, pregnancy, abortion, sex counseling, and Yale services were written by the students and based on our lectures given in the sexuality course, plus their own readings.

Sex and the Yale Student was a successful venture. The booklets were paid for by money collected in the course. They were then distributed to every Yale undergraduate and graduate free of charge. In all, over 16,000 copies were eventually given away. The response of students, faculty, and alumni was and continues to be positive.

Not surprisingly, the publication and distribution of *Sex and the Yale Student* was picked up by the news media. As a result of the publicity and the positive reaction of those involved at Yale, the booklet eventually was re-written as *The Student Guide to Sex on Campus,* which sold over 100,000 copies, primarily to other schools who distributed it to their students. By 1974 the material was outdated. A revision was done and the booklet renamed *Sex at Yale.* It continues to be distributed to incoming students free of charge.

The booklet provides an opportunity for students to learn about sex on campus. They don't have to read it but over 90 percent do.

A survey of 300 randomly selected students, done in 1974, showed that almost all found it to be of some personal value. They appreciated being given something they could read in private when and where they chose. They also appreciated a source of information that was reliable and which helped them to know the issues confronting a student population. An important aspect of the book was that it described the sex counseling and sex education program and let students know what services were available to them. As one student said, "My reaction was that I didn't think I would need any of your services, but it was important to know you were there in case I ever did!"

Another program has been a student-to-student counseling service. Similar to programs which have been successful at other schools, the students who wish can call or come in to speak to a trained undergraduate counselor. The program has been on a relatively small scale. Most students using it either feel they don't want to bother a professional person with what they consider to be a minor issue or simply that they are more comfortable talking to some one of their own age. Still, most students prefer the professional services offered by the University Health Plan—their individual physicians, the gynecology clinic, and the mental hygiene division which provides individual psychotherapy and group therapy in addition to our own sex counseling services.

"Topics in Human Sexuality"—One Model

The sex course, called "Topics in Human Sexuality," is a noncredit series of lectures followed by small group discussions. Students register for the course and pay a $5.00 fee to the Student Committee on Human Sexuality. At the present time at Yale, registration is limited to 250 students. The students in charge of the course's organization strive to have as close to a 50-50 balance of men and women as possible. The course is open to all undergraduates and to a limited number (usually enough for one small group discussion) of graduate students. (Medical, nursing, public health, and divinity students have sex courses of their own.)

The "topics" lectures are titled: "Female Sexuality," "Male Sexuality," "Sex as a Medium of Exchange," "Contraception and Abortion," "Pregnancy and Birth," and "Potpourri." The last is a discussion of subjects suggested by the students during the course. Before the course begins, the students are asked to reserve the entire evening each week that the course is held. We have found in recent years that if the six evenings are fitted into three weeks of the semester it is easier for students to arrange the time without interfering with other obligations. The lectures usually last an hour to an hour and a half. The question period adds another half hour. For the remainder of the evening the students are in their small discussion groups. The lectures are audio taped and tapes are available in the university language library.

At the time of registration students are given a choice of whether or not they wish to participate in a small group. Over 80 percent usually choose to join such a group. Each group is made up of six to eight students as well as a male and a female group leader. The group leaders are students themselves. Usually one is a first-year medical student and the other an undergraduate who has taken the course in a previous year. Generally speaking, the medical students have also participated in a previous course as we now find that about one third of the first year class at the medical school have taken our course either at Yale or at one of the other colleges where we have initiated this program.

When registering for the course, each student is given a questionnaire about sex information, attitudes and behavior. They are asked to fill it out in private and submit it anonymously. They keep the questionnaire but turn in their answer sheet one week before the course begins. When they return the completed answer sheet they are given their admission pass to the course. In this way close to 100 percent of the course participants are able to contribute basic data for use in the course. When they are given the questionnaire, an attached information sheet explains that the rationale for the questionnaire is to provide up-to-date sex information about students. If the answer sheets are returned by one week before the start of the course, there is time to process the data and present it in the course. As students have done this each year for ten years, it is also possible to compare present knowledge, attitudes and behavior with the past.

The weeks before the course begins are a busy time. The Student Committee on Sexuality meets weekly. Student group leaders are found (usually 20 male and 20 female) and arrangements are made for their training and supervision. On the week-end before the course begins one day is set aside for group leader training and orientation. After the Student Committee has dealt with organizational details, we talk about the history of the sex course, its goals, the principles behind the format, the use of films, and any innovations we plan to try.

The bulk of time in training focuses on the small groups and the role of student leaders or "facilitators." In the undergraduate course, leaders are not meant to be expert in the subject matter or in small group dynamics but simply to deal with practical aspects of organization and encourage a level of discussion which avoids over-intellectualization on the one hand and too much personal revelation or "therapizing" on the other. We recommend that the male-female team of facilitators borrow a concept from co-therapy (as used in Masters and Johnson sex therapy)—that the female leader should pay attention to the needs, questions and group participation of the females in the group while the male leader does the same for the male contingent. Apart from this degree of facilitation and organization, the leaders participate as regular group members.

After a discussion of the purposes and philosophy of small groups and the role of the leaders, there is a simulation of an evening in the course. We give a mini-lecture, show a film, and the student leaders divide up into two or three small groups which are led by faculty advisors, ourselves or a psychiatric resident. The faculty advisor can use this mini-group experience as a springboard for demonstrating and teaching about group interaction. Role-play is sometimes used as well.

The first night of the course is an important one. The students are keenly interested, but anxious. They represent a fairly wide spectrum of knowledge about and experience with sex. The kick-off lecture should contain solid information and should confront emotionally charged material, but it shouldn't overwhelm. Although content matters, a sex course is one place in which Marshall MacLuhan's famous dictum strictly applies—"The medium is the message." The general tone and style of presentation *is* the message. Over and over again students say that the most important and helpful thing about the lecture series—but especially this first lecture where they simply don't know what to expect—is the ease, humor and humaneness with which sex is discussed.

In 1975, for the first time, the kick-off lecture was on female sexuality rather than male or the even older first lecture topic of "Anatomy and Physiology." We believe that a female should lecture about female sexuality partly as a safeguard against male chauvinist bias and partly because of the subjective nature of some of the material to be presented. Our gestures in the direction of Womens' Liberation—having the first lecture by a female, about females—led to a standing ovation at the start of the 1975 course! We have continued to start the series with the female sexuality lecture. By 1979, however, although this remains the best way to begin, it doesn't seem to be such a "big deal" to anyone anymore.

The material covered in "Female Sexuality" focuses on normal development from birth through adolescence, touching on subjects such as children's sex play, the little girl's concepts of penis versus her own anatomy, how society can give girls negative attitudes towards themselves and their sexuality, and so on. The material on adolescence is put in the framework of our concept of "sexual unfolding" and includes material about private body experiences such as feelings about breasts, menstruation, vaginal secretions, and masturbation. Normal genital anatomy and the physiologic changes that take place when a female responds sexually are always included.

Along with all this useful information we are, of course, using words; technical words like *clitoris, vulva,* and *orgasm* as well as juicier words like *come* or *wet pants.* We don't use words like *fuck* or *screw* or *prick* instead of saying *intercourse* or *penis;* it's just not our style. But we often manage to talk about the words that can be used in describing sex and then we do say *fuck.*

On the first night a film is also shown. The best course opener has been a film entitled *Looking for Me*. It is a film made by a dance therapist working with normal and disturbed children. There are a number of relationships between the film and the course in sexuality. Its depiction of the body and the basic freedom of body expression that children have, and which is so often lost as we become socialized, highlights a basic concept in sexology: Sex is a natural function. Adults can give up control and let their bodies re-establish their own natural rhythms unaltered by performance demands or cultural dictates of what their bodies should do. Later on, when we discuss spectatoring in sexual dysfunction, we will stress the centrality of this idea of the need for spontaneity in body expression. The film also tackles the issue of developing trust between people on a body level. After ten years of using many films in sex education courses, "Looking for Me" remains our favorite and the one we feel has the most impact on the most students.

There is another film we have used on the first night which has elicited enough varying reaction so that we no longer use it at the very beginning of the course. This is a scientific film about female sex response. It shows the anatomy and the different changes in female physiology which accompany sex response. We think it is a unique and excellent film. However, there are two reasons why it might be held until after the first night. First, the confrontation with the anatomy. Students are all curious about female anatomy. Despite previous sex education courses or films many students—female and male—are not familiar and comfortable with female genitalia. Seeing vulvas and vaginas on the screen, in color and during sex response can be a shock. The second reaction is to the mechanical dimension of sex that can be identified in the film. Students write afterwards that they've had enough of mechanical sex. Ninety-five percent of them have seen a film with intercourse in it before coming to college. What they were looking for—and said so very clearly when other films depicted it—was a human relationship, a message about sex which included tenderness, affection, and caring. Interestingly, the film to be described shortly, which students felt showed these qualities most clearly is a film called *Vir*

Amat, a film of a male homosexual couple. The female sex response film is now part of an optional "film night" which follows the lecture series.

Immediately after the question period, the students go to their assigned groups. The two student leaders and the eight to ten student members usually meet in one of the student leader's rooms. The male to female balance is sometimes equal but more frequently is a ratio of six to four owing to the much greater number of male students at Yale. After people have introduced themselves, the group leaders explain that the same group will meet each time. They ask for an understanding that whatever is discussed in the group be regarded as confidential.

Groups usually meet for about two to three hours. Invariably, the discussion starts with some referral to material presented in the lecture. The tendency, at first, is to intellectualize. The group leaders are aware that, although a warming up time is necessary, eventually people need to get to talking about their feelings—feelings brought to the course, feelings arising in the "sexuality" classroom, and feelings generated in the group. Students who have never talked to anyone about their sexual experiences and attitudes find that they can do so and that it is rewarding to share with others. There is a wide range of experiences, attitudes and values with which others sometimes identify and sometimes question, and it is the process of mutual recognition and questioning which makes the groups worthwhile. Not infrequently students will write after the first few group meetings, that, although they haven't said much, the meetings have been personally important to them. One or two students usually drop out of each group.

The main feedback about the course from its students is in the form of a written statement; a Post-Meeting Reaction (PMR) form. Students are asked to write about the most and least helpful aspects of the lecture, the films when they are used and the discussion groups. They are also asked to make suggestions for material to be included in the next lecture. The PMR's are filled out each night by each student, collected by the members of the committee and returned to us by the next day for our review. We find that we are frequently given ideas to discuss in the subsequent lectures and that the PMR's help us to have a "feel" for the group we are teaching. The following quotes are taken from PMR's filled out after the female sexuality lecture in response to the question "What was most helpful?"

Quotes from females
"It was all very helpful. Really, that is, females *need* to know about females."

"The masturbation material."

"Recognizing the feeling of the woman trying to catch up in the face of such an obvious sign of excitement in her partner's erect penis—and that actually both partners are equally excited."

"Factual information on female response."

"How to avoid hurting men in certain areas."

"The negative effects of achievement anxiety."

"Thoughts about pressure, competition and other counter-productive elements."

"Oh! When you talked about teaching your daughter about her anatomy. I called my mother and bawled her out for neutral or negative messages."

Quotes from males
"The easy, warm style."

"The stories and information about the wide range of normal. It makes me feel more normal—as if I'm not the only one who worries about sex."

"Honesty, interest, straightforwardness."

"The feelings and moods of the growing, developing sexual human."

"Even information I already knew was helpful."

"Things that make the process more personal."

"The talk on vaginitis and the clitoris. Could much better understand what a woman's genital area looked like."

The male sexuality lecture is in many ways similar to the female so far as the outline is concerned—factors in development which affect sexual attitudes and behavior, early masturbatory and interpersonal experiences including homosexuality and body feelings. Then there are the more specifically male "themes" in relating to females—competition, performance, anxiety, confusion and humiliation; the pressure to have sex and the loneliness of the campus scene. Males have misconceptions about their own bodies. They are often confused about or simply ignorant of the female body. Male sex response is similarly misunderstood despite exposure to an ever-growing list of resource materials.

In recent years we have woven material relating to homosexuality into the first two lectures on male and female sexuality. We feel that so many students are dealing with the emergence of their sexual identity, whether it is to be homosexual, heterosexual, or bisexual, that discussing homosexuality together with everything else seems more appropriate than segregating it in a separate lecture. Thus, in the female sexuality lecture, there is discussion of homosexual experiences in adolescence along with other comments about physical and emotional development. The main presentation of homosexual material, however, is held for the second course meeting. It is a tough subject for students to deal with, the working out of sexual identity being one of the primary tasks they face at their stage of development. The goal of the first night is to start to get students comfortable talking about sex. By the second night, they can deal with a more anxiety-provoking subject.

Homosexuality is presented in three ways: in the lecture material, by a homosexual panel discussion, and by a film about a homosexual couple. In our lecture we draw on case material to present a realistic picture of issues which confront homosexuals who see us. We also describe the homosexual feelings and experiences which are so much a part of everyone's development.

Another picture of homosexuality is presented by the panel discussion. Men and women from the Gay Alliance come to the course and talk about themselves becoming aware of their homosexuality, the problems these feelings create with regard to family, friends, and careers and their feelings about "coming out." For most students this is a very important communication with the homosexual community. Many of the myths about homosexuality—who they are, what they do with each other, what being homosexual means—are dispelled. Ignorance, fear, and hostility can be and often are replaced by an understanding and non-judgmental attitude.

The film we show during the male sexuality lecture is called *Vir Amat* [3]. It is a film of a male homosexual couple who live together. It is explicit in its portrayal of the way in which the two men share with each other—in and out of bed. We include a number of quotes from students' reactions to this film, for, as one might imagine, there is a wide spectrum of response.

Male Response to Film
"My reactions to begin with were surprising for me in that what I was seeing created few negative feelings, but as the film progressed I saw things explicitly that I have only considered superficially before I was uncomfortable and I think that a great many defense mechanisms took over and I think I stopped myself from feeling a lot."

"Helped give me different perspective on homosexuality."

"No better way could have been found to deal with male sexuality or with homosexuality."

"I did not like this film. Although gay organizations are 'normal,' I still have my doubts."

"A good way to confront the issue—creates no problem for me—it's nothing I haven't seen or done on occasion here at school."

"I wasn't sure how I would react, to my surprise I wasn't disturbed at all, but rather felt 'that's cool.' "

"Very upsetting—found myself at one point fantasizing that the police ought to come into their room and break things up. Eye-opening cause I thought homosexuality didn't 'bother me'."

"The film of the two gay lovers was very touching. People should be more tolerant of gays. It's hard to admit if you are."

"Found it repulsive."

"Good film—honest—not my cup of tea."

"Unlike *Behind the Green Door*, there was a feeling of warmth in this film. I could see many so-called heterosexual attributes in their relations and was really a little jealous."

"Terrible—The only type of sexual affairs I can't watch is male homosexuality."

"It kind of floored me. I have to admit that I would have preferred not to see it. I guess I'm not as liberal in my attitudes as I thought I was and the film really made me feel uncomfortable because I really can't conceive of the situation as a love relation as I perceive it."

"It was good for me to see. I am male and I was surprised to see myself getting aroused."

"Uncomfortable to watch but probably worth the experience."

"Hard to take but worth it (probably)?"

"Very incredible. I could respond to the film because I recognized things I have done with women but I still have problems thinking about doing them with another man."

"I feel empathy for the sensual pleasure (though I am not into oral contact to such a degree), I did not feel that it was unnatural—though I felt some queasiness because homosexuality is socially unacceptable, i.e. I should have felt repulsed according to the mores of society, but wasn't."

"Easier to take intellectually than in my gut."

Female Response to Film

"Interesting to note some sort of tender non-exploitative relationship and to see sex without clearly defined sex roles—dominant/submissive, male to female, etc."

"I guess I'm just not quite as liberal as I tend to give myself for being. I guess I'm looking for some sort of beauty in sex and films on masturbation and homosexuality—don't show me that."

"I felt very uneasy watching; first of all, I felt like I was an intruder. Secondly, the way they were interacting seems very unnatural. I can't even visualize myself having intercourse with another woman. *Oral* intercourse seems very repulsive to me. How common is oral intercourse? In oral intercourse, when the male ejaculates, does the female swallow it or spit it out? Is it complicated for a man to stick his tongue into the *tiny* opening of a female's vagina?"

"Excellent, beautiful. Such a tender relationship. Nice to see someone else's mechanics in sex, just to know you're doing all right."

"Very interesting—good film, somewhat shocking but a good shock to have."

"Excellent—wish you would show one with gay women."

"Really enlightening—they had a more loving relationship than nearly all that I've been involved in."

"A little shocking at first but we've been discussing homosexuality in our room lately so it wasn't as shocking as if I had seen it a year ago."

"I thought the film was very beautifully presented. My previous conception of the gay experience was certainly changed—one loses the realization that there are two *males*, rather feeling that these are two people in love, expressing their love."

"Very enlightening—I liked it."

"At first kind of threatening, but as it went on, it became less so and even erotic—is there a female counterpart?"

"Turned me off but that's just my problem."

"I definitely got to the plateau watching it."

The comments quoted are selected from more than 300 different student reaction forms. We don't believe we have omitted any category of response or overemphasized any particular type of reaction. It seems to us that regardless of the reaction type, this film invariably helps students get in touch with their feelings about themselves and about homosexuality.

The third evening focuses on sex as a medium of interpersonal exchange. This lecture is given by both of us. In it we describe the need for negotiation when two people come together sexually. Each brings a sexuality made up of attitudes, beliefs, and past experiences which are reflected in their personality. The process is a learning one, a give and take to meet emotional as well as physical needs. The basic concepts developed by Masters and Johnson and presented to couples in sex therapy are presented and explained to the entire class. These principles include: Sex is a natural function; there is no such thing as an uninvolved partner; sex will not yield to a goal orientation; spectatoring; feelings are facts; give-to-get; touching for one's own pleasure; etc. The communication guidelines which we give in therapy are described, e.g., that couples are asked to begin their sentences with "I" statements; and that they verbally protect themselves when they feel physically or psychologically uncomfortable. The basic message is that sexual exchange involves developing trust between two people and that to develop trust, people must be willing to assert themselves and be vulnerable—physically and psychologically—to those with whom they wish an emotional bond. To more fully appreciate the meaning of these communication guidelines the students are asked to use them in their small group discussions.

After the third lecture the stage has been set to talk about some of the issues and decisions students face. Contraception, abortions, pregnancy and venereal disease are the major topics discussed. Recent studies are presented. Findings which relate particularly to college students are explored. For example, Zelnik and Kantner found that most college students have intercourse at sometime without contraception and that many students regularly have intercourse with no protection. The Yale students are usually shocked to hear the statistics. Indeed, their own statistics are quite different (as we described, p. 285 in Chapter 9 on contraception). Contraceptives are brought to the classroom and circulated during the lecture. The pros and cons of each method are described. We don't say too much about venereal infection because, although there has been a virtual epidemic of venereal disease among young people, this has not been true among Yale students. We mention gonorrhea and syphilis and the signs and symptoms of these diseases, and we let the students know whom to see when they are worried about having a disease.

The lecture which has turned out to be one of the most popular with students is the one on pregnancy and childbirth. This is discussed on the fifth evening that we meet. The basic facts about fertility, conception, biological and psychological changes during pregnancy, sex life during pregnancy, and prenatal care are presented. A film shows the last moments of labor and the process of childbirth. In it the husband is present throughout. He and his wife are able to watch the delivery. The first breast feeding is also shown.

After the film, two or three couples who have recently had a baby, and who have brought their baby with them, come to the front of the lecture hall and describe their experiences to the students. Not infrequently, the husbands dominate and it starts to sound as if they had the baby. It is not unusual for one or more of the women to breast feed the baby in front of the class. The students always have many questions about body changes and how that feels, pain in labor and delivery, natural childbirth and anesthesia. The couples have often openly discussed the effects that pregnancy and having a baby have had on their sex lives.

There is a continuity between the early lectures and the lecture on pregnancy. The messages are that sex is good, that sex between two people can be something special, that it is not without trial and error, and is a learning process. And there are rewards. A baby is one. But, "more" important is the experience of emotional sharing between two people and the bond that results from that sharing.

The last night of the course is more loosely structured than the other nights. Students ask questions. Areas already covered may be gone over again. New topics are covered, such as menopause, talking to children about sex and appropriately for this "potpourri" lecture, drugs and their effects on sex. There is an open discussion about the course—the lectures, the films and the discussion groups. At the end, each of the students writes a brief summary of what the course has meant to him or her and what suggestions he or she has for improving it.

The group leaders and the faculty advisors meet one last time to discuss the course and make their own recommendations for the future. As faculty in our college, we have felt that giving the course was part of our job. As a result, all of the money taken in could be used for projects such as the *Sex at Yale* booklet.

Why Give a Human Sexuality Course on Campus?

We have never stopped believing in the value of the course for students and our experience over the years on many campuses has, if anything, strengthened our belief. Students today are not totally ignorant of the facts of biology, psychosexual development, or birth control, but they aren't as informed or thoughtful as many adults presume. There are important lacunae in their concepts, myths and old wives tales still abound, and the latest books on sex have given rise to new and up-to-date *mis*-information. High school sex courses have sometimes imparted mixed messages along with facts.

The students who sign up for the sex course are not less well-informed than their peers. When we contrasted their scores on the sex attitude and knowledge questionnaire with a random sample of students who did not take the course, we found that course-takers were less sexually experienced but *more* knowledgeable than their peers. They seem to represent a sub-group of students who like to use their intellect to cope with and prepare for life experiences. Blos has noted that adolescents do have (in contrast to acting-out tendencies) a growing capacity to use thought as trial action and as a bridge between present and future [2]. The sex course capitalizes on this growing capacity. (Those who choose not to take it will perhaps read the booklet or pick up information from roommates in post-course discussions, as well as learning through their own trials and errors.)

In addition to supplying needed facts and concepts the course also weaves facts and feelings together. The lectures are never just cerebral. We include actual student experiences and their feelings about experiences (obviously disguising the identity of the students if we use student material). We also talk some about ourselves, our children, our own feelings and doubts and, in general, try to communicate about sex as a life-long human experience that includes humor, irony, pain, confusion, joy, guilt, i.e. *feelings*. One student wrote on her post-meeting-response, "I knew the facts. You put them together with the feelings. That's what was most helpful for me."

The films are extremely useful in helping students to recognize what they do feel about such things as lesbianism, oral sex, or the birth process. They are sometimes surprised by what they feel, perhaps concerning a prejudice they never suspected or a level of easy acceptance when they anticipated a negative reaction. There is no doubt that the films can produce strong affective responses, ranging from disgust to sexual arousal, and students must be prepared for this before viewing sexually explicit films. We also feel that small group discussion immediately afterward is vital, providing an opportunity to ventilate, to correct misperceptions caused by the high feeling level, and to hear the wide range of others' responses.

Because college students are such a varied group, with differing levels of maturity and experience, a course in sexuality should have flexibility and put a minimum of pressure on the individual. The fact that the course is noncredit means that students can attend or not on an entirely voluntary basis. Students seem to find ways of using the course to meet their own needs. A few drop out. More than a few take the course twice, for example, as a freshman and again as a senior. Some small groups continue to meet for months after the course has ended.

Within the small groups, no one is pressured to participate if he or she wants to take a listening role. Hearing others talk about their experiences and feelings can be an important step in learning about sex for the relatively inexperienced, as Anthony Powell has described it in his novel series, *A Dance to the Music of Time*. The 17-ish protagonist has just heard about his friend's sexual experience with a pick-up in London: "This was a glimpse through that mysterious door, once shut, that now seemed to stand ajar. It was as if sounds of far-off conflict, or the muffled din of music and shouting, dimly heard in the past, had now come closer than ever before."

The small groups meet a wide variety of needs. In them males and females are talking together about sex, developing the capacity to communicate with one another, to use sex words and express feelings about sex, to listen. The socially isolated student can fill in some of the blanks caused by a paucity of ordinary peer interactions. One graduate student from a foreign country was very relieved to hear that other young males' experiences were at least roughly similar to his own. His lack of close friends with whom he could share and compare had led him to fear he might be way-out or freakish. The small groups are also a social experience—a way to meet people, and that is not an unimportant value on a campus where the number one student distress is said to be loneliness.

Initiating A Sex Education Program on Campus

We have assisted more than 30 different colleges and universities in their development of sexual health services including sex education. In all instances we have had personal contact with students and staff from the institution and have been able to learn about the particular situation. As a result of this consulting experience, as well as the opportunity to teach complete courses at Yale and 12 other schools, we offer the following advice to those considering initiating a program.

Form a committee of interested administrators, faculty, students, health and campus ministry personnel. If they are not represented on the committee, then the Dean's Office, the campus health service and the campus ministry should be informed of what is happening. Students who are willing to devote their primary extracurricular energies to the project are best-suited. A balance of male and female students representing the three upper classes usually means the participation of six to eight students. Let the students suggest faculty people who have already shown an interest in students and who could help in the creation of the course either as teachers or to pave the way with the campus administration.

A good starting activity for the committee is a campus survey to ascertain the level of student interest and willingness to participate in a sexuality course. The survey can also ask for volunteers who feel they have had some special training which could be of value during the course. For example, we are now finding that many students are interested in sex education or in group dynamics and have participated in workshops or other courses which have prepared them to be more helpful in the sexuality course.

The details of organizing the course, registering students, getting data, etc., have already been described. Choose the faculty from existing community resources. More and more sex educators are becoming available and many professionals are now getting training in sexuality—ministers, social workers, teachers, doctors, and nurses. It is best to have a small faculty, two or three lecturers, from the local scene.

The course should not be compulsory. By keeping it as an elective you respond to student needs to deal with sexuality as they decide for themselves. In the few instances we know of in which courses have been made compulsory, there has been an ensuing controversy which set back the entire program, in at least two instances, permanently.

We know that the course we have described can be transplanted. We originally brought it to Yale from Mt. Holyoke. At least a dozen of the 30 schools we helped have now had an on-going program for more than five years. As clearly documented in a recent publication, *Sexual Health Services for Academic Communities*, [4], the need is there, and the times finally permit educators to provide sexuality education in an open and honest fashion.

References

1. Pomeroy, Wardell B., *Dr. Kinsey and The Institute for Sex Research,* New York, Harper and Row, 1972, p. 61.
2. Blos, Peter, *On Adolescence,* New York, Free Press, 1962, pp. 124-125.
3. *Vir Amat,* a film produced by the National Sex and Drug Forum, San Francisco, 1971.
4. *Sexual Health Services for Academic Communities,* National Liaison Committee of the American College Health Association Planned Parenthood Federation of America, Inc. and SIECUS, Philadelphia, George F. Stickley Co., 1976.

Appendix

Sexual Decision-making: Some Questions

The decision to have or not to have intercourse for the first time is a serious decision, faced by almost every young woman today. Many students and student couples ask our advice about having intercourse. We always say to them, no one can tell you whether you should or not, but perhaps we can help you think it through by suggesting these questions to ask yourself.*

Do you know why your parents and/or religion have taught that intercourse should wait until marriage? Do you accept these ideas? If so, then you would be creating a lot of inner turmoil to go against your own beliefs.

If you do not accept these beliefs you were taught, is it only at their intellectual level? Do you feel really comfortable and firm in your own beliefs? Try to imagine how you would feel about losing your virginity. Would it make you feel less valuable, less lovable, less good? If so, it is a bad "bargain." This is not to say that an emotional reaction to first intercourse is a sign of trouble. On the contrary, it is a very important moment and an outpouring of feelings can be expected—feelings of joy and sadness, pleasure and disappointment.

Have you said no to intercourse not out of moral consideration but out of fear? Many women have fears about sex, especially first intercourse. Do you fear pain or bleeding? Do you think there is

* As we indicated above, p. 58, these questions were originally posed in our magazine column and were directed to women. In truth, however, but for the wording, they are equally applicable to both sexes.

some reason you would have an unusually difficult time? Are you afraid you would be unable to respond sexually? Are you afraid your parents would find out? A moral decision made out of fear or ignorance is not really moral. You must understand your own feelings and try to find someone (perhaps a doctor) who can hear your concerns and help answer your questions.

Are you yielding to group pressure from your friends against what you feel is right for you? Don't dismiss this question lightly. Most people don't recognize the full extent of the influence exerted on them by peers. It is easy to feel you are "hung up" or abnormal when your way is against most of the people around you. Remember also that some friends may be giving the impression they are more sexually experienced than they actually are.

Are you expecting too much from intercourse? If you believe that intercourse will transport you to the stars, make you overnight into a "real" woman or other over-blown fantasy, it won't. Try to get your expectations down to earth before you decide.

What does intercourse mean to you—permanent commitment for life? Fidelity for both partners? Love?

However you answer the previous questions, does your current relationship meet these criteria? Does he understand what it means to you and do you understand his feelings?

Would you feel comfortable being naked with a man, touching his penis and having him touch your genitals, seeing him ejaculate, allowing yourself to respond sexually with him? If not, slow down and go through the stages of physical intimacy at a pace that feels right to you before having intercourse.

Is your current relationship emotionally intimate and open? Could you tell him if you were scared or if something hurt? Could he tell you he never had intercourse before and was really nervous? You are much more likely to have a satisfying experience if the relationship is at this level before you have intercourse.

Can you and he get effective contraception and will you both use it faithfully and correctly?

Are you prepared to face a pregnancy should your contraception fail?

Do you and he have the opportunity for uninterrupted privacy, free from the fear of being heard or intruded upon?

If, after asking yourself these questions, you still feel confusion and doubt, try to find a trusted person with whom you can talk it out—a religious counselor whose ideas you respect, an older sister, a woman you are close to or a doctor who cares enough to spend time talking with you.

INDEX

Index